RESCUED FROM OBLIVION

A VOLUME IN THE SERIES

Public History in Historical Perspective

EDITED BY

Marla R. Miller

RESCUED FROM OBLIVION

HISTORICAL CULTURES IN THE EARLY UNITED STATES

ALEA HENLE

UNIVERSITY OF MASSACHUSETTS PRESS
Amherst & Boston

Printed in the United States of America

ISBN 978-1-62534-499-1 (paper); 498-4 (hardcover)

Designed by Jen Jackowitz
Set in Adobe Caslon
Printed and bound by Maple Press, Inc.

Cover design by Frank Gutbrod
Cover photo: Woman's Shoes, originally owned by Mary Ledyard, made by Jonathan Hose and Son, about 1750–60, handstitched leather, silk brocade, and linen, with silk-covered wooden heel; gift of Dr. John L. Comstock, 1840.3.2ab, The Connecticut Historical Society

Library of Congress Cataloging-in-Publication Data
Names: Henle, Alea R., author.
Title: Rescued from oblivion : historical cultures in the early United States / Alea Henle.
Other titles: Historical cultures in the early United States
Description: Amherst : University of Massachusetts Press, [2020] | Series: Public history in historical perspective | Includes bibliographical references and index.
Identifiers: LCCN 2019044528 | ISBN 9781625344984 (hardcover) | ISBN 9781625344991 (paperback) | ISBN 9781613767443 (ebook) | ISBN 9781613767450 (ebook)
Subjects: LCSH: Societies—United States—History. | History—Societies, etc. | United States—History, Local.
Classification: LCC E172 .H45 2020 | DDC 369/.1—dc23
LC record available at https://lccn.loc.gov/2019044528

British Library Cataloguing-in-Publication Data
A catalog record for this book is available from the British Library.

A portion of chapter 3 previously appeared in "The Means and the End: Letters and the Work of History," *The Edinburgh Companion to Nineteenth-Century American Letters and Letter Writing*, ed. Celeste-Marie Bernier, Judie Newman, and Matthew Pethers (Edinburgh: Edinburgh University Press, 2016): 103–18.

This work is dedicated to Ellen Nickenzie Lawson,
my historian mother
(this apple didn't fall too far from the tree)

Contents

Acknowledgments

ANYONE UNDERTAKING A RESEARCH PROJECT of this magnitude incurs extensive research and writing debts. Several institutions supported my research and writing through grants and fellowships, including the Library Company of Philadelphia (twice), the McNeil Center for Early American Studies, the Andrew W. Mellon Foundation, the University of Connecticut Humanities Institute, the Massachusetts Historical Society, the Historical Society of Pennsylvania, and the member institutions of the New England Regional Fellowship Consortium. My employers, Miami University (Ohio), University of Wisconsin-Madison, and Western New Mexico University also provided support during research, writing, and revision phases. As for research assistance, I am indebted in particular to the (many!) librarians and archivists at (in alphabetical order) the American Antiquarian Society; the American Philosophical Society; Houghton Library (Harvard); the New England Historic Genealogical Society; the Pilgrim Society; and the historical societies of Connecticut, Georgia, Maine, Maryland, Massachusetts, New Hampshire, New York, Pennsylvania, and Rhode Island.

In addition, numerous individuals commented on drafts of chapters and whole manuscripts. Richard D. Brown provided guidance while this project was a dissertation. Marla Miller and two anonymous reviewers for the

University of Massachusetts Press offered comments that helped refine, reorganize, and improve the final version. Others sources of insight, suggestions, and support include Jessica Linker; Cornelia Dayton; Christopher Clark; Robert A. Gross; Jim Green; the leaders and attendees of the Mellon Early American Literature and Material Texts seminars from 2010 to 2016; and attendees at Society of Early Americanists and American Historical Association panels.

And, of course, thanks to my family for their support and historical and editorial advice!

RESCUED FROM OBLIVION

Introduction

BOSTON MINISTER JOHN ELIOT AND nine other men established the first historical society in the United States, now known as the Massachusetts Historical Society, in the late eighteenth century. Eliot acknowledged the existence of other learned organizations in Boston, not least the Academy of Arts and Sciences, but argued the new society would be different. Rather than encompassing all arts and sciences, the new Historical Society would "pursue one particular subject." He and the other founders intended to "confine our attention to this business of collecting things which will illustrate the history of our country." Other historical society founders throughout the nation used similar terms to describe their intention to collect, gather, preserve, protect, save, snatch, or, more poetically, "rescue from oblivion" all manner of historical materials.[1]

The Massachusetts society founders considered its establishment a progressive action—and one desperately needed. The new nation deserved preservation of its historical materials. At the time, no other learned societies took history as a primary or even secondary object. The older, Philadelphia-based American Philosophical Society did not actively pursue historical collecting for another quarter century. National, state, and local governments maintained collections of materials, but for legal purposes rather than historical. Unfortunately, government records were ill organized and ill kept. Many public officials, historians, and collectors mingled personal and government materials in their collections. Historical Society founder Rev. Jeremy Belknap, credited as the major force behind the organization's existence, obtained a number of New Hampshire records while writing a history of the then-colony—and never returned them. Few libraries and academic institutions gathered and preserved historical matter.[2]

Members of the Massachusetts Historical Society toiled alone for its first decade, but within sixty years the number of active historical societies increased exponentially. States and territories from Maine to Louisiana and Georgia to Minnesota boasted historical societies, as did several cities and counties. Historical organizations served as a mark of civilization and allowed founders to affirm particular views and interests—although many societies failed or endured long periods of dormancy. The society officers and memberships drew almost exclusively from the ranks of wealthy, professional, Protestant men of European descent. Their activities emphasized history in the image of their shared lives and experiences. Their female equivalents had influence on societies' collecting, but this did not translate into active accumulation of things documenting women's lives and labors. Officers overlooked the histories of laboring classes and racial and ethnic minorities.

Collecting and preserving historical materials mattered on multiple levels, including affirming importance and ensuring inclusion within the broader historical record. Active efforts to preserve the histories of specific places and peoples generated concerns among others who saw their accomplishments and those of their ancestors diminished or rewritten, or their presences overlooked. Many people vested in ideas of progress and innovation valued historical materials as a means of measuring how much generations improved on one another. Amid competition within and between states, historical documents fueled claims for achievement.

Rescued from Oblivion uses close examination of historical societies to explore historical cultures and consciousness in the early United States. Eliot's description of the new society's mission identified core concepts which characterized historical cultures over the succeeding generations: "this business of collecting things which will illustrate the history of our country." Founders and members had to organize and establish operational procedures. Officers decided what to collect. They did so in service to ideas of national history, but their rhetoric exceeded their reach.

With respect to organizational culture, founders' decisions persist in many historical institutions to this day. The men who established historical societies followed existing organization practices: elected officers, held regular meetings, published volumes, and kept records. The earliest societies were voluntary entities reliant on members. They took the form of gentlemen's clubs pursuing goals with public benefits. Successful applications for state charters recreated the societies as quasi-public organizations. The two identities coexisted uneasily, particularly with respect to fiscal matters as most historical societies endured precarious finances and relied to varying degree on government support. State charters laid the groundwork for the bulk of early societies to organize around geopolitical identities: cities, counties, states. Over the second half of the nineteenth century, these close relations furthered development of a "Western" model of historical societies wherein some societies organized as effective arms of state governments and received regular financial assistance.

The process of reconciling society officers' differences over what to collect contributed to the emergence of primary sources as building blocks of history. At first, officers described collection objectives in terms of content: desired facts and information. Inherently subjective, content-based collecting allowed imposition of conscious and unconscious biases. Preservation processes thus facilitated minimization of materials reflecting the experiences of racial and ethnic minorities, laborers, and women. Officers gradually shifted collecting objectives to circumstances of creation and use, for example, valuing items as historical because they had a connection to a particular place, person, or time.

Preserving historical materials involved balancing complementary and competing activities. Historical societies embraced collecting, organizing, preserving, and educating alongside entertaining and promoting social interaction. The organizations and members shared a common vision and sought to preserve history in their image: the Anglo-American world of the professional elites. Although historical societies embraced national rhetoric, officers built their collections through local action, with a focus on local and regional information. From the first, officers pursued preservation through publication as a means of preserving documents and information. Publication efforts, although laborious and expensive, reaffirmed collecting interests and served as an additional means of outreach to potential donors and supporters.

Several officers endorsed rhetorical appeals to the general public, but society publications focused on the interests of the members. Disagreements about what to publish were resolved in favor of miscellaneous publications instead of themed, geographical, or chronological arrangements, undercutting societies' ability to engage broader support for their publications.

Yet historical collecting and publishing were rife with differences of opinion over what to preserve and how, not just between officers of any given organization, but among different organizations and the people who were and were not in elite circles. Historical society founders understood the nation in relation to the local. They embraced bipartisanship and extended membership to Federalists, Republicans, and Whigs, the better to draw on governmental support regardless of political party—yet in turn they consciously minimized documentation of slavery. Print culture offered opportunities for challenges to historical society authority. The expansion of printing during the Early Republic encouraged contributions from historical society members who opted to publish external works amid the rise of popular histories. Likewise, print offered opportunities for members of disadvantaged groups to rewrite history to include themselves and their peoples, albeit contingent on sufficient monetary support. Other venues for historical activity included public commemorations, expeditions, and performances.

The historical society founders organized around local (city, county) and state identities that they described in nested, relational terms, whereby officers pursued narrower and broader ambitions simultaneously. Most societies endorsed documenting national history but did not contribute to popular history initiatives. Officers restricted their spheres of action to within learned, scholarly circles, apart from a few notable exceptions. Early historical society activities were largely secular. Officers gathered religious materials primarily documenting churches and denominations within the public sphere. This contributed to the establishment of separate religious historical societies, particularly around the midcentury.

Historical collecting and preservation activities reflected and affirmed identities and connections. Through attention to the past, participants emphasized the importance of particular places, peoples, and activities. Inclusion mattered, deciding which people, places, and events were important, what warranted remembrance and, the other side of the coin, what should be forgotten. Participants put the past to the service of the present to justify land claims and control. Society officers, members, and other historically minded individuals collectively documented a multiplicity of Americas for their descendants to contemplate and preserve.

Chapter 1 surveys the establishment, organization, successes, and failures of early historical societies. Eliot, Belknap, and other founders created the Massachusetts Historical Society in response to chaotic, piecemeal preservation of historical materials. They established a separate, specialized society in the face of a general lack of action on the part of governments, learned institutions, and the public. Historical societies relied on the efforts of middling-upper-class professional men not inside the top echelons of politics and business. With few exceptions the societies struggled to attract monetary support and as a consequence relied heavily on government assistance.

The second chapter showcases the complex relationships between historical societies and governments. Most early historical societies organized around geopolitical identities: cities, counties, and states. In the process, they reflected and contributed to nested identities wherein individuals understood larger identities (state, nation) in relation to smaller (city, county, state). The proliferation of geographical societies reflected dissatisfaction with existing organizations and tensions between locales. Historical society officers assumed proactive roles with respect to protecting government records in government hands. They petitioned local, state, and national governments to obtain copies of European archival documents, organize and publish colonial records, and erect fireproof buildings.

Chapter 3 highlights how the problem of defining what to collect contributed to the shift toward primary sources as the building blocks of history. At first historical society officers described their collecting interests in terms of information, in particular about the public world members shared. Yet the problem of describing this in sufficient detail to prompt contributions, combined with differences among members, led to alternative methods of valuation. By midcentury, many described collecting interests in terms of circumstances of creation alongside or instead of topical information. Historical society officers also re-assessed the place of natural history within their collections, given the rise of separate natural history societies, exhibiting interest predominantly in gathering textual materials. Exceptions for non-textual items were few, most notably Native American artifacts. Ironically, several members chastised society leaderships for focusing heavily on the past and ignoring opportunities to preserve contemporary documents.

Historical societies pursued publication as a means of preserving documents and information, but their actions in this regard undercut and overlooked opportunities to appeal to broader publics. Chapter 4 demonstrates how historical societies' publication committees emphasized publication as preservation rather than as an opportunity for popular appeal. The publication committees repeatedly ignored chronological or topical organization in publications, despite criticism from reviews and from historical society officers.

Chapter 5 explores the divide between historical societies and popular history. Several historical societies held lectures open to people able to afford admission fees. Likewise, officers organized public commemorations of historic events, with distinct differences between those who watched processions through the streets, attended the actual ceremonies held in churches or government buildings, or celebrated at the festive banquets afterward. The Connecticut Historical Society proved a notable exception, as its varied collection attracted a diverse clientele of visitors ranging from well-heeled businessmen to mothers with young children to laborers, suggesting early historical societies' unrealized potential with respect to class and gender.

Finally, chapter 6 examines what historical societies did *not* collect and what tactics women and disadvantaged populations used to challenge or subvert historical organization authority. Mini case studies of two notable donations highlight ways women of wealth and station, female equivalents to the male membership, ensured acceptance of items documenting women's lives and labors. African Americans and Native Americans faced higher bars to inclusion. Despite occasional inclusive rhetoric, society leaderships largely excluded documentation of slavery and enslaved peoples through chronological and geographical distancing. Officers expended far more attention on Native American peoples but stressed documentation through European American accounts and affirmation of Native nations as dying or vanishing peoples. Discussions of the discovery of America overlooked Native American claims in favor of European, and Spanish in favor of Scandinavian.

A growing cohort of women, African American, and Native American historians challenged historical society preferences through the power of the press by the mid-nineteenth century. Historical society members and historians dissatisfied with the secular bent of most historical societies also challenged the status quo. They preserved and disseminated alternative narratives and documents through publications and established new historical societies to collect and preserve the histories of particular religious denominations, races, and ethnicities over the second half of the nineteenth century. Attempts to preserve particular histories thus contributed to the preservation, in varying degrees, of other histories.

Chapter One

"The Lumber Yard of History"

The Organization, Progress, Successes, and Failures of Historical Societies

THE OHIO-BASED LOGAN HISTORICAL SOCIETY described its purpose as "to collect, stack up, to keep and season the materials out of which, in future, a most useful and accurate history may be constructed." Its short-lived, mid-nineteenth-century publication, *American Pioneer*, became a "lumber yard of history." Historical society officers and members saw themselves as middlemen, gathering and protecting materials for the sake of future generations in the face of general inaction. The federal government did little to collect and preserve historical materials apart from funding the purchase of early presidential papers for the State Department. Congress did not allocate funds for the Library of Congress to purchase manuscripts, or establish the National Archives until the twentieth century. State and local governments provided assistance but initiated few preservative actions. Libraries and academic institutions likewise did little. In contrast, early historical societies amassed collections of early books, pamphlets, newspapers, manuscripts, artifacts, indigenous antiquities, and natural specimens.[1]

General inaction to preserve historical materials mattered. State and national governments' inattention to their records contrasted with known use of historical documents for research purposes. Historical society founders also recognized the value of historical documents for citation in court cases, justification for legislative bills, and to ensure the inclusion of particular peoples and places in local, regional, and national narratives. For example, Boston historian Hannah Mather Crocker suggested that prudent matrons such as herself might save a nation "by preserving the records and certain documents that shall be sufficient evidence to prove the boundaries of the nation." At the time, the northeastern border between Canada and Maine was in dispute.[2]

To date, most research on historical societies in the United States appears as individual institutional histories. Complementing these, recent scholarship focuses on historic preservation in specific cities (e.g., Philadelphia, Pennsylvania, or Deerfield, Massachusetts) or analyzes individual historic sites (Independence Hall, Plymouth Rock) over an extended timeframe. With few exceptions, scholars have failed to compare historical societies. In 1934 historian Julian P. Boyd defended historical societies by recounting a narrative of their rise and progress to answer criticism based on their apparent decline following the establishment of the American Historical Association in 1884. Later, historian David Van Tassel highlighted the importance of the historical societies' dual roles as preservers and creators even as they became centers of localism. Historian and librarian Walter Muir Whitehill's *Independent Historical Societies* (1962) and the North Caroliniana Society's *Historical Consciousness in the Early Republic* (1995) address societies by state and region, mirroring the local bias of institutional and location-oriented scholarship. Only Leslie W. Dunlap, a mid-twentieth-century librarian, examined multiple societies. Historiographical developments since Dunlap's work call for this examination.[3]

By the mid-nineteenth century, professional men of station, predominantly Protestants of Anglo-American descent, organized more than fifty historical societies in the United States to preserve historical materials. They relied on volunteer labor to gather and protect materials, and often failed or had periods of sporadic activity punctuating stretches of dormancy. The members sought to document the history of the nation but understood it through the lens of the local. Few historical societies received large-scale donations. Officers relied on membership fees or assistance from local and state governments, which increased affiliations with local and state identities.

"Food for Worms": Preserving Historical Materials before Historical Societies

Founders of the first historical societies created organizations focused on collecting and preservation in no small part because earlier efforts to gather and preserve historical materials on a large scale met with failure or limited success. Today, historians have numerous repositories available for consultation, from government archives to quasi-public societies to academic libraries. Massachusetts Historical Society founders had far fewer options, despite access to informal networks of correspondents throughout the states. Indeed, they recognized insufficient action or support for gathering and protecting historical materials on the part of governments, learned organizations, private individuals, and the general public.

Colonial historians used government records as a primary consultation point in researching the history of the colonies and their peoples. New York colonial official Cadwallader Colden based his early eighteenth-century history of the Iroquois on access to official documents. Later in the century, Rev. Jeremy Belknap acknowledged in the first volume to his *History of New Hampshire* a debt to New Hampshire and Massachusetts officials for providing him with access to public records.[4]

Such straightforward acknowledgments masked a complex situation in which government records were incomplete, dispersed within colonies, located in Europe, or insufficient alone as a source for writing history. Records were vulnerable to fire and other disasters, with notable losses. Thomas Hutchinson worked on a history of Massachusetts while in the colonial government. He held multiple government offices, serving at various times as lieutenant governor, chief justice, a probate judge, and councilor, and therefore had access to the colony's "ancient" public records. Unfortunately, many were lost, forcing him to seek materials for his history elsewhere. A year after the first volume was published, a mob protesting the Stamp Act looted his house and destroyed historical materials in his possession. Afterward, some radicals implied the destruction was an attempt to keep Hutchinson from continuing his history. Hutchinson's friend, Rev. Andrew Eliot, rescued some of Hutchinson's papers, allowing him to complete the second volume.[5]

Record-keeping practices allowed officials to keep government records in private establishments and refer to both private and public matters in correspondence, blurring the lines between public and private. Colonial governments preserved records for administrative use, not historical. Often officers and elected officials did not turn over documentation to their successors. Connecticut exemplifies how government records at the time were not under consistent governmental control. In the mid- to late eighteenth century, the Connecticut General Assembly repeatedly directed state officials, including

Governor Jonathan Trumbull, to collect colonial documents. Trumbull gathered many, but kept them in his home even after retiring from office. Historian Christopher Bickford suggested Trumbull made two collections: a personal collection, which his family offered to the Massachusetts Historical Society in 1794, and one of documents gathered in compliance with the General Assembly's request, which the Trumbull family returned to the State of Connecticut much later.[6]

Trumbull intended the collection for a library accessible by the public, for the use of future historians. His heirs did not consider Yale a suitable recipient for his collection of Connecticut colonial records. His son David offered the collection to the new Massachusetts Historical Society in 1794, believing his father would have preferred the quasi-public Society over a "Collegiate or other Library, where they probably would soon become 'Food for Worms.'" While Europe enjoyed more than 2,500 libraries with extensive holdings in the mid-eighteenth century, colonial citizens had far fewer options. In 1756 Oxford University's Bodleian Library received its largest single donation, which contained more than five thousand volumes, to date. Neither the College of William and Mary nor Yale College boasted as many works at the time of the Revolution.[7]

Drawing on English precedents, editor Ebenezer Hazard of Philadelphia sought assistance from the Continental Congress for an ambitious project to collect and publish American colonial records. Congress voted to allocate funds to Hazard's enterprise and provided an endorsement which facilitated access to colonial state papers. Whether he received any monies is unclear. Despite assistance from friends, he completed copying materials for only Massachusetts and New Hampshire. Publication of the first two volumes of his collection in the early 1790s left him in debt.[8]

Most historians relied primarily on private and family collections. While Thomas Hutchinson found his own family papers proved helpful in writing his history of Massachusetts Bay, he acknowledged a debt to his brother-in-law Samuel Mather for free access to Mather's library. Hutchinson believed earlier Boston historian and minister Thomas Prince also collected "the greatest and most valuable part" of his history from the Mather library. Similarly, William Stith, a retired president of the College of William and Mary in Williamsburg, Virginia, owed much of the contents of his mid-eighteenth-century history of the colony to the manuscripts and books in the library of planter William Byrd II.[9]

Unfortunately, private and family collections posed problems of care and preservation over generations. Individuals with historical materials often willed these to their heirs. This allowed for sale or disbursement. Boston minister Cotton Mather's library passed to his son, rather than being sold to pay his debts, possibly through lifetime gifts from Mather to his son or legal finagling after Mather's death to ensure lineal passage. The library and associated materials largely remained in the family for nearly a century afterward. Virginia collector William Byrd II left his library to his son, William Byrd III, who sold it. Rev. Thomas Prince bequeathed his historical and religious libraries to the Old South Church, but the contents were neglected even before British depredations during the occupation of Boston. At least one historical collector directed his materials to a younger, kindred spirit: former town clerk and Governor Stephen Hopkins left his historical manuscripts to fellow historian Theodore Foster rather than a family member.[10]

Rev. Jeremy Belknap drafted a letter in 1774 proposing Harvard College Library become a repository for historical materials. At the time, the thirty-year-old Boston-born and Harvard-educated minister served the First Church in Dover, New Hampshire. He began researching the history of New Hampshire and became convinced of the importance of the active collection and preservation of documents. Aware of growing unrest in the colonies over matters of governance, Belknap pondered how future historians might view the times in which he lived. He imagined the Harvard library as a place to collect "such authentic Documents as may enable some future historian to delineate the present times in as full and perfect a manner as possible."[11]

Nothing came of Belknap's suggestion, but later English-born Boston minister and historian William Gordon proposed a similar plan. Gordon was then working on a history of the American Revolution (published 1788) and conscious of the difficulties of locating and accessing historical records. His idea involved appointing a committee to gather historical materials. Harvard leaders chose Gordon to carry out the project, but he did nothing and returned to England leaving the matter unaddressed.[12]

Trustees of Harvard College took the proposal under consideration again and approached Belknap, who had recently moved to Boston. He agreed to lead Harvard in collecting historical matter, reflecting that he "often experienced that, where there is much labour and little profit, I am not out of employ." He urged owners of important collections to donate them to Harvard and attempted to arrange for Harvard to purchase a valuable collection of newspapers and pamphlets from pioneering historical editor Ebenezer Hazard of Philadelphia. Within twelve months, Belknap became convinced college officials lacked the will to collect and preserve historical materials. Belknap never donated from his own collection to the project, probably suspecting the plan would fail.[13]

Belknap and other historically minded individuals in Massachusetts recognized the limitations of governments, learned institutions, and private collectors in collecting and preserving historical materials by 1790. Scholars place the establishment of the Massachusetts Historical Society in the context of the specialization of learned culture and the extension or adaptation of European practices. The founding of the Society also commented on the failures of other institutions and organizations. The founders determined the best way to ensure preservation of historical materials was through a society focused solely on this objective.[14]

"The Honourable Example": Establishing Historical Societies

At the outset, early societies embraced grand ambitions. Over time, their expectations declined and they restricted their spheres of potential action. Americans founded more societies as the nineteenth century progressed. New Yorkers created the New-York Historical Society thirteen years after establishment of the Massachusetts Historical Society. Massachusetts citizens organized the American Antiquarian Society after another decade. By the twenty-fifth anniversary of the Declaration of Independence, men established societies in Pennsylvania and all New England states except Vermont. Behind these points lay a tale of successes—and failures.

"A Safe Repository": From One to Few, 1790–1820

New York City businessman and philanthropist John Pintard called on Belknap in 1789 to suggest forming a Society of Antiquaries. The following year, Belknap drew up such a plan. For inspiration, he probably looked to European historical and antiquarian societies, which were largely affiliated with royalty and organized along national lines. He also had domestic examples: the American Philosophical Society in Philadelphia and the American Academy of Arts and Sciences in Boston. Instead of emphasizing the United States, he put forward the broad, mandate "of collecting, preserving, and communicating the antiquities of America." Under such a goal, the proposed society would begin to redress the imbalance of historical resources between the Old World and the New—and lead to the development of a network of historical societies throughout the country.[15]

When the founders met and agreed on a constitution for the new society, they chose a more limited plan. They described their mission in terms of "the United States" rather than the more expansive "America." Belknap had suggested a small, active residential membership of seven, limited to individuals willing to contribute time, money, and materials, but his fellow founders set the number of resident members at thirty, meeting quarterly and led by a cohort of officers elected on an annual basis. They did not actively encourage the establishment of similar societies in other states. The founders chose to call the new organization the Historical Society. They sought to preserve the country's history "from the ravages of time and the effects of ignorance and neglect," but specifically they valued promotion of "historical knowledge of our country" in developing an educated, republican elite. While the founders' conceptual rhetoric stressed the nation, their logistical steps focused on Boston and Massachusetts.[16]

Officers sought an act of incorporation from the state three years later, much as the Society of Antiquaries in London had earlier. Incorporation brought practical advantages. As a corporation, the Historical Society attained a legal existence apart from its members and could sue, be sued, and own property. The Commonwealth of Massachusetts did not grant incorporation as a matter of course. Petitioners first demonstrated they offered public value and served the common good. At the time, the Commonwealth used incorporation of government-sanctioned societies to promote desired objectives. The Massachusetts Medical Society received an act of incorporation as a means to regulate the medical profession. In granting incorporation, Massachusetts officially recognized the Historical Society as offering a public service, putting it on equal standing with the American Academy of Arts and Sciences and the Massachusetts Bank. The act established a relationship between the Historical Society and the Commonwealth. Members of each branch of the legislature should enjoy "free access to the Library and Museum." In turn, Historical Society members obtained access to the legislature and legislative facilities; officers arranged to hold the first meeting after incorporation in the State House.[17]

The act of incorporation changed the number of residential members to sixty and added "Massachusetts" to the Historical Society's name. Although the preamble to the act established the Society's goals as "collection and preservation of materials for a political and natural history of the *United States*," the name change linked the Society's existence and actions to the state. Incorporation remade the Society into *Massachusetts*'s Historical Society.[18]

Despite the name change, society officers attempted to collect materials documenting the nation as well as the state and region. As corresponding secretary, Belknap drafted a circulating letter soliciting donations from "every Gentleman of Science in the Continent and Islands of America," and sent it to European correspondents as well. The Massachusetts Historical Society boasted a geographically diverse membership and received donations for their library and cabinet from around the nation and Europe. Yet the Society's publications in the early volumes related almost exclusively to New England, which citizens of Massachusetts had long understood as a larger version of their state. A few articles reflected other parts of the nation, such as a topographical description of Prince George's County in Virginia, an account of Bacon's rebellion, a letter about early eighteenth-century Georgia, and items regarding eastern portions of Canada in which Massachusetts and New England had long-standing interests.[19]

Belknap's grand plan for a network of societies did not materialize during his lifetime. The nation's second historical society was founded in 1804. By that time, the Massachusetts society was well established and identified with the state, although its sphere of action centered on Boston. With this example before them, founders of the second society associated their organization with their own state and established the New-York Historical Society.

The New York society followed Massachusetts society precedents. Founders set quarterly meetings and annual elections. The first president, treasurer, both secretaries, and all but one of the seven initial standing committee members remained in their positions for at least eight years, and many served for longer terms, giving the Society a durable beginning. Both New York and Massachusetts societies drew their members from the ranks of educated white men, predominantly those practicing professions rather than trades. Resident members, whose numbers were not capped, needed to live in New York and pay admission and annual fees. Both Massachusetts and New York societies waived fees for out-of-state and honorary members. The New York society incorporated under state law five years after its foundation.[20]

The New-York Historical Society recognized "the honourable example of the Massachusetts Society." The two organizations were not rivals, but founders foresaw the potential for competition. Soon the societies went their separate ways with little communication except for exchanges of publications. When New York society officers published a circular soliciting materials and information, they did not limit their ambition "to a single State or district, but extend[ed] to the whole Continent." Founders understood their objectives in terms of "history of the United States in general" and the history of the state of New York "in particular." True to this creed, the New York society published volumes of *Collections* concentrated on New York. As in the case of the Massachusetts society, national and continental interests proved subsidiary to the city and state.[21]

The third successful society organized in the United States had stronger national and hemispheric ambitions. Isaiah Thomas and five other men petitioned the Massachusetts legislature for permission to incorporate an American Antiquarian Society in 1812. On hearing the news, minister Timothy Alden—who had previously served as the Massachusetts society's librarian and cabinet keeper and was creating a catalog of the New-York Historical Society's library—could not imagine anything the antiquarian society could do "which ha[d] not already been anticipated by the industrious Mass[achusetts] His[torical] Soc[iety] whose praise is in every part of the civilised world." He was not alone, for Massachusetts industrialist John Lowell similarly "thought the Historical Society quite enough for one State." Lowell maintained his opinion after the antiquarian society's establishment, but Alden concluded that more societies would result in more success.[22]

The American Antiquarian Society's founders assured the Commonwealth of Massachusetts their society would pursue objectives "essentially distinct from any other [society] in our Country." As the "American Antiquarian Society," it harked back to Pintard and Belknap's first discussions about collective action to preserve historical materials—and suggested an affinity with national organizations in Europe. Society president Isaiah Thomas of Worcester encouraged this, ignoring the two older American historical societies when composing an account of the Society's creation and compared the American Antiquarian Society to European societies of antiquaries. The historical societies became affiliated with states, but he intended the antiquarian society to be national in orientation.[23]

Philadelphia-area historians and antiquarians followed a similar arc: adopting a broad mission in their first endeavor only to quickly narrow to a state focus. Belknap years earlier had asked historical editor Ebenezer

Hazard of Philadelphia about establishing an antiquarian society in the Quaker city. Hazard replied that "perhaps the thing might be considered as falling within the [American] Philosophical Society's department." The American Philosophical Society, founded in Philadelphia decades before the Revolution, divided into six committees or classes focusing on physical and mathematical sciences. Learned gentlemen in Philadelphia did not take any additional steps to gather and protect historical records until three years after the establishment of the American Antiquarian Society. The philosophical society added a seventh committee or class to study history, undoubtedly inspired by the loss of the Library of Congress when British forces burned Washington the previous year. Formally designated the Committee of History, Moral Science, and General Literature, it was more often described as "the Historical and Literary Committee."[24]

Being part of the American Philosophical Society provided the committee with benefits not available to other historical organizations. The mother society already had a schedule of regular meetings, financial accounts, a building (Philosophical Hall), a library of books and manuscripts, a cabinet of curiosities, a record of producing publications, as well as a network of national members. It even boasted a librarian, the Philadelphia bibliophile and wine merchant John Vaughan, who acquired and organized materials. The committee did not place any limit on the number of members, describing the membership as "indefinite." Any Society member, regardless of residence, could join, and thirty-five Philadelphia men promptly did so.[25]

The committee's small roster of officers were all Philadelphians. Lawyer William Tilghman served as chair, Vaughan as recording secretary, and lawyer Peter Du Ponceau as corresponding secretary. These officers, along with the American Philosophical Society president, physician Casper Wistar, and "a few zealous members," immediately began holding meetings and "publish[ed] an appeal to their fellow citizens" for contributions. They "offer[ed] the archives of the Society as a safe repository" in which to deposit books, manuscripts, correspondence, and "every thing" of historical or related interest. The request bore little fruit, so the committee adopted a "more direct method" of obtaining donations—targeting individuals. This approach proved "more successful than they had anticipated" and relied on the labor of French-born polymath Du Ponceau as corresponding secretary.[26]

These Philadelphia-based officers were aware of active societies pursuing similar objectives in Massachusetts and New York. They effectively ceded collecting in and about those states. Instead of acting nationally, the officers centered their attention on Pennsylvania and "other states where no analogous establishments have been formed." They did not confine their correspondence to their state, but as citizens of Pennsylvania they were particularly interested in materials relating to "the history of our own state." Officers declined to compete with the Massachusetts and New York societies in collecting New York and Massachusetts materials. Pennsylvania documents were a different story, as the committee considered means to obtain valuable documents and prevent them from being donated to other area institutions, particularly the well-established Library Company of Philadelphia, a cross-town circulating library. Unfortunately, the committee's reliance on Du Ponceau contributed to its slide into inactivity when he turned his interest to linguistics.[27]

Amid the natural outbreak of historical interest and national sentiment leading up to the Declaration of Independence Jubilee, some Philadelphian men organized the Historical Society of Pennsylvania. The Society had a state-oriented mission, and several founders were members of the largely dormant Historical Committee of the American Philosophical Society.[28]

Most early historical society founders and officers were Federalists, with aspirations to collect and preserve historical materials in national terms. Dedicated to the idea of the United States, their imaginations ran ahead of the integration of the disparate colonies, states, and territories into a whole. The material, communication, and distribution networks necessary to create and support a unified national identity were still in stages of infancy. Even as officers engaged in the development of a strong national government, they understood the nation through the lens of the local. Many gentlemen attempted historic preservation at the national level but succeeded primarily on local and state levels.[29]

"Doing Justice to Themselves, Their Forefathers, and to Posterity": From Few to Many, 1820–1850

Before the 1820s, men founded five historical societies three states—two in Massachusetts, one in New York, and two in Pennsylvania. Over the following decade, eleven more states and territories created thirteen new societies in anticipation of the Declaration Jubilee. Citizens in Tennessee, Ohio, Maine, Rhode Island, New Hampshire, and Connecticut, organized state historical or antiquarian societies, although Tennessee, Ohio, and Connecticut didn't survive long. In Massachusetts, residents of Plymouth and Salem founded local historical societies, the Pilgrim Society and Essex Historical Society respectively. Men in other states and territories followed suit. The number of historical societies kept pace with, and even exceeded, growth in population and number of states in the Union. By the mid-nineteenth century, twenty-four of thirty-one states had a state historical society, as did one territory (Minnesota). Although a number failed early on, several were reestablished.[30]

Puzzlingly, citizens in only one southern state tried to found an early historical society. This was Tennessee, and the attempt failed. Virginians did not organize the Virginia Historical and Philosophical Society until 1831, and the impetus came from outside the state. The three primary founders hailed from New Hampshire, Kentucky, and Bermuda.

TABLE 1. States by Date of First Historical Society Establishment or Attempt, 1791–1850

1791	Massachusetts
1804	New York
1815	Pennsylvania
1820	Tennessee
1822	Maine, Ohio, and Rhode Island
1823	New Hampshire
1825	Connecticut
1827	Illinois
1830	Indiana
1831	Virginia
1833	District of Columbia and North Carolina
1835	Louisiana
1836	Kentucky
1837	Arkansas
1838	Vermont
1839	Georgia
1843	Iowa
1844	Maryland and Missouri
1845	New Jersey and Wisconsin
1849	Minnesota
1850	Alabama

Most early Virginian historians wrote about events in which they had participated or been interested bystanders and thus had little or no need to gather information on earlier times and places. Before the Revolution, a number of gentlemen in Williamsburg included history among the interests of a new learned society, but within a year the society reorganized without reference to history. The cultural and economic elites lived spread throughout the state. They lacked any sense of urgency in collecting and preserving historical materials, perhaps due in part to the repeated loss of colonial statehouses and records in Jamestown and Williamsburg to fires. Moreover, Virginia was uninvolved in historical rivalries among New England and mid-Atlantic states over Revolution-era contributions, depriving the state of another reason to actively preserve historical materials. In addition, the state had no public school system, contributing to low literacy rates.[31]

A venue for historical commemoration and preservation in Virginia involved public ceremonies and physical proximity to the Jamestown settlement. Virginians celebrated the first settlement at Jamestown in 1807 with an event answering Massachusetts's similar anniversary commemorations of Plymouth Colony, which Bay State citizens began celebrating during the Revolution. The 1807 Jamestown Jubilee offered Virginians a chance to assert their claims as the first settlement and leaders in the cause of independence and constitutional government. Three more took place before the Civil War, in 1822, 1834, and 1857. These featured trips to the ruins at Jamestown and were always well attended if not necessarily well planned. Gentlemen from various eastern Virginia towns formed organizing committees who rarely cooperated. Members of planning committees from Williamsburg and James City County nearly came to blows in 1834 while directing favored guests to separate events.[32]

The celebrations did not satisfy teacher Jonathan Cushing, who became concerned about Virginia's "deficiency" in learned societies within a few years of settling in there. Born in New Hampshire, he received his education at Dartmouth before ill health sent him south in the 1820s in search of a warmer climate. Passing through Richmond, he met leading Presbyterian clergyman John Holt Rice, who encouraged the Yankee to take a position as tutor at Hampden-Sydney College in Farmville, Virginia. Cushing soon became the college's president, serving until his untimely death at age forty-two in 1835.[33]

Cushing wrote an article under the pseudonym "A Country Correspondent" in 1824 asking "why is there no *Antiquarian* or *Historical Society* in

Virginia?" Such organizations, he observed, fostered literary achievements, stimulated intellects, and encouraged interest in the country. By connecting "new generation[s]" with the past, historical societies promoted the development of "an intellectual and highly moral people." Moreover, a lack of reverence for the past resulted in people living for themselves alone, which in turn would ultimately result in moral deterioration as people acted without considering the impact on other generations. Although a transplanted Yankee, he valued Virginia's history and expressed a desire "to see the people of the South awakened from their long slumbers; and doing justice to themselves, their forefathers, and to posterity."[34]

Initially wary of establishing a historical society, Bermuda-born Professor George Tucker advised Cushing that any organization would not last long. Virginians had established many learned societies only to watch them "languish and decay." Not dissuaded, Cushing argued even a society lasting "some six or seven years," could still accomplish quite a bit. The argument swayed Tucker, who referred to the exchange in his address at the organizational meeting of the Virginia Historical and Philosophical Society in Richmond in 1831. The Society's name reflected its multiple interests, but the "first object . . . [wa]s to collect the materials for a complete and authentic history of the State."[35]

Tucker correctly predicted the demise of the first Virginia historical society. Early Virginian histories, written by participants and interested bystanders, developed and promoted a master narrative of Virginia's past that flattered white men descended from white male colonists. This satisfied many elite Virginians, leaving little need to collect and preserve historical materials. Finances were also a problem, as many members neglected to pay dues and the Commonwealth provided no aid. Yet Cushing was correct in his view that even a short-lived society could accomplish something. After a period of dormancy from 1840 to 1846, the Virginia Historical and Philosophical Society was reestablished as the Virginia Historical Society. The name change reflected the Society's focus on historical collecting, although it continued to accept artifacts.[36]

The Virginia society was part of the multiplication of geographically named societies, reflecting narrowing visions and scopes. The New-York Historical Society and American Philosophical Society's committee each recognized prior claims. New Yorkers acknowledged the Massachusetts society's activities in New England. Philadelphians in turn ceded collecting in

Massachusetts and New York to those states' respective societies. Likewise, the state historical societies formed between the 1820s and the 1850s conceived of their missions in terms of states as central spheres of action. Of the societies established before 1850, only the American Antiquarian Society survived with a nationally oriented name and some degree of national objectives.[37]

The Business of History: Who, Where, How, and How Much

Early historical society founders adopted and adapted existing practices of learned organizations. They drafted constitutions, laws, and regulations and established regular meetings, with officers elected annually. Officer ranks included presidents, treasurers, and standing committees of individuals who met regularly and provided the officers with guidance and support, a pool of men available for assignment to lesser committees. Recording secretaries took minutes and kept the society records, while corresponding secretaries handled communications. Librarians organized written and printed materials, and cabinet-keepers oversaw artifacts.[38]

"No Particular Party or Sect": Professional, Protestant, Anglo-American Men of Wealth

Officers and members formed the core of historical societies. Massachusetts Historical Society founders created two membership classes. Residential members resided in the state and paid a five-dollar admission fee—raised to eight within a few years—plus two dollars annually. The fees restricted membership to merchant, landowning, and professional classes. Belknap was one of the few to take advantage of a lifetime membership option, bartering donation of a portion of his library in lieu of hard currency. Anyone elected to membership who lived outside the state became a corresponding member, as did any residential member who relocated out of state. Essentially honorary, corresponding membership had no fee requirements. Later historical societies established similar arrangements, although some, including the American Antiquarian Society, created only one membership class.[39]

Societies elected members from the ranks of professional white men with education, wealth, and standing. Individuals who did not fit neatly into these ranks had to demonstrate historical interest and scholarship before being elected to residential membership. Isaiah Thomas of Worcester gave the Massachusetts Historical Society several gifts of newspapers and periodicals.

A wealthy printer and businessman, he did not have a college degree and practiced a trade. Despite his donations, the professionals who led the Society did not elect him as a member until shortly after he published a two-volume *History of Printing in America* in 1810. By that time, he was on the cusp of organizing the American Antiquarian Society, claiming for himself and that society the term "antiquarian" in contrast to the more professionally restrictive "historian."[40]

Historical societies relied on elected officers more than other members. These men served as gatekeepers to the societies, disseminating ideas of appropriate collections and accepting donations. As a group, they formed a narrow subset of society at large. They were primarily college-educated, American-born white men of Anglo-American descent practicing law or serving as ministers. The Massachusetts Historical Society benefited from a core of doers, particularly in the critical position of corresponding secretary. Belknap was the first to fill this office, from 1791 until his death seven years later, and set a high standard for activity. Boston minister John Eliot succeeded him and maintained an active correspondence with members and contacts, in addition to playing a role in the Society's continued publication program, serving on the Publications Committee, and contributing a number of items for the *Collections*. He served in the position for fifteen years. His successor, Rev. Abiel Holmes, filled the position for an even longer term of twenty years. This stable leadership helped keep the Society from failing after under any one leader who might die or move away.[41]

New England society membership rolls had a particularly homogenous character. Massachusetts Historical Society founders and officers generally shared a place of birth (Massachusetts), alma mater (Harvard), and religion (Congregational). More than two-thirds of the twenty-six men elected to society office before 1820 were lawyers or Congregational ministers, serving the established church in the state although favoring liberal Unitarian doctrines over conservative Trinitarian. The American Antiquarian Society's founders and officers likewise mostly hailed from Massachusetts, attended Harvard, and were Congregationalists, later Unitarians.

Early New England historical societies boasted a sizable share of clergy—at first. Then the clergy became too politically partisan, aligned with the Federalist Party due to shared condemnation of the French Revolution and concerns over democracy. The clergy largely retreated from public guardianship of the political sphere by 1820 to organizing public order through the development of a domain of moral citizenship. This move from politics and order to morality caused some New England historians to reevaluate the place and influence of ministers in historical societies. Shortly after helping found the New Hampshire Historical Society in 1823, lawyer John Kelly noted "our clerical brethren seem to wish that they may have more of their order as associates." Kelly was concerned this would give the ministers "control of the Society" and preferred "to have a due proportion of the members from different professions."[42]

The founders of both the Massachusetts Historical and American Antiquarian societies came of age before or during the American Revolution and were committed to the idea of the nation. The historical society founders were in their thirties and forties when they established the Society. The average age at first election to office was thirty-seven. The youngest of the Massachusetts society officers, lawyer Josiah Quincy, was elected a member at the age of twenty-four. He was a counselor and treasurer for over twenty years, while also holding state and national elective offices. Sixteen other men also held historical society offices for more than ten years, eleven of those for more than twenty years, and three (lawyers John Davis and James Savage and physician Redford Webster) for approximately forty years. On average, the antiquarian society founders were a decade older than the historical society founders, and the officers served shorter terms.[43]

The New-York Historical Society boasted a more diverse membership than Massachusetts with respect to religion, education, and profession. The New-York society included Episcopalians, Lutherans, Presbyterians, and Quakers. Five of the founders had traveled to New York from Europe, and other founders and officers originally hailed from portions of the Northeast outside New York. They received their education at a variety of institutions including Columbia (formerly King's College), Princeton, Harvard, Yale, Pennsylvania, Aberdeen, and Edinburgh. While the founders featured relatively equal numbers of ministers and lawyers, the latter dominated the officer ranks over the first sixteen years. Half of the officers served for more than ten years, but only three did so for twenty or more years (lawyer Anthony Bleecker, physician David Hosack, and merchant John Pintard, all founders). Thus not only was the New York society more diverse, but officers served for shorter durations.[44]

Befitting the relative heterogeneity of the mid-Atlantic elite, the American Philosophical Society's Historical and Literary Committee and

Historical Society of Pennsylvania were more like the society of New York than Massachusetts. Two of the three Historical Committee officers were born in Europe: Du Ponceau in France and Vaughan in England. The short-lived, Philadelphia-based Religious Historical Society included Baptists, Episcopalians, Presbyterians, and Reformed Dutch ministers. The vast majority of members across the societies were professional white men of Anglo-American descent affiliated with Protestant denominations.

The Massachusetts and New York societies each boasted state and nationally elected officials among their founders and officers, but societies enjoyed at best little political influence. Had the founders been able to shape state or national policy to achieve their aims, they probably would not have established societies in the first place. Several members of each society served in state legislatures and Congress. Others held statewide offices (attorney general, secretary of state), and a few became state governors including James Sullivan and Christopher Gore of the Massachusetts Historical Society and DeWitt Clinton of the New-York Historical Society. Sullivan and Clinton were Jeffersonian Republicans who disagreed with Federalist society officers on many political matters, but societies were bipartisan. Boston historian Hannah Mather Crocker described the ideal historical society as "consist[ing] of no particular party or sect" dedicated only to "preserving and extending knowledge to future generations." For practical purposes, having highly placed allies in both parties increased the odds of obtaining governmental assistance.[45]

Officers endorsed political bipartisanship but did not extend membership across racial or gender lines. They excluded Americans of African, Asian, or other non-northwestern European descent from membership for decades, even centuries. This contributed to Pennsylvanians of African descent eventually forming the Afro-American Historical Society in 1897.

Society laws did not bar women from membership, but social customs restricted them to supporting roles. Lawyer William Rawle Sr. of Philadelphia opened the door for women's involvement in the Historical Society of Pennsylvania, albeit in a limited fashion. A member of the American Philosophical Society's Historical and Literary Committee, he attributed the committee's failure to its restrictions limiting membership to American Philosophical Society members. Rawle proposed the Historical Society of Pennsylvania establish three membership tiers: one for individuals living in or near Philadelphia, a second for other Pennsylvanians, and a third, open to all Americans, into which "females may be admitted." Rawle had a specific female in mind for the third-class membership: local antiquarian Deborah Norris Logan. She controlled an important cache of the papers of her husband's grandfather, early Pennsylvania statesman James Logan, once secretary to colony founder William Penn. Rawle did not consult her in advance. Logan heard a rumor that she had joined the Society a few months after his amendments passed. Expressing surprise, she wrote to a friend that she believed the Society "ha[d] no Honorary Members and if they had they do not want women." Moreover, she did not consider women members in keeping with "the retirement and modesty which I think we ought never to loose sight of." A few years later, her name appeared on the list of honorary members, but the Historical Society of Pennsylvania did not extend membership privileges to women for almost forty more years, in 1862, at which time it also welcomed foreign-born members.[46]

The Massachusetts Historical Society elected a female member in 1849, one year after American women first demanded the franchise at the historic Seneca Falls Convention, but with important caveats. James Savage, then president, oversaw election of Connecticut historian Frances Caulkins as a corresponding member in no small part due to Savage's admiration for her work. The election was likely unsolicited on her part, as she did not visit the Society, attend meetings, or contribute to publications. The Massachusetts society did not admit another woman as a member for more than a century, until 1966.[47]

While society members came from among the European American elite, most did not rank among the highest echelons of politics, religion, or money. Few of their names were known far and wide in their own time or after.

"For the General Benefit of Society": Accumulating Collections

Historical societies lacked sufficient financial resources to accumulate large collections by purchase and instead relied on donations. Society officers therefore had to offer donors sufficient value to justify their entrusting the societies with valued materials. Historical societies offered their contributors a variety of benefits including public acknowledgment, affirmation of historical value and ancestral importance, and assumption of care and housing for contributed items. Many donors, particularly individuals and families, accepted these as fair exchange. In turn, motivated donors in control of desirable gifts could affect the development of collections.[48]

Society officers also served as arbiters of historical value. Donors' letters often deferred to societies determination of whether items should be included in society collections. While rhetorical, the deferrals contained a layer of truth for societies often reviewed materials and selected some for accession while returning others. By accepting materials, societies affirmed historical value, confirming collectors' discernment and reassuring family members of their ancestors' historical importance. For their part, societies published lists of donors in newspapers and their own publications, naming donors, describing their gifts, and publicizing their generosity. Corresponding secretaries or other officers regularly wrote personal letters of acknowledgment.

In addition, society officers assumed responsibilities to care for donated materials: housing gifts, organizing them, and making them available through publications or library visiting hours. Finances constrained societies' ability to do this; nevertheless, officers proclaimed their interest in taking "custody" of materials so as to preserve them "for the general benefit of society." Officers welcomed both donations where ownership was transferred to the receiving society and deposits wherein societies undertook custody and care of items but the depositing individuals retained ownership. The Rhode Island Historical Society received a silver sword hanger from a donor who believed his uncle had used it during the Revolution—on the condition that it would be returned should the giver "Ever be Called uppon to Fight the battles of My Country."[49]

The societies collected a vast array of materials. Print and manuscript items for societies' libraries predominated, although societies also accessioned indigenous artifacts and natural history specimens for their cabinets. Even societies with limited existences accumulated resources during their periods of activity. The larger the collections, the greater need for space and care in housing.

"A Plain, Economical Style": Rooms, Buildings, and Furniture

Societies faced a variety of expenses, not least obtaining facilities, furnishing them, and caring for their collections. While in-kind support addressed some needs, others required cash. Many societies' annual meetings included addresses from invited lecturers, often prominent members, followed by elaborate banquets. Officers also hosted lectures, participated in historical celebrations, and bore the cost to print and distribute publications.

Space was a primary need for societies, to house libraries and cabinets. Boston businessmen William Scollay, Charles Bulfinch, and Charles Vaughan donated a room in a new Boston building in 1794 for the Massachusetts

Historical Society's use. Forty feet long, twenty-five feet wide, and twenty feet high, it belonged to the Society "for ever" on payment of a token fee of five shillings. The Society remained there for nearly forty years. The American Antiquarian Society received the title to its building, Antiquarian Hall, as part of a bequest on the death of founder Isaiah Thomas. The American Philosophical Society's historical committee enjoyed its parent society's hall, while the New-York Historical Society relied on government assistance for rooms in government buildings.[50]

While it helped to have rooms or whole buildings, this was not enough. These required finishing: painting and other refinements, along with furnishings such as shelving, tables, and chairs. The Massachusetts Historical Society appointed a committee to finish their new rooms in "a plain, economical style." Thomas had a building erected for the American Antiquarian Society, but the Society was responsible for finishing it with "alcoves and other accommodations" for the library and cabinet. In some instances, the rooms holding libraries and cabinets were not suitable for members to meet. The American Antiquarian Society held three of four quarterly meetings in Boston during its early years and in the first year paid at least fourteen dollars to rent rooms in Boston's Exchange Coffee House. Similarly, the Massachusetts Historical Society's facilities were primarily a storage space, and it rarely held regular meetings there before 1833, preferring members' houses.[51]

The process of arranging and moving into new facilities often took years from start to finish. The Massachusetts Historical Society decided in 1825 to relocate due to a lack of storage space and concerns about vulnerability to fire. Eight years passed before officers arranged a new location, in turn sufficiently crowded within ten years to set the Society searching for more space. Similarly, the board of the Rhode Island Historical Society noted the lack of space and dangers of fire in 1839 but required six years to finance and raise a new building. In the early 1840s, American Antiquarian Society librarian Samuel F. Haven recognized the risk of storing materials in the cellar while Antiquarian Hall rotted around them. The Society's Council admitted the need for a new and improved situation a few years later.[52]

Newer, younger, and smaller societies did not require their own buildings. In the western portions of the nation, the young, Jefferson-based Missouri Historical and Philosophical Society was granted room in the state capitol building after organization in 1844. The legislature also assisted the Society in furnishing the rooms, albeit with a spending limit of ninety dollars—a boon to the Society, which had less than twenty dollars in the treasury. At much the same time, wealthy Connecticut art patron Daniel Wadsworth decided to erect a gallery of fine arts in Hartford. Educator Henry Barnard persuaded Wadsworth to add space for the Connecticut Historical Society and the Hartford Young Men's Institute (which became the Hartford Public Library). The building also housed the Natural History Society.[53]

In addition, historical society collections required care. Often societies spent money to bind newspapers, periodicals, and pamphlets as a preservative measure. Isaiah Thomas recorded instances where he paid to have newspapers and pamphlets bound for the American Antiquarian Society library, and considered the expense part of his many contributions. For the most part, societies sought to keep their expenditures within their means. They relied on officers and members for unpaid, voluntary labor to process and arrange libraries, cabinets, and publications, with a few exceptions. No society had enough money to fund all desired initiatives.[54]

"Generous, Well-Heeled Patrons": Benefactors, and the Lack Thereof

Money equaled power for historical societies. Financial resources, or the lack thereof, constrained officers' ability to carry out society objectives. Societies had two primary sources of funding: members and governments. In both cases, they competed with other organizations and had to prove their requests deserved the money they asked for.

Although many individuals donated large amounts to learned organizations in general, most historical societies received limited assistance and were forced to rely on members for operating funds. In Britain, popular and fashionable societies drew contributions from large numbers, particularly societies organized around religious purposes. British societies able to attract wealthy patrons willing to give sizable donations also fared well financially, while American historical societies went begging for large or small donations. The Massachusetts Historical Society and American Antiquarian Society typically had less than two hundred dollars on hand for use during the first decades of the nineteenth century, while the New-York Historical Society teetered on the edge of bankruptcy.[55]

Unfortunately, American historical societies had comparatively few benefactors willing to contribute cash. Any gifts of coins and currency specimens were intended for preservation in collections. The Massachusetts Historical Society's first president, lawyer and commonwealth attorney general James

Sullivan of Boston, gave the Society two hundred dollars he received for the copyright to his history of Maine and later donated the copyright to his history of Massachusetts land titles. Philadelphia editor Ebenezer Hazard donated twenty dollars in response to Belknap's plea for support, and member Elias Boudinot of New Jersey and non-member merchant Samuel Eliot of Boston each gave the Society fifty dollars. These were the exceptions, not the rule. Out of over one thousand gifts mentioned in the Massachusetts society's minutes or acknowledged in its *Collections*, less than 1 percent included cash for the Society treasury.[56]

Historical societies' youth and lack of status were factors in their receiving limited philanthropic support. Eliot donated fifty dollars to the Massachusetts Historical Society, but gave twenty thousand dollars to Harvard to support classical Greek studies and an additional five thousand dollars for the college library. The Massachusetts Historical Society conducted a subscription to pay for new and larger facilities in 1832 and 1833. The subscription raised the targeted amount, thanks in part to major contributions from member James Bowdoin and non-members Samuel Appleton, Peter Chardon Brooks, and Jonathan Phillips, each of whom gave three hundred dollars. In stark contrast, Harvard College, partly because it was more than a century old and had very high status, received numerous gifts exceeding five thousand dollars in the previous quarter century. Wealthy merchants supported the Massachusetts society more as it grew in age, stature, and connections to Harvard.[57]

Isaiah Thomas was the exception to the lack of large-scale benefactors, but even he did not give the American Antiquarian Society, which was largely his creation, extensive cash support while alive. When the Society set out to publish its first volume of *Transactions*, Thomas loaned the necessary amount. Similarly, he constructed a building at his own expense when the Society proved unable to raise sufficient funds but retained title to the property. He encouraged other supporters of the Society to donate money to a hire a librarian rather than paying for one himself.[58]

On the other hand, Thomas was generous to the American Antiquarian Society in his will. He left the Society its building, cash, and income-generating property, valued at more than thirty thousand dollars. Thomas also gave three hundred dollars in cash or books each to the American Philosophical Society, American Academy of Arts and Sciences, Harvard University, and the historical societies of Massachusetts and New York.[59]

Without major beneficiaries, the most dependable income for historical societies came from membership fees. Many societies required newly elected resident members to pay an initial fee, after which came annual dues, generally assessed at the rate of two dollars. These constituted a burden for the less wealthy. The New-York Historical Society doubled their annual dues in the 1820s, from two to four dollars, to help relieve the pressure of growing debts. Other societies maintained the original rate of two dollars per year. On occasion, the Massachusetts Historical Society temporarily increased the dues by fifty cents for the new library catalog in 1811, and two years later by one dollar and fifty cents for the newest volume of *Collections*. Otherwise, officers did not change dues until 1839, when the charge rose to three dollars. Corresponding and honorary members were exempt from such fees.[60]

Since most societies operated on shoestring budgets, they could not afford salaried librarians. There were a few exceptions. The American Antiquarian Society paid librarians following Thomas's death thanks to his generous bequest. The Massachusetts Historical Society voted in the 1830s to pay an assistant librarian one hundred dollars to spend six months arranging materials, and nine years later gave Rev. Joseph B. Felt, librarian, only a little more for a year of his services. In New York, librarian George H. Moore kept the New-York Historical Society library open for several hours beginning in the 1840s. Also in that decade, Connecticut Historical Society officers arranged to hire bibliophile Rev. Thomas Robbins. The Connecticut-born Robbins was a pastor of a church over the border in Massachusetts at the time of his hiring. He had served in Connecticut parishes and was pleased to return to the state. He negotiated payment of six hundred dollars per year on the condition that he would leave his library to the Society. Robbins's pay was in keeping with his standing as a minister, as many of his contemporaries received between five hundred and a thousand dollars. The Connecticut society used a variety of means including membership dues and subscriptions to cover costs.[61]

Most organizations, including some churches, had to deal with absentee members and unpaid dues. Historical society officers often complained of members failing to pay assessments. The Massachusetts Historical Society approved an addition to the laws and regulations in its first decade stipulating failure to pay the annual assessment for three years meant forfeiture of membership, although this was not necessarily carried out. The Massachusetts society voted to have the treasurer report the names of members who failed to pay their annual assessments, almost two decades later, when they decided it was time to enforce the requirement. The American Antiquarian Society passed bylaws offering a diploma of membership as a reward for prompt payment of annual fees, and advised that members who did not pay the six-dollar membership fee, after a one-year warning, would be removed from the rolls. Members Rejoice Newton and Edward D. Bangs suggested abolishing the annual fee entirely and lowering the admission fee for life membership after four years, in hopes it would raise more revenue, but the recommendation was tabled. Despite the difficulties of collection, membership fees were the bedrock of society finances.[62]

"For the Encouragement of History": Government Support

From the outset, societies petitioned the federal government for support. One of the earliest petitions involved requests for copies of public documents. Officers of the Massachusetts Historical Society asked Congress for copies of government publications shortly after the Society was established. The request went through Society member Congressman Peleg Coffin Jr. of Boston. The petition failed, but the officers turned their attention to the Executive Branch with greater success. The Society sent copies of its first *Collections* to Connecticut-based corresponding member Oliver Wolcott Jr. who, as secretary of the treasury, donated copies of congressional journals and committee reports, presidential messages, financial documents, and reports of the secretaries of state, war, navy, and the treasury. Massachusetts Congressman Josiah Quincy and New Hampshire Senator William Plumer Sr. also gathered government documents.[63]

The American Antiquarian Society likewise collected government documents. The Society considered itself a national organization, but incorporated at the state level out of concern the national government lacked the power to grant an act of incorporation, at least outside the District of Columbia. In its petition, the American Antiquarian Society "ask[ed] for no other aid" from Massachusetts than the benefits of incorporation. As it turned out, the Society did solicit additional assistance from the Commonwealth, requesting copies of state laws and publications. The Society requested laws and publications from other states in the nation, and most obliged.[64]

While the Massachusetts Historical Society was unsuccessful in getting Congress in its first decade to donate documents, the American Antiquarian Society's timing was better. In response to the American Antiquarian

Society's request, Congress ordered two hundred copies of legislative materials printed in addition to the regular copies for members of Congress. Twenty-five were reserved for the Library of Congress. State and territorial executives, state and territorial legislature branches, universities, colleges, and historical societies each received a copy. The antiquarian society's request in the early nineteenth century contributed to the dissemination of government documents to local institutions in the nineteenth, twentieth, and twenty-first centuries, late nineteenth-century creation of the Federal Depository Library Program, and similar preservation of state government publications.[65]

Governments supported societies through a variety of means, allowing the use of rooms within city or state buildings, giving permission to run lotteries, and allocating land grants. Most historical societies benefited from government assistance. Some would not have survived without it.

The New-York Historical Society and the Edge of Bankruptcy

The New-York Historical Society received extensive governmental support, yet faltered and nearly failed. Most historical societies operated on shoestring budgets, but according to the sesquicentennial history of the New York society, "it didn't even have a shoestring to begin with." Instead, the Society benefited from DeWitt Clinton, then mayor of New York City, and John Pintard, clerk of the city corporation, being among its founders. Orphaned shortly after his birth, Pintard's merchant uncle Lewis Pintard raised him in New York. Educated at the College of New Jersey (now Princeton), John Pintard served as his uncle's assistant, provisioning American prisoners of war during the Revolution, and later established himself in New York City as the kind of man entrusted with day-to-day organizational roles. Between 1787 and 1791 he was New York City alderman, a trustee of the New York Society Library (a subscription library), secretary of the New York Manufacturing Society, first sagamore of the Tammany Society (a political organization), New York agent for the sale of Belknap's *History of New Hampshire*, and an active mason.[66]

Before establishing the New-York Historical Society, Pintard negotiated permission for the Tammany Society's American Museum to be lodged in City Hall. In a similar fashion, he and Clinton arranged for the historical society to occupy a room in the Old City Hall rent-free for five years. Even societies with separate facilities occasionally conducted their meetings within government buildings. The Massachusetts society held its first post-incorporation meeting in the Massachusetts State House in 1794.

Other learned organizations also benefited from government-subsidized accommodations.[67]

Under Clinton New York City hosted numerous cultural organizations in government buildings. The city provided space and furnishings on several occasions. The New-York Historical Society needed new rooms in 1809. The American Academy of Arts, which obtained use of the second floor of the city-owned Government House through Clinton's support, offered a room to the New York society. The College of Physicians later occupied a portion of the building as well. The Society had little money, and the city partly provided the furnishings of the room. Pintard found several mahogany tables in City Hall that once belonged to Congress and secured permission to put them to the Society's use. The city further supported the Society by permitting it to use a room in the city hall for a discourse by Rev. Samuel Miller on the two-hundredth anniversary of Henry Hudson's discovery of New York, while the city comptroller paid for refreshments served at the event.[68]

The New-York Historical Society sought incorporation and financial support from the State of New York in 1809. The State passed an act incorporating the Society for a term of fifteen years, a sharp contrast to the acts of incorporation that Massachusetts granted to the historical and antiquarian societies, which didn't include term limits. As a state senator, Clinton led efforts to pass a bill to further support the Society in the New York Senate, then dominated by fellow Jeffersonian Republicans. The Senate paired the measure to aid the New York society with one for "killing the wolves and panthers" in the still partly wild state, thus combining the interests of frontier Republicans and city elites. Clinton was successful and the bill passed the Senate unopposed. Both Pintard, a Federalist, and fellow member Samuel L. Mitchill, a Tammany Republican, New York assemblyman, and naturalist, lobbied the Federalist-dominated assembly, but neither fared as well. Mitchill was "mortifi[ed]" to admit the assembly had rejected the bill "for the destruction of wild beasts, and for the encouragement of history."[69]

Despite its failure to obtain state funding, the New York society expanded its library and cabinet and outgrew the room in Government House. Pintard cast a covetous eye on the city Alms House and on Bridewell prison. When the city planned to move the inmates to newer quarters at Bellevue and abandon the buildings, Pintard suggested to Clinton that cultural institutions, such as the Society, be allowed to take over one of the buildings. Before departing as mayor, Clinton helped Pintard petition the city and the old Alms House was renamed the New York Institution, housing the New-York Historical Society, American Academy of Fine Arts, and the Literary and Philosophical Society of New York—all organizations connected with Clinton and Pintard.[70]

New York and Massachusetts both assisted historical societies without handing over cash. The New York legislature allowed the New-York Historical Society to conduct a lottery to raise twelve thousand dollars. Massachusetts gave the Massachusetts Historical Society an early grant of unsettled lands, as well as copyright to a map of the state that the Massachusetts society was authorized to produce. Societies could not, however, assume that states would provide assistance. The American Antiquarian Society petitioned the Massachusetts Commonwealth for permission to run a lottery in 1814, which was denied.[71]

While the New-York Historical Society enjoyed extensive government aid, it wound up deeply in debt. The Society depended in part on Pintard, a cash-strapped founder whose resources did not live up to his philanthropic desires. He offered the Society his sizable collection of books on American history but was not wealthy enough to give his library to the Society outright and instead proposed to sell it at cost. The Society agreed and, in 1809, managed to gather enough funds to make an initial payment and acquire the library. It did not pay him in full, and thus one of the Society's first debts was owed to Pintard.[72]

New York society officers lived beyond the Society's means. Although they had few financial resources, members celebrated the two-hundredth anniversary of Hudson's trip to what became New York with an address and a lavish dinner. A year later, the New York society celebrated St. Nicholas Day in a similar fashion. The dinner took place at the Washington Hotel, where "a table was most sumptuously spread for them . . . both as to choice wines and delicate viands." Officers repeated the combination of annual meeting, dinner, and celebration of Saint Nicholas Day yearly, regardless of ongoing debt issues. Members paid for their meals and drinks, but the New York society covered any differences between the dinner costs and member subscriptions. In contrast, the Massachusetts Historical Society celebrated the tricentennial of Columbus's arrival in the Americas followed by a feast but otherwise did not have annual celebrations and lavish meals. While the dinners by themselves did not put the New York society in a hole, they contributed to rising debts.[73]

In addition, the New-York Historical Society officers spent money they couldn't afford on lasting materials: books and manuscripts for the library and artifacts and specimens for the cabinet. Most of the Society's accessions at the time came from gifts, but it purchased some materials. The Society also published a volume of *Collections*, an expensive undertaking that rarely turned a profit.[74]

Financing these required taking out loans, which in turn began accruing interest. The Society's delicate financial position helped motivate the successful 1814 petition for aid from the state. Because the grant took the form of a lottery, the Society did not receive the money immediately. Rather than holding off until funds trickled in, the Society borrowed more money, which officers spent on books, manuscripts, and publication of two volumes of *Collections*, along with its first library catalog. Once the Society moved into the New York Institution, leaders opted to emphasize collecting natural history specimens, which entailed purchasing display cabinets. At the same time, the Society became the first historical society with a paid staff: a sub-librarian was hired at one hundred dollars per year to keep the library open twice a week for three hours at a time.[75]

Alas, money from the lottery was slow to arrive. Dr. John W. Francis, then the New-York Historical Society's librarian, assumed a loan on the Society's behalf. Debts remained, accruing to the point the Society sold the lottery to Union College for $8,000 in the early 1820s. Despite the sale, the Society carried debts totaling more than $10,000. Officers instituted cost-saving measures including closing the library. They renewed efforts to collect overdue funds, and raised the annual membership fee from $2 to $4, measures that reduced the debts to $7,500. One-fifth of that sum was owed to the Washington Insurance Company for an old loan, two-fifths to Francis, and two-fifths to Pintard, although the latter two had already forgiven substantial debts.[76]

Surveying the situation, a New-York Historical Society committee recognized the existence of a prime asset and circulated a notice offering for sale at public auction the "choice and rare Library." The committee hoped other New York City learned societies would come together to purchase the collection as a whole, rather than allow "the scattering" of the contents through sale in lots. After all, earlier in the year, the New York Athenæum, City Library, and historical society discussed combining their collections into a single library. The *New-York American* and *New York Spectator* published articles suggesting that, since the library might "be purchased cheap," the Athenæum directors should step in. Failing this, newspapers along the Atlantic seaboard wondered if New Yorkers might donate money to prevent the sale. The Philadelphia-based *National Gazette* hoped wealthy New Yorkers would not allow such an "evil" to come to pass, as the dispersal of the library would be "a public misfortune." The New York City *Spectator* considered the situation "highly discreditable to the city." Citizens of other cities would "laugh at us," and Bostonians would find the sale amusing, for if the Massachusetts Historical Society faced "the same circumstances, [we believe] the money, for its redemption would be contributed in seven hours."[77]

The news prompted members of at least one other historical society to worry about the impact on society collecting. "What security will there be to future donors that their donations shall be sacredly preserved, if societies can dispose of such gifts without the consent of the donors?" antiquarian John Farmer of Concord, New Hampshire, asked fellow New Hampshire Historical Society member John Kelly. Farmer concluded future gifts would come with additional strings attached to prevent such occurrences. At the same time, he wondered if the New Hampshire society should send a committee to the sale. Kelly, however, considered the proposal "nothing more than an attempt to arouse those who have a regard for the literary honor of their state to a little needed liberality." They need not send a committee to the sale because it wouldn't take place.[78]

Tension over debts exacerbated differences within the New-York Historical Society membership over its nature and purpose. Physician David Hosack, a founding member and Society president from 1820 to 1827, favored increasing dues yet again to raise revenue. He and several fellow officers considered the Society as a quasi-public organization with a responsibility to gather and protect historical treasures as a public trust. Another faction, led by Charles King and William Gracie, viewed the Society as a private gentlemen's club with embarrassing financial difficulties which should be settled by selling resources. In March 1825 King and Gracie proposed giving the debts committee power to sell the library and cabinet with the condition that they be purchased whole and deposited with another learned institution in the city. This answered the Hosack faction's primary objection, against scattering the collections, but did not please them. Members quarreled over whether to sell only nonessential materials or the library, differences rising to the point that officers and standing committee members walked out of a committee meeting. The split Society did not sell the library, but neither did officers hold another meeting for nine months.[79]

Second vice president John Trumbull attributed the split to a conflict of interest. Nine of the ten members of King and Gracie's faction belonged to the New York Athenæum, which wished to acquire the New-York Historical Society's library. In this light, the articles circulating in New York City newspapers at the time about the proposed sale—and hopes that the Athenæum might step in and purchase the library "cheap"—may have reflected lobbying for the King-Gracie faction. Trumbull had other objections as well. Even if there were no conflicts of interest, he considered sale of gifts held in trust illegal.[80]

In addition, the New-York Historical Society's act of incorporation expired a year before the crisis. The terms of the original act prohibited use of Society funds for any purpose not "contemplated by this act." If the Society were found to have violated the specification, its property "vest[ed] in the people of this State." The clause left open to interpretation the legality of the Society's potential sale, even to the New York Athenæum, despite the act's expiration. Other states did not include similar clauses in historical society acts of incorporation.[81]

The State of New York came to the rescue, affirming the New-York Historical Society as a quasi-public organization chartered to serve the public good. After extensive discussions, the state renewed the act of incorporation, reinstated the Society's previous slate of officers, and found a way to justify granting funds to the Society. State senator John C. Spencer acknowledged a popular "repugnance to appropriate monies from the treasury" but argued the Society's case was unusual and required action. Surely the legislature and people of New York would not "suffer one of the proudest monuments of our enterprise to perish for the want of the very small sum." No individual could accumulate collections of books and manuscripts on the scale of the Society, for "*public institutions* alone are competent to the object," and with its official charter, the Society acted on behalf of the state and its people—and therefore deserved rescue with public money. The legislature and governor imposed one condition: that the Society manage to discharge all remaining debts, which it did, save for one. Pintard was unable to produce documents to back up his claim for approximately $1,400, and the Society refused to pay. In effect, the Society balanced its books at Pintard's expense.[82]

Dealing with the New-York Historical Society's debts threw into sharp relief different ideas about the nature of the Society. Through renewal of the incorporation and the state's gift of funds, the Hosack faction affirmed the Society as a quasi-public organization intended to contribute to the public good. The process exhausted the officers. At the next annual meeting, all but two officers and members of the standing committee declined to stand for reelection. The Society went into eclipse.

"Like Lazarus 'It Sleepeth'": Failures and Partial Successes

The New York society's period of dormancy was not an exception. Many early societies did not remain active long. Some became inactive for periods of time while others failed entirely. These warrant consideration alongside successes, for they litter the first decades of organized historical preservation in the United States.

The first attempt to pair historical protection with a learned organization highlighted two problems: low number of active supporters and shifting or conflicting ideas about means and goals. Shortly after discussing the possibility of an historical organization with Belknap in 1790, Pintard created the American Museum to carry out the work in New York City. He was a trustee of the American Museum, its first secretary, and the force behind its creation. Rather than organize a stand-alone society in his first attempt, he "engrafted an antiquarian scheme of a museum" on the flourishing Tammany Society.[83]

The American Museum was intended to serve many functions, but high on Pintard's list was preservation of historical materials: "every thing relating to the history of America." He sufficiently impressed city officials to obtain a room for the museum in City Hall. The Tammany Society printed and circulated a broadside proclaiming the museum's creation and purpose, and soliciting contributions to be sent to Pintard's care, and donations began to roll in. As secretary, Pintard was well positioned to influence the development of the museum. He did not create the museum alone; Tammany Society member Gardner Baker, a natural-born promoter, joined Pintard in organizing it. Baker served as the museum's day-to-day keeper, in charge of depositing donations in the museum and admitting visitors at appointed times.[84]

In less than a year, external events separated Pintard from the museum. First, as a Federalist, he was concerned with the Tammany Society's shift in favor of Jeffersonian Republican politics. He left the Society over the matter, although he remained friends with Baker, a Republican. Second, Pintard was involved with New York financier William Duer, who manipulated stocks with the assistance of Pintard and others. Duer defaulted on his debts. Pintard, who had cosigned many of Duer's notes, fled to New Jersey amid the panic following Duer's default and arrest. He remained there for many years, resigning or forfeiting all his positions in New York organizations. After his return he spent a year and a half in debtor's prison.[85]

Baker took over the museum, without Pintard's support and patronage. The Tammany Society had originally intended the museum to be free to visitors, but soon recognized the cost of maintaining the collection. Visitors could pay an admission fee of two shillings per person per visit or pay a dollar for a year's entry. To attract visitors and make the museum self-supporting, Baker emphasized the sensational rather than the historical. He advertised the "Museum & Wax-Work," now located at the exchange rather than city hall, as a place to see curiosities including an "Ourang Outang" and "East-India Porcupine." The Tammany Society relinquished all claim to the museum in 1795, acknowledging Baker's labors—or paying their debt to Baker—by giving him the museum in lieu of wages. After leaving debtor's prison a few years later, Pintard regained standing and influence in New York City, but he did not attempt to establish another American Museum. Instead, he joined with other New York City gentlemen to form the New-York Historical Society.[86]

Similarly, in Philadelphia the Historical and Literary Committee of the American Philosophical Society's overreliance on Peter Du Ponceau's labors led away from general historical collecting. While conducting correspondence on behalf of the committee, Du Ponceau, a gifted linguist, became interested in Native American languages. The committee's first volume of *Transactions*, published in 1819, consisted almost entirely of articles relating to languages. The second volume, published when the committee was largely moribund, featured a treatise on languages presented in the form of a letter from Du Ponceau to Vaughan.[87]

Du Ponceau's preoccupation with languages contributed to the decline of the committee. Philadelphian philanthropist Roberts Vaux wrote to local historian and antiquarian Dr. John F. Watson in 1824, advising him not to donate to the Society. Vaux, a member of the Society and the committee, described the Society as "sluggish" while the committee "ha[d] collected much material for History, which will *sleep the sleep of death.*" The Society revitalized, but the committee became defunct.[88]

Further north, the Connecticut Historical Society failed within two years due to loss of prime movers. Judge John Trumbull and other Connecticut leaders petitioned the state for permission to incorporate the Society in 1825. The organizers—staunch Connecticut Federalists—viewed history as a means to oppose the rise of Jacksonian democracy through affirmation of Connecticut's previous virtue as a "land of steady habits." They also responded to the upwelling of commemoration connected to the Marquis de Lafayette's tour of the United States before the fiftieth anniversary of the Declaration of Independence. Unfortunately, Trumbull departed the state soon afterward and the Society became inactive.[89]

Many historical societies failed, and even active societies included periods of dormancy. The American Antiquarian Society appeared to be so inactive in 1829 that New Hampshire member John Farmer inquired if it was dead. No, replied its aging founder Isaiah Thomas, the Society was "not dead, but like Lazarus 'it sleepeth.'"[90]

Documenting Historical Societies

Historical societies did not give their own records the care and attention spent on older materials. Most surviving societies have holes in their archives. The American Antiquarian Society records reflect different hands and interest or time for record-keeping between founder Isaiah Thomas, librarian Christopher Columbus Baldwin who took over after Thomas's death, and Baldwin's successor Samuel Foster Haven. Indeed, many societies failed and left little to no evidence of their existence. Other historical society collections contain the records of some defunct societies. The Massachusetts Historical Society and New England Historic Genealogical Society each hold some of the Dorchester Historical and Antiquarian Society's records.[91]

As a preservative medium, print played an important role in documenting the existence of failed societies. Addresses reprinted in newspapers, pamphlets, and printed ephemera offer the clearest indication some societies existed. References to the Religious Historical Society, established in Philadelphia in the late 1810s, include articles in a local periodical and a printed circular with manuscript additions in the collections of the Library Company of Philadelphia.[92]

The Religious Historical Society embraced an even bigger objective than national history, nothing less than the whole of Christianity. Founded in Philadelphia in 1816, the Society affiliated with a local Presbyterian weekly. Nevertheless, in keeping with Philadelphia's religious diversity, the Society was interdenominational with "each [member] collecting the historical fragments of the section of the Church of Christ to which he belongs." Early officers included Presbyterian ministers Samuel B. Wylie, Ezra Stiles Ely, and Jacob J. Janeway, Dutch Reformed minister Jacob Brodhead, and Baptist minister William Staughton, all of Philadelphia, as well as Episcopalian divine James Milnor of New York. The Society also had members and officers who were not ministers, including merchant Robert Ralston and lawyer Nathaniel Chauncey.[93]

The Religious Historical Society may have originated in response to the organization of the American Philosophical Society's Historical and Literary Committee. In the first annual address given before the religious society, Wylie celebrated missionary and bible societies, and mentioned in passing "two species of history"—civil and religious. While illustrative of one another, "mere civil history" was only "the external shell, or visible machinery" compared to religious history. The Society's very breadth of mission contributed to its undoing. Those historical societies that did survive focused on narrower missions.[94]

Successful historical organizations left far more documentation than those who failed. The Religious Historical Society and the Historical and Literary Committee offer a sharp contrast with respect to surviving documentation. The parent society retained and preserved committee-related materials. The Religious Historical Society left little in contrast. Other individuals may have attempted to organize around the preservation of historical materials and either failed or left behind little to no known documentation of their labors.

Citizens began to establish historical societies organized around specific religious sects toward midcentury, to complement those centered on civil identities. Methodist minister Rev. James B. Finley called for a historical society in 1839 to preserve documentation of Methodism. Finley's call appeared in the *Western Christian Advocate*, a Methodist publication produced in Cincinnati. At the time, Cincinnati was one of the largest cities in the nation: the Queen City of the growing Northwest. Located on the Ohio River, it was at the center of immigrant and commercial networks stretching throughout the western states and territories. Although less than 5 percent of Cincinnati's population was Methodists, the sect located many of its activities in the city. More than a quarter million Methodists lived west of the Alleghenies in the Jacksonian era.[95]

The *Western Christian Advocate* played a key role connecting distant, isolated congregations, and editors supported Finley's call for a denominational historical society. Within a few months, a group of Cincinnati ministers and laymen gathered and established the Western Methodist Historical Society. Western Methodist founders considered other historical societies worth imitating; however, secular societies "collected the histories of civil society." In contrast, the Methodist society would gather materials for the history of the church. It was "a *moral duty* which we [the church] owe to God," harking back to colonial Massachusetts minister Cotton Mather and other Puritans' providential histories of New England colonies.[96]

Editors of the *Western Christian Advocate* mentioned other efforts as an added incentive for Methodists to spring into action. A Virginian minister had more than six hundred pages relating to the Protestant Episcopal church in that state. Baptists had collected information as well. The editors did not mention, and likely were unaware of, the Universalist Historical Society organized in Boston around 1834. To the faithful, it was not sufficient to include accounts of religion in broader works of American history. Denominations deserved attention in their own right as records of past sacrifices and services and as inspirations for present and future generations. Shortly after 1850, Presbyterians and Baptists each created historical societies in Philadelphia (Presbyterian Historical Society, 1852, and American Baptist Historical Society, 1853), with additional denominations following suit over the latter half of the century.[97]

The Western Methodist Historical Society suffered the fate of many related societies, surviving under a new name as the United Methodist Historical Society of Ohio. Subsequent officers deposited the Society's library and archives at Ohio Wesleyan University but did not include institutional records of the earlier periods. The Society produced a printed pamphlet in 1839. This and the *Western Christian Advocate* articles document the Society's early existence.

Early historical society founders and officers shaped the historical landscape. Their existence and successes, however narrow, stood in stark contrast to decades of individual actions. Quasi-public organizations maintained collections despite periods of dormancy. The societies collectively affirmed secular, nongovernmental action, in close affiliation with governments, as an operative means of historical preservation.

Equally, their successes reflected the potential for small groups of active individuals to make long-lasting decisions as to inclusion and exclusion. In setting precedents and becoming arbiters, society officers laid the organizations open to challenges from outside individuals who did not agree with their priorities—and internally from members with different ideas as to the societies' missions and functions. Historical collecting reflected the fractious macrocosm of the United States.

What early historical societies chose to collect and save determined, in great measure, the primary sources modern historians of early America use. The societies petitioned governments for financial support and encouraged state and federal involvement in the collection and preservation of public records as historical documents. Likewise, they amassed collections of early books, pamphlets, newspapers, manuscripts, artifacts, native antiquities, and natural specimens. These facilitated the production of documentary collections, dispersing copies of historical materials throughout the growing nation, the hemisphere, and the Atlantic world. Their publications disseminated and commented on ideas of history, underwriting the genre of local history. Further, their petitioning prompted governments to undertake some preservative measures.

Chapter Two

"So Divided and Subdivided"

Preserving Local Histories and Government Records

INSPIRED BY NEW ENGLAND HISTORIANS, New Orleans citizens organized the Louisiana Historical Society in the Jacksonian Era. Anglo-American men predominated on the membership rolls, but Society officers took a particular interest in documenting the state's diverse history, not least Louisiana colonial records located in Europe. In the process, they created a partnership of sorts with the state. When the Louisiana legislature appropriated two thousand dollars to obtain copies of Spanish records, the Society oversaw the project. Officers hired a Spanish agent who eventually sent important papers to the Louisiana secretary of state, historian Charles Gayarré.[1]

The Louisiana society similarly paired with the state to gather French records. Judge John Perkins Jr., a cotton planter and Society member, carried official letters from both the Society and the Louisiana governor when he visited France. Perkins found archival materials in disorder but managed to obtain two volumes of transcribed records comprising more than a thousand pages. The state purchased another thousand pages of extracts made by Felix Mange, editor of *L'Abeille de la Nouvelle-Orléans*, but Perkins advised the governor as many as sixty-one thousand pages of relevant archival materials remained. Perkins recommended that anyone deputed to undertake the project "receive his instructions from the [Louisiana] Historical Society, and have his commission signed by the Governor." The combination of state and Society would ensure the agent "ha[d] every facility extended to him."[2]

In effect, officers of the Louisiana Historical Society set themselves up as a quasi-independent state agency, blurring the lines between society and state. Other societies had more distant relations with state and local governments. Societies petitioned governments for support and preservative action, with varying success. The close affiliation between historical societies and governments reflected the import of political and civic or civil history in the eyes of society officers and government officials.

Most early historical societies organized to protect the histories of cities, counties, states, and nation—in short, civic polities. Anthropological scholarship on antiquarian and historical pursuits in Western culture indicates a strong connection between interest in historical and land- and place-based identities. Historical society officers prioritized political and civic or civil history, which fueled societies' advocacy on behalf of government records located within the United States or kept in European control. Petitions from societies also contributed to increased governmental action to preserve records, particularly at the state level. Officers encouraged federal and state governments to fund missions to European archives, surveyed state and federal record-keeping practices, and petitioned many of the thirteen original states to publish colonial records.[3]

Local and state identities fueled the proliferation of historical societies in the first half of the nineteenth century. Many societies came into being due to civic fears of being forgotten or overlooked. Although society members participated in collaborative actions and sometimes enjoyed membership in multiple historical organizations simultaneously, each society sought to ensure the history of a particular place and people was preserved and remembered. Societies' close affiliations with governments and government-based identities in turn fueled advocacy to gather and protect government records.

"An Authentic History of This Part of the Commonwealth": Fostering Local and State Identities

The second quarter of the nineteenth century witnessed a boom in historical society creation. Before 1819 five historical societies existed in three states (Massachusetts, New York, and Pennsylvania). During the 1820s alone, gentlemen from eleven states and territories established a total of thirteen new societies. The expansion of historical societies kept pace with and even exceeded the growth in population and number of states in the Union. Twenty-four of thirty-one states had a state historical society by midcentury, as did one territory (Minnesota). Although a number failed early on, several were reestablished. In addition, men organized county, city, and sect historical societies.[4]

American historical society founders may have known of developments in Europe, where provincial, county, and city historical societies proliferated over the first half of the nineteenth century. Antiquarians organized five county and local historical societies in England in the 1830s and three times as many the following decade. The number of historical organizations in Germany had a similar surge between 1833 and 1846, from at least twenty-four to sixty.[5]

Nevertheless, the growth of societies in the United States was as much an internal phenomenon as a response to external developments. Scholars have offered various explanations for the dramatic growth. Centennial and bicentennial celebrations of colonial settlements contributed, prompting organization of several societies. The jubilee of the Declaration of Independence intensified public interest in the American past. Aging veterans of the American Revolution were fading from the scene, providing another impetus for society establishment. Further, historical societies became signs of civilization in far-off frontier territories, especially as these organizations facilitated European-American assertions of control over the lands of Native American nations. Some settlers established societies even before territories gained statehood.[6]

Likewise, historians noted that early successes in New England reflected ideas of historical societies as means to affirm identities in the face of changes. Society founders and active members used the societies to maintain continuity and connection with the past for those remaining in New England as family members emigrated west. Historian Julian Boyd and librarian Leslie Dunlap posited Yankee migrants as the Johnny Appleseeds of historical societies, planting groups in Indiana (1830), Virginia (1831), Kentucky (1836), and Georgia (1839). Western and southern historical societies forged their own identities, incorporating local preferences and elevating their importance.[7]

Yet a broader range of institutional missions flourished than existing scholarship has considered, demonstrating that citizens founded historical societies to ensure different identities and histories were remembered. Most new societies—local, state, national—focused on places and governments, and their establishments reveal discontent with existing historical societies. People in various parts of the nation did not want others to collect, preserve, or write their histories. The spread of historical societies formed part of an ongoing discussion about what types of history and historical materials should be collected and protected, how historical materials should be gathered, and who should be involved with these processes. Or, at a more basic level, whose histories mattered.

"Within Our Own Reach": State Historical Societies

From the establishment of the second historical society in 1804, officers began to negotiate their fields of action. The New-York Historical Society, based in New York City, proclaimed a particular interest in materials documenting United States history generally but their state's history in specific. Similarly, the American Philosophical Society's Historical and Literary Committee readily ceded Massachusetts and New York to the existing historical societies and opted to focus on Pennsylvania and "other states where no analogous establishments have been formed."[8]

New England rivalries offer a clear example of the proliferation of historical societies organized around state identities to preserve local histories, affirm each state's importance, and claim state contributions. New Hampshire printer and historian Jacob B. Moore recommended the establishment of a local historical society in 1821, "rather to keep our materials . . . within our own reach, than to offer them to neighboring institutions." He no doubt had Massachusetts in mind, as the only New England state with historical and antiquarian societies at the time. The following year founders of the Rhode Island Historical Society warned that societies in nearby states, namely Massachusetts, "are every year draining this State of the historical documents and memorials with which it abounds." The creation of new societies offered members a means to affirm their states' history, identity, and importance against the overwhelming primacy of Massachusetts's historical narrative.[9]

State and territory residents were concerned that this lack of historical action might result in their absence from history. Establishing historical societies helped boost awareness of places' good qualities. The Rhode Island society founders worried other societies, namely the Massachusetts Historical Society, had acquired and preserved documentation pertaining to Rhode Island's revolutionary services but misinterpreted it "to the establishment of their own fame." James David Butler, a professor at Vermont's Norwich University, spoke before the Vermont Historical and Antiquarian Society in 1846 and raised similar concerns. A recent account of the taking of Ticonderoga in the American Revolution had described the action solely in terms of Connecticut and Massachusetts forces, while in truth "all but one sixth" were Vermonters. If his fellow state residents did not take action "it will be the play of Hamlet with the part of Hamlet omitted."[10]

In addition, civic leaders concerned about their state's character used historical societies to affirm and shape future generations. The founders of the Vermont Historical and Antiquarian Society believed history and awareness of Vermont's past contributions would help renew citizens' commitment to Vermont's moral character. Although the Society was weak, early members developed historical myths about Vermont, effectively fashioning a state identity that lasted for a century.[11]

As New England states struggled to find their historical voices, migrant New Englanders carried expectations of historical collection, preservation, and identity with them to other states and territories. The primary founder of the Indiana Historical Society, lawyer and editor John Hay Farnham, was born in Massachusetts, as were a quarter of the Society's founders. Massachusetts-born physician Edmund Jarvis was the first librarian of the Kentucky Historical Society, founded in 1838. Judge Benjamin Tappan, also Massachusetts born and raised, was the first president of the Historical and Philosophical Society of Ohio, and a fellow expatriate, Judge Henry A. Bullard, first president of the Louisiana Historical Society.[12]

Other expatriates carried loyalties to their prior residences and histories. For most of the 1830s, the New-York Historical Society was barely active. After moving to New York City, Rhode Island–born merchant and banker John R. Bartlett suggested the Rhode Island Historical Society turn its attention toward New York. "There is yet a wide field for Historical research," he noted, adding that "if other Societies leave their own field of operation untouched there is no impropriety in that of other States, turning up their furrows for them." Ironically, the Rhode Island society's stance against out-of-state acquisition of Rhode Island artifacts and manuscripts did not deter Bartlett from recommending officers take advantage of New York's period of in-operation, although they evidently declined to follow the suggestion.[13]

Historical societies established layered identities which allowed officers and members to reconcile interests in the histories of their respective states, regions, and the nation. The Georgia Historical Society proclaimed its "primary object" as documenting the "*History of the State of Georgia in particular, and of America generally.*" Most state and local historical societies used similar rhetoric to claim their spheres of action outward from city or county to state to nation to hemisphere. Virginia lawyer William C. Rives welcomed the reestablishment of the Virginia Historical and Philosophical Society as the Virginia Historical Society in 1846. Speaking before the Society, he argued that appreciation for a larger identity (national) depended on appreciation for the smaller (state), for "the more we love our State, the more we shall love the Union of which it forms a constituent and honored part." Amid growing sectional tensions, such proclamations reflected willingness to elevate state interests over national but also recognition that citizens belonged simultaneously to states and nations.[14]

"The Oldest Settlement": City and County Historical Societies

In addition to state historical societies, men founded local societies to affirm smaller identities in relation to the state and in negotiation with nearby or rival towns—to boost their fame and repute. They sought to ensure inclusion of their histories on multiple levels. Scholarship on historical societies in the early United States has focused on state societies, understandable given the influential collections and activities of those located in the Northeast and mid-Atlantic. Nevertheless, many early societies focused on local places and identities instead of states.[15]

Several New England towns followed or accompanied commemorative celebrations with formation of historical societies, part of a local history movement that supported an expanding array of local history publications. After celebrating the Plymouth landing in 1820, local men organized the Pilgrim Society to affirm the Plymouth colony's place "among the first lines of history of New-England, and of these United States." The Pilgrim Society incorporated historical objectives but placed an emphasis on veneration and defense of their ancestors' place in broader histories. A year later, twenty-six Essex County gentlemen looked ahead to a similar anniversary for Salem and launched the Essex Historical Society to honor and preserve the history and place of Salem and Essex County—and to address Boston's claims to preeminence in the history of the Bay Colony. Seven also belonged to the Massachusetts Historical Society but saw no conflict of allegiances. The Essex society had one brief, the state another, and the similar institutions could cooperate.[16]

Honoring local heritages did not require focusing on local actions. Founders of the Essex Historical Society announced the intention to gather "ample materials for an authentic history of this part of our commonwealth," that is, their county on the northeastern corner of the Bay State. At the same time, they looked beyond local boundaries when convenient. Officers claimed an expansive mandate to solicit "original letters, documents, and papers . . . connected with the public history of this county, *or of this commonwealth*." Collecting and preserving state history provided resources through which the county society could make claims on the history of the larger state. Preserving history on the state level also enhanced the Essex society's ability to define and position its locality and its history in relation to other counties and towns. Their petition presented the county "as the most ancient settlement" in Massachusetts. This was a form of local patriotism, affirming allegiance to nation through state and state through locale.[17]

Similar interests were aroused in Worcester, Massachusetts. The nationally oriented American Antiquarian Society was located in the town, but by the mid-1820s lawyers and historians William Lincoln and Christopher Columbus Baldwin embraced local history. While in their early twenties, they established the Worcester County Historical Society following the centennial of the town's incorporation in 1722. They also published the *Worcester Magazine and Historical Journal*. Without explicit reference to Boston, Plymouth, and Salem, the two made a modest claim for their area's significance. Worcester County, the men proclaimed even as they faced the likelihood of suspending the publication, was "of no inconsiderable consequence among the sister sections of the Commonwealth." Unfortunately, either few citizens of Worcester County shared that view—or were willing to take their hard-earned money and pay for its diffusion. The journal lasted less than two years, while the Worcester society struggled on for another decade. Despite the failure of these pet projects, Lincoln honored his hometown and bequeathed an important legacy to posterity by producing one of first deeply researched town histories in 1837. The Worcester example did not deter citizens elsewhere. Inhabitants of Dorchester inaugurated a fourth Massachusetts local historical society in 1843, to preserve and affirm the history of their community, settled in 1630, the same year as Boston and on that larger town's doorstep.[18]

Other states also hosted multiple local historical societies. Ohioans established several in the late 1830s and early 1840s, with a speedy proliferation showing not only a bent toward preservation but the need to tell competing and complementary stories. As early as 1822, nine Ohio men petitioned the Ohio state legislature to incorporate its first historical society. The legislature granted their request, but for unknown reasons the original petitioners never followed through. A new coalition of citizens from around the state succeeded nine years later. The founders of the Historical and Philosophical Society of Ohio pieced together disparate local histories to construct the state history they and their forerunners had long desired. "We may not be extensively acquainted with the history of the State," lawyer Benjamin Tappan admitted to the Society in 1832, but "each one of us has knowledge of some facts, concerning the civil, or Natural History of the State, not known to all, yet worth communicating."[19]

Ohio boasted six historical societies, spread from Ashtabula in the northeast to Cincinnati in the southwest, within a decade. These included the Marietta Historical Association, organized in 1841 to commemorate "the oldest settlement" in the Buckeye State. Located in the southeastern corner of Ohio, Marietta was settled in 1788 by a group of Revolutionary War veterans. The community had already marked its jubilee when men formed the Marietta Historical Association, just as its earliest settlers were dying off. Its mission went beyond the local. Proud of Marietta's role in opening up the Old Northwest, the group aspired to collect materials "illustrative of western history" generally and aligned its interests with Ohio much as the Plymouth Society did with the interests of Massachusetts: as the first among many.[20]

Educator, cattle dealer, and real estate speculator Ephraim Cutler was the Marietta society's first president. Born in Massachusetts, Cutler moved to the Ohio in the 1790s and was elected to the territorial legislature. One of the few Federalists at the Ohio Constitutional Convention in 1802, he helped lead the effort to keep slavery out of Ohio while maintaining friendly relations with slave states. He made a sizable profit moving cattle into Virginia to fatten them up before selling them to eastern cities. He conducted a wide correspondence on the subject of early Ohio history and was himself in demand as a living source of Ohio history before his death in 1853.[21]

Other Ohioans formed the Logan Historical Society, which they named for an eighteenth-century "Indian philanthropist and friend of the white man" mythologized as a good victim. Thomas Jefferson had memorialized Logan, a Mingo, as an exemplar of Native American eloquence, and Logan society founders wished to follow Jefferson's lead. The first twenty pages of their publication recounted Logan's character and speech, contrasting his life with present conditions and affirming the idea of Native Americans as vanishing peoples. The founders' objectives extended beyond Logan and native antiquity to embrace Western history in general and Ohio in particular. Pickaway County, Ohio, where the Logan society was located, owed its existence to emigrants from the Old Dominion.[22]

The Marietta and Logan organizations were potential rivals, and the Marietta society commented that the Logan society's "projects, from their scope, interfere somewhat with ours." The sons of Massachusetts and Virginia would face each other on the battlefield in the Civil War, but in the 1840s the respective Cavalier and Yankee society founders promoted harmony to celebrate their respective contributions to the making of Ohio. On behalf of the Marietta society, Cutler encouraged "the formation, every where, of like associations, holding friendly correspondence and rendering mutual aid." In this spirit, he and his fellow members extended good wishes to the Logan society. The Logan society "cordially reciprocate[d]" the Marietta society's good wishes and reprinted that group's circular in the *American Pioneer*, the Logan society's publication. "The sons and descendants of old Virginia," the Logan society averred, would gladly aid "their more northerly brethren" and had "the fullest confidence that the sons of the pilgrims will acquit themselves to the credit of their parentage."[23]

The Logan society ceased within a few years with the failure of the *American Pioneer*, though the supporters did not give up the ghost. Efforts to revive it were under way at midcentury. The Marietta society outlasted the Logan group by eschewing time-consuming publications and concentrating on building a library of rare books, old newspapers, and manuscripts. Meanwhile, another group, located in the northeastern county of Ashtabula, on the border with Pennsylvania, compiled roughly seven hundred manuscript pages relating to the history of the Western Reserve and northern Ohio.[24]

The Historical and Philosophical Society of Ohio endorsed the existence of local branches, fostered by a central association, to gather historical facts about their respective areas of the state. The Ohio society encouraged citizens throughout the state to form local historical societies. The Ashtabula, Marietta, and Logan groups were already in motion when the Historical and Philosophical Society of Ohio called for more such ventures. In this case, a local group proved hardier than the statewide association. The Columbus-based state society helped establish the Cincinnati Historical Society. When the state society ran into financial troubles in the late 1840s, it ended up relocating to Cincinnati to merge with the local society.[25]

In contrast to Ohio's federal approach, the New Jersey Historical Society, launched in 1845, discouraged local societies lest they take detract from its own efforts. Perhaps in Ohio decentralization was necessary, but in New Jersey citizens could regularly travel from all parts of the compact state to attend common meetings. One statewide New Jersey association could build a single repository of books and manuscripts, unlike local groups on the Ohio model, which scattered materials in multiple locations.[26]

In Baltimore the Maryland Historical Society, also founded in 1845, preferred to foster local societies. Founders limited resident membership to people within fifteen miles of Baltimore and encouraged corresponding members outside this circle to form chapters of the state organization. They advocated the strategy as an answer to the same geographical problem that plagued the Buckeye State. Given the extent to which historically minded individuals were scattered, officers of the Maryland society could not expect them to attend meetings in Baltimore. Attendance at local chapters was more feasible, and the proposed chapters would extend the work of the state organization. Their presidents were ex officio vice presidents of the central Society. By this means, the Maryland society aimed to join its far-flung members in a common effort of historical collecting and research and avoid concerns that one part of the state was favored over another.[27]

Local historical societies proved as susceptible to failure as state societies but several prepared for the possibility. The Cincinnati Historical Society's constitution specified in the event of dissolution its property would be go to Cincinnati, with the exception of items donated under the condition of return in the event of failure. Worcester County Historical Society members had more options. William Lincoln reported to the American Antiquarian Society in 1827 that the Worcester County Historical Society and Worcester County Lyceum of Natural History each wrote into their constitutions to transfer property to "some public incorporated institution, established in the town of Worcester" should they dissolve. A member of the Worcester County Historical Society as well as the American Antiquarian Society, Lincoln assured fellow antiquarian society members that "although it may be painful to anticipate the decease" of such societies, "we may derive consolation . . . from the consideration that the American Antiquarian Society will, in all probability, become the residuary legatee of their considerable acquisitions." This reassurance was limited as the American Antiquarian Society entered a period of relative inactivity at much the same time.[28]

If the American Antiquarian Society struggled to remain active, then surely local initiatives were destined to fail, at least so reasoned Bostonian Joseph Willard, a member of the American Antiquarian Society and Massachusetts Historical Society. In an 1831 exchange with New Hampshire antiquarian John Farmer, Willard expressed skepticism regarding proposals to publish works of local history and antiquity. The audience was simply too small to sustain such efforts. Only New England men, Willard insisted, could value the region's history, for "what care the men of New York & Pennsylvania for it"? The problem arose "because we are so divided and subdivided into States, that whatever is of interest to and is considered of value in one part of the Community in another and no distant part is looked upon with indifference." And not just states: counties, cities, and towns splintered the audience for history still more.[29]

Local historical societies reflected coexistent local or "sectional" intrastate loyalties and interests. The ways in which such societies defined their mission, particularly in New England, reaffirmed locales' historical importance and may have contributed to shifts toward veneration of the past. In the second half of the century, local societies proliferated. The historical society phenomenon began with national and state orientations, but decentralization predominated.

National and International Ambitions

In contrast, few societies focused on the national level. For the first half of the nineteenth century, the American Antiquarian Society was the only national historical society in the United States, although organized at the local level and inconsistently active. In the 1830s citizens in the District of Columbia founded a national historical society that did not survive long. Given this absence, historical preservation became a matter for local and state initiatives.

Despite the difficulties attendant on wide-scale visions, the American Antiquarian Society attempted to organize and operate on a national level and create an international network. From the first, officers spoke of developing a network of hemispheric correspondents. In addition, they established a national structure intended to build on representatives in other states. Neither succeeded, but the failures were notable for their rarity.

The American Antiquarian Society's organization largely resembled other learned societies. The Society did not limit the number of members, but had a single membership class open to white men of standing. Three of the Society's four quarterly meetings were to be held in Boston close to members who lived in or near the city. The organizers decided to base the library and cabinet in the small, inland town of Worcester, Massachusetts, the residence of founder Isaiah Thomas, rather than metropolitan Boston or New York City, so as to avoid hazards associated with large cities and seaports: fire and war. The Society was founded even as the United States declared war on Great Britain, a conflict deeply unpopular in largely Federalist New England.[30]

As the force behind the American Antiquarian Society, Thomas contributed to its differences from other historical societies. Born in Boston to a poor family, Thomas apprenticed to Boston printer Zechariah Fowle at age seven and worked for Fowle before buying him out by 1770. Thomas published the *Massachusetts Spy*, a radical Boston Patriot newspaper. Moving his press to Worcester in 1775 for safety, he avoided the British occupation of Boston. He expanded his initial business into multiple printing and book selling partnerships, often with former apprentices. At the age of fifty-three, he retired from business and devoted the remainder of his years to collecting, philanthropy, and other pursuits. Thomas supported the Massachusetts Historical Society, but the American Antiquarian Society was a ruling passion. The first president of the Society, he remained in office until his death in 1831.[31]

Thomas led the petition effort to incorporate the American Antiquarian Society with a pledge to give the new Society his personal library. Even before the bequests he left on his death, he was the most active and generous donor, defraying most of the Society's principal expenses including erecting a building as well as gifts of books, manuscripts, and artifacts, not least his first printing press. He did not limit his involvement to donations and presidential duties—he personally corresponded with members and potential donors in search of additional contributions. New Hampshire antiquarian and genealogist John Farmer mentioned possessing a rare volume, *Ligon's History of Barbados*, which was not in the Society's library. Thomas repeatedly suggested it would be a welcome donation until Farmer finally sent it to Worcester.[32]

As a printer and historian of printing, Thomas built the American Antiquarian Society on the tradition of printing as the art that preserved all other arts. He understood the "Antiquarian" element of the Society's name as potentially encompassing anything and everything. Quoting Sir William Jones of Calcutta, founder of the Asiatic Society, Thomas presented the American Antiquarian Society's objects as "Man and Nature—whatever is, or has been performed by the one, or produced by the other." The Society focused on "American Antiquities," which included attention to "modern productions" that would pass on to future generations information about "literature, the arts, manners, customs and discoveries in our time with accuracy." For Thomas, collection and preservation of the past entailed attention to the present.[33]

Nevertheless, the Society's interest in the present did not preclude the distant past. At the Society's first annual meeting, minister William Jenks of Bath, Maine, gave an address wherein he identified several preservation priorities for the Society. First, investing in unearthing ancient American history. Investigation of the mound-builders, at the time considered a separate race from the Native American peoples, ran a close second. The Society pursued both. *Archaeologia Americana* (1820), the Society's first major volume, published during Thomas's lifetime, consisted primarily of articles describing mounds and antiquities discovered in the "old" northwestern states and territories. The Society's goals included collection of indigenous antiquities and materials documenting the history of all European settlements on the continent, implicitly distinguishing it from the Massachusetts Historical Society, whose officers expressed interest in Native Americans primarily in relation to its members and correspondents within the boundaries of the United States in general and Massachusetts in particular.[34]

Although Thomas and other members interpreted the "American" portion of the Society's name in terms of the United States, they also invoked it in hemispheric terms. At the time, colonies throughout Spanish and Portuguese America resisted colonial rule and declared independence. The Society's original laws, passed in 1813, presupposed selection of honorary members from Spanish America. Thomas reaffirmed this while recommending election of members from Europe, China, and the Indies, asking "should it not be one of our first endeavours to extend membership to gentlemen of distinguished characters in Spanish and Portuguese America?"[35]

Thomas stressed the need to have "members in all the principal cities and towns in the United States, and some in the interiour of every state" so as to warrant the name the "*American* Antiquarian Society." Adding international members was one of several suggestions he made based on member comments. He also recommended more frequent meetings, but of equal or more import he desired to raise the Society's stature. To this end, he suggested an investigation into whether the Society might obtain some form of recognition from Congress "to make the Society appear respectable as a National Institution."[36]

In response, the officers reorganized the American Antiquarian Society so as to become more national in scope and action. Following Thomas's suggestion, they revised Society laws in 1815 to create an ambitious and complex governance structure which vested power and responsibility in local members while encouraging involvement throughout the nation. Previously, the Society's Council had seven members, not including the president, who had full voting privileges, and vice presidents, who were ex officio members. Under the new system, the number of councilors depended on the number of states in the Union. They were not equally distributed. Five residing in or near Worcester formed a subcouncil, which was to meet monthly and have responsibility for managing the library and cabinet. Another five residing in or near Boston formed a second monthly subcouncil to offer general advice. Additionally, each state in the nation would have a resident councilor, as would the district of Maine and "Plymouth Old Colony."[37]

The reorganization granted distance members influence, but power remained vested in officers residing close to Worcester. The regional councilors had "a right to a seat, and with the power to act, in the meetings of the Council" but were not required to attend. Their duties were primarily to correspond with American Antiquarian Society officers in Worcester and to gather information and articles about antiquities. The number of corresponding secretaries was raised to three in expectation of increased correspondence. The Society also created the position of receiving officers in the various states, to accept donations and forward them to Worcester. The Worcester and Boston councilors were elected annually alongside the Society's officers, even as the Massachusetts and New York historical societies elected members of their standing committees. The president and Worcester subcouncil were empowered to appoint other councilors and the receiving officers, due to the distances involved. The arrangement emphasized appointment of men known to Society officers or who were brought to their notice.[38]

Officers bowed to actual experience fifteen years later and reorganized as a Worcester-based institution with nationally oriented collections. The regional arrangement had not produced the hoped-for results. Members throughout the nation agreed to serve as state councilors and receiving officers but did little to contribute to the American Antiquarian Society's governance. At length, the Society officers revised the laws. All references to regional councilors and receiving officers were removed. The subcouncils combined into a single council of ten members to meet quarterly in Worcester. The Society would have two meetings a year, one in Worcester and one in Boston. The number of corresponding secretaries was reduced. The Society also voted to limit the number of members to 140.[39]

Insufficient communication networks undermined efforts to establish national periodicals and likewise contributed to the failure of the American Antiquarian Society's attempt at a nationally representative council. Regional councilors had loyalties to their respective locales. New Hampshire statesman William Plumer Sr. accepted appointment as councilor in 1821, but became the first president of the Concord-based New Hampshire Historical Society shortly thereafter. Despite the American Antiquarian Society's failure to create a national organizational structure, it collected materials nationally. A large proportion of donations came from New England, but the Society managed to solicit contributions of government documents, newspapers, and other items from across the growing nation. The Society's leaders stressed its importance and value as a truly national institution.[40]

Following Thomas's death, Worcester-native Christopher Columbus Baldwin actively enhanced the Society's collections on a national level. Thomas's will included funds to pay for a librarian. Having previously served as an unpaid librarian, Baldwin gladly took the paid position with a patriotic pride in the Society's mission as "a national institution." He wrote letter after letter to individuals across the republic to carry this out, asking organizations and individuals for donations, bragging he "ha[d] begged and stolen to the number of near Five Thousand [pamphlets and volumes]! Bravo!" On learning that nephews of elderly Boston antiquarian, collector and Massachusetts Historical Society founder Thomas Wallcut expected to inherit his collection and were willing to donate materials, particularly pamphlets, to the American Antiquarian Society, Baldwin claimed the donation at the earliest opportunity. The Massachusetts Historical Society librarian at the time, Joseph Willard, complained that Baldwin "had his 'huge paw'" on Wallcut's pamphlets "unknown to me" and was "loud in his praises of the *more than four horse wagon load* treasure." Willard conceded that "they are preserved, and that is the chief thing." Despite only five years' service as the antiquarian society's librarian before dying in a carriage accident, Baldwin's activities helped put the Society on the road to realizing its ambitions in terms of collections, particularly newspapers.[41]

As a sign of gathering national consciousness, a group of gentlemen in Washington, D.C., organized another national historical society in 1835. The American Historical Society echoed state historical societies' objectives, lauding their "gratifying progress" while pointing out that the state societies focused on "the acquisition of facts relating to their respective States." The founders observed a need for "a more comprehensive range of inquiry" and elected to organize in the nation's capital. Where state historical societies looked to gather materials documenting the history of the new nation in general and given states in specific through the records of specific colonies and states, the American society's mission encompassed the continent in general and American republic in particular. Some of the organizers of the new society believed national history offered a means to promote continental unity. States had cooperated for their mutual benefit during the American Revolution, making the past an example for the present to follow.[42]

One of the American Historical Society's stalwarts was Washington, D.C., printer and editor Peter Force, a source for the Society's interest in history as a tool to promote interstate cooperation. Force grew up in New Jersey and New York. At the age of sixteen, he left school to apprentice to a printer in Manhattan. Force began collecting books and manuscripts on American history at an early age. He moved to Washington, D.C., then still recovering from its burning by the British, to print under a government contract and never left. As a nationally minded printer, he cultivated interests in the country's history. He purchased the documents, pamphlets, and newspapers Ebenezer Hazard had assembled in the Revolution from Hazard's son Samuel, incorporating it into his own growing collection.[43]

Force's collecting supported his interest in encouraging a national historical society. Over the late 1820s and early 1830s, he cultivated federal subsidization of the *American Archives*, a monumental documentary history of the United States, including colonial settlement and the American Revolution. In conjunction with lawyer and congressional clerk Matthew St. Clair Clarke, he convinced Congress to appropriate money. United States Secretary of State Edward Livingston signed a contract with Force shortly before Force helped organize the American Historical Society. A committed nationalist,

Force hoped to counteract rising sectional tensions by showing cooperation among the states during the Revolution. He assembled the first volumes of the unfinished *American Archives* during the Society's short existence.[44]

The American Historical Society held at least two annual meetings, gathered donations, and issued a volume of *Transactions* but failed in less than a decade. The state of national distribution and communication networks may have hampered the Society's success. Although facilities for transportation and communication had improved since the turn of the century, most of the historically inclined individuals whose aid the Society required were scattered across the nation and involved in local pursuits. Ironically, the Society ceased operation just as railroads began knitting the nation together. The Society's constitution specified resident members pay a five-dollar admission fee along with three dollars annually, and members may have hoped for financial assistance from Congress. Congressional members were already questioning federal support for the *American Archives*, so Congress was unlikely to provide aid to the Society. The *American Archives* also increasingly occupied Force's time and attention, depriving the Society of his active leadership and contributing to its failure.[45]

The absence of a successful national society proved a mixed blessing for other societies. It permitted greater scope, inasmuch as local and state societies sought to fill the national gap within their spheres of influence. Massachusetts, Rhode Island, Virginia, and other states had more freedom to make competing claims on colonial and revolutionary events and contributions. At the same time, lack of national leadership decreased the societies' potential to act in concert on matters of mutual concern, raising the burden on any given society or member desirous of promoting national action on issues.

"The Want of Materials": Preserving Government Records

Despite division into separate organizations, several early historical societies made an attempt to influence the federal government in support of preserving historical documents, particularly colonial records located in European state archives. The Library of Congress did not acquire manuscripts at the time due to funding issues. The State Department purchased some presidential collections but otherwise overlooked the matter, The National Archives, founded 1934, was not even a glint in legislators' eyes. Although the societies failed at the federal level, historical society encouragement contributed to several states' acquisition of copies of European colonial documents. States, particularly the original thirteen colonies, turned more attention to their records, often following actions and petitions on the part of historical societies.[46]

American History in European Archives

Americans recognized relevant European archival holdings early in the century, particularly after the Treaty of Ghent and the end of the Napoleonic wars made travel to Europe attractive. Philanthropist John Pintard composed a memorial to the State of New York in 1814 requesting financial aid for the New-York Historical Society. Nearly half of his request contained speculations on the variety and extent of New York–related materials in European government archives, the library of the Society for the Propagation of the Gospel in America, and Canadian public records offices. His memorial implied the state's assistance might be partly spent pursuing these, although the Society did little to nothing in that vein at the time.[47]

Editor Jared Sparks stressed the importance of English colonial records for United States history a decade later. Connecticut-born and Harvard-educated, Sparks spent time as a tutor and Unitarian minister before finding his niche as an editor and historian. By the mid-1820s, he was the publisher and editor of the *North American Review*, had negotiated with George Washington's nephew and heir, Bushrod Washington, to publish the general's papers, and arranged with President John Quincy Adams and Secretary of State Henry Clay to collect, edit, and publish the *Diplomatic Correspondence of the American Revolution*. To support his historical projects, Sparks traveled to state archives in search of materials.[48]

Returning to New England after a tour of southern states, Sparks wrote an essay putatively reviewing the Historical Society of Pennsylvania's first volume but also raising awareness of the vital importance of assembling historical manuscripts and archives and making them more accessible. Historians' failures were not always their own fault, Sparks suggested, but sometimes due to "the want of materials." In the United States, historical materials were scattered across the landscape with many lost and others inaccessible. Historical societies worked to redress the situation through collections and publication programs. Nevertheless, Sparks argued, historians faced a nearly unsurmountable problem: "the colonial history of America [wa]s shut up" in English archives. Obtaining copies of colonial records relating to the United

States was not a project for individuals or societies to undertake; rather, "the government is the proper organ for managing this business." He did not mention records in other European countries relating to the United States, but many historians and historical societies recognized that French, Spanish, and Dutch archives also held important colonial records.[49]

Sparks's suggestion that the federal government should take action struck a chord with members of the Rhode Island Historical Society, who soon approved a resolution desiring the state's congressional delegation support funding a mission to copy English records. Before Rhode Island's interest even reached Congress, the U.S. House of Representatives instructed the Committee on Libraries to investigate the matter. Nevertheless, Rhode Island Representative Dutee Jerauld Pearce warned the Society that he could not give them much encouragement for "I know the temper of the house too well to even indulge the hope." He soon changed his mind based on news the New Hampshire Historical Society had expressed interest as well.[50]

The Massachusetts Historical Society also joined Rhode Island in petitioning Congress, although this represented a departure from existing practices in that it asked to fund an external project which would not add to the Society's collections or publications. The Massachusetts society's quarterly meeting took up the matter after receiving a request from the Rhode Island society. The Massachusetts society's earlier petitions to the federal and state governments involved soliciting assistance for the Society to carry out collecting and publication goals. For the most part, such efforts had involved government assistance to the Society, which then produced a product (publications) or service (preserving and providing access to government documents and portraits as historical materials).[51]

The committee of the Massachusetts Historical Society drafted a lengthy memorial to Congress stating that the Society worked to support future historians' research. Officers had produced twenty-one volumes of *Collections* relying on voluntary labor and member-provided financial support but were concerned over the lack of colonial records in the nation. Members and their dues would not suffice to make a difference, an implicit admission of the limits of voluntary associations. Bringing copies of all relevant English documents to the United States would probably require "the intervention of the National Government."[52]

Moreover, committee members pointed out that having such copies would enable historians to write the full history of the nation. As a result, American citizens would feel an "exhilarating sentiment," possessed of a history "free from the uncertainty of tradition, and the degradation of fable." The Society also argued that other (European) governments materially supported preserving and publishing their early records. The United States had so far made no contribution, but funding a mission to copy European colonial records would support "the principle of national honor."[53]

Although the Joint Library Committee of Congress's usual business involved selecting books for purchase and drawing rules and regulations governing the library, members passed a resolution in favor of the proposal. The committee recommended funding for the project come from the foreign relations contingency fund. When reported to the House, the matter was read and tabled. The Rhode Island society later concluded that Congress would have appropriated the funds if the recommendation hadn't been reported late in the session.[54]

The Rhode Island Historical Society was overly optimistic, for Congress was reluctant to spend money on books and repeatedly turned down opportunities to purchase rare works put up for sale as notable European libraries were dismantled. Congress purchased a few manuscript collections in the 1830s and 1840s, namely presidential papers. Both House and Senate passed a bill acquiring George Washington's public papers for twenty-five thousand dollars in 1834. Government officers had consulted Washington's papers on numerous occasions because the government's copies of some of the documents had been destroyed in the War Office fire of 1800. George Corbin Washington withheld papers he considered private, but Congress later purchased these for an additional twenty thousand dollars. Congress also approved purchases of two other presidents' papers over the second quarter of the nineteenth century: Thomas Jefferson and James Madison. Legislators otherwise did not invest in acquiring historical documents.[55]

While historical societies petitioned Congress to obtain English records, they also appointed agents in Europe to pursue subjects dear to society members' hearts. The agents were often traveling society members and their acquaintances. The Rhode Island society asked their agent in England, Thomas R. Hunter, to locate information about Roger Williams, including his birthplace, parentage, and education. In addition, Hunter was to check any libraries he visited for any writings of Williams or other Rhode Island settlers. He was further charged to discover whatever he could about the state's first settlers "& such other information relative to the history of this state as it is the object of this Society to collect and perpetuate." Despite the breadth of the last charge, the Society primarily requested Hunter to pursue specific information and resources, not to copy colonial records.[56]

Undaunted by earlier failure to get congressional funding for copies of European documents, lawyer and historian William R. Staples urged the Rhode Island society to try again in 1830. Officers promptly appointed him to a three-member committee to consider the matter. Not content with merely petitioning the state's legislature to raise the matter with Congress, Staples drafted a memorial, which the committee proposed the Rhode Island legislature adopt and send to Congress. The committee created a related document and distributed 150 copies to the president of the United States; Department of State; state and territorial governors; historical societies; university and college presidents; and prominent public figures, asking them to petition Congress to act. The Society received encouraging replies, including a communication from Colonel Henry Cruger of South Carolina, who had just returned from England. There, at the State of South Carolina's request, he had investigated the feasibility of obtaining copies of the colonial records, concluding it was impossible to estimate the cost. He sent back a list of documents relating to South Carolina's history and wished the Rhode Island society success in their petition.[57]

In addition, Georgia, North Carolina, and Virginia obtained materials from England in the 1820s and 1830s. Historians in North Carolina (Archibald DeBow Murphey) and Georgia (Joseph Vallance Bevan) initiated the contact with England before Sparks's essay appeared in print. However, Georgia and the Carolinas only received lists of materials relating to their colonies, such as indexes intended to aid the states or their agents in determining which documents to have copied. Georgia Governor George M. Troup urged the state legislature to fund an agent to obtain actual copies. The legislature declined and instead requested the state's congressional delegation arrange for Congress to fund such a mission.[58]

Apart from Congress's general disinclination to invest in books and papers, conflicting ideas about the value of colonial records undermined the petitions. Rhode Island Senator Nehemiah Rice Knight brought the Rhode Island Historical Society's second memorial before Congress. Although many congressmen favored the project, he reported it unlikely to pass during the current session. He had misgivings as to whether it would succeed after hearing, incorrectly, that Virginia, Georgia, and South Carolina "have copies of all they need." States outside the original thirteen colonies "do not feel any interest in the measure & therefore I conjecture will not lend a helping hand." The northern historical societies and at least one southern state desired action at the national level but could not overcome lack of interest on the part of western states that were never colonies.[59]

With congressional action lacking, states took the lead. Georgia was the first to appropriate funds to copy English documents. The legislature had the impression that South Carolina and some New England states were moving forward with similar efforts, suggesting a degree of rivalry. Georgia's appointed agent, Charles Wallace Howard, embarked for England in 1838. When he returned the following year with twenty-two manuscript volumes copied by clerks, they were deposited for a period with the newly formed Georgia Historical Society. At much the same time, the New-York Historical Society successfully petitioned the state legislature to fund an expedition not only to English archives but French and Dutch ones as well. New York's agent, John Romeyn Brodhead, returned with eighty volumes of transcripts. He described his mission as "the child of this [the New-York Historical] Society."[60]

New York's mission had ripple effects. Benjamin Penley Poore, a Massachusetts-born clerk working for Brodhead in France, alerted Massachusetts legislators and influential historians to the wealth of materials in that nation touching Massachusetts history. Aware that travel delays would prevent legislative consideration of the matter until the next session, Poore was willing to risk not being paid for his labors. "Firmly convinced of the value of the Documents," he wrote Jared Sparks that he "only wait[ed for] *your approval* to go on and copy them." The Massachusetts legislature eventually voted funds for copies to be made for deposit in the state archives.[61]

Historical societies in other states also expressed interest in the growing collection arriving in New York. Vermonter Henry Stevens set up shop in London by 1845 and made good money providing copies of colonial documents to various states, antiquarians, and historical societies. After failing to convince the New Jersey legislature to have English documents transcribed, the New Jersey Historical Society commissioned Stevens to create an index to British records connected with that state, an inexpensive but necessary preliminary step. Over the remainder of the nineteenth century, many other states and historical societies sent similar missions to Europe.[62]

Of Filing Systems and Fireproof Buildings: The State of Domestic Public Records

Historical societies also expressed interest in the care of physical government publications. The societies desired to supplement government archives, not replace them. Society repositories helped ensure survival of government materials, a concern of heightened importance given the destruction of federal archives during the British burning of the nation's capital.

Interest in domestic public records, as opposed to the copying of European archival documents, often took the form of members themselves copying excerpts from state or town records for donation or publication. Antiquarian Redmond Conyngham donated transcriptions of Commonwealth records to the Historical Society of Pennsylvania. Benjamin Howland of Newport likewise copied town records for the Rhode Island society. He began the transcription a year after the Society resolved to investigate obtaining copies of materials from the state's original five town clerks. The Rhode Island society paid Massachusetts and Connecticut clerks for copies of state records relevant to Rhode Island. The New Hampshire society expressed similar interest in Massachusetts records relating to New Hampshire. After obtaining copies, the publication committee included excerpts in the next volume of the New Hampshire society's *Collections*.[63]

Society members approved of individual actions because document preservation rarely constituted a legislative priority at state or national levels. New Hampshire Senator William Plumer Sr. learned in 1802 that congressmen were "entitled" to copies of congressional documents including statutes and committee reports but had to review and select what they wished to take. This provision applied to documents remaining after all the people who routinely received copies were supplied and to materials left behind at the end of a session. Spares were kept in a lumber room located above the Senate chamber. John Beckley, the clerk of the House of Representatives and newly appointed librarian of Congress, controlled the key to the room. Plumer and Beckley feuded during Beckley's tenure as librarian. According to Plumer's account, Beckley at first indicated the documents belonged to the government. After observing one of Beckley's "favorites" among the representatives selecting documents, Plumer determined to do the same. While in Washington, he tried to accumulate a complete set for himself. He gathered documents for the Massachusetts Historical Society and for a Massachusetts friend, Ichabod Tucker of Salem, but noted in his diary they were not "half so large & extensive as mine—tho' as much so as I was able to make them."[64]

Plumer considered his actions a preservative measure. Beckley kept the documents in abominable conditions: unorganized and "covered & mixed up with dirt, plaster and rubbish." The roof did not adequately keep out rain. Workmen entered the room to retrieve other items stored there, such as "glass in basketts with straw—window sashes, &c.," regularly walking over the old statutes, committee reports, and other printed products of congressional labor. Plumer found the whole scene "unhealthy" due to the "water on the papers, the dirt & filth in the chamber." Newer sets of documents, including journals of recent Congresses, were likewise neglected. "It is really a pity," he mourned, "that documents, some of which are so valuable, should be suffered thus wantonly to be destroyed." On the other hand, most public servants probably considered the documents well preserved, as they were extra copies above and beyond those distributed to congressmen, the president, and department heads. Moreover, abysmal treatment of government records was hardly an American invention. The British House of Commons appointed a Record Commission to investigate documentary disorder in Britain in 1800, based in part on the argument that continued mistreatment would be a national disgrace.[65]

Congressman Josiah Quincy, a Massachusetts Historical Society member, perhaps took inspiration from the Society or the British example. He proposed in 1810 that the House of Representatives order an investigation into "the state of the ancient public records." He was appointed to the committee, which subsequently reported that documents lay "in a state of great disorder and exposure; and in a situation neither safe nor convenient nor honorable to the nation." Secretary of State Robert Smith advised Quincy and the committee that "ancient" papers brought from the previous capitals at Philadelphia and New York were voluminous and had never been "properly" arranged. This rendered searching through the records difficult, although they were important and "often closely connected with the immediate interests and rights of individuals."[66]

Unfortunately, Quincy's report set no precedents. Smith suggested allocating additional storage space in a fireproof building, and providing a full-time clerk to arrange papers. Quincy and the committee concurred. They recommended devoting a building to organization and store public records, which would require relocating federal and city government offices currently occupying the building. The general post office should move because it was open all night, potentially exposing records to fire and robbery. The patent office, too, should move, so as to allow space for "the keeper of patents to make an useful and accessible arrangement of th[e]m." Congress took no immediate actions, and the burning of Washington by the British a few years focused congressional attention on rebuilding.[67]

Historical societies also took an interest in the care and organization of state and local records. In some cases, officers established their collections as safe repositories for materials previously in government hands. Thomas petitioned the Worcester Circuit Court of Common Pleas in 1816 to entrust to the American Antiquarian Society a volume "relating to Land Bank Titles" held in the County Register of Deeds office. Although irrelevant to any current business before the court, the manuscript "may hereafter become a matter of some curiosity." The court agreed and turned the book over to the Society for safekeeping.[68]

The Rhode Island Historical Society used a different approach to protect at-risk public records. The Society learned in 1834 that an old volume in a Newport court clerk's office contained valuable records documenting the late seventeenth-century government under Sir Edmund Andros. The Society did not ask for the volume itself as a deposit or donation. Instead, officers requested the General Assembly have the volume copied and keep both the copy and the original in the secretary of state's office.[69]

One of the most notable efforts to motivate governments to take better care of their records originated in New Hampshire. Richard Bartlett, a member of the state historical society, conducted a survey of public records in the United States in the 1830s "to induce the legislatures of the States, where it may be necessary, to provide for the more safe and perfect keeping of the publick archives." He summarized his results in a brief pamphlet, which the Society distributed throughout the nation. While the impact of Bartlett's report on government record-keeping practices is difficult to ascertain, the fact of the report, its contents, and dissemination made it an important moment in historical society-government relations.[70]

Bartlett's appreciation for public records was less evident at the start of his career in law and public service than at the end. Born in New Hampshire, he became a clerk to New Hampshire Secretary of State Philip Carrigain at the age of fifteen, thanks to his fine handwriting. Carrigain put Bartlett and another clerk to work labeling old records. In later decades, Bartlett remembered the two "abandon[ing] the task in despair" and "covering the ends . . . with papers neatly marked." When he became secretary of state, he undertook to reorder the records, although he was unable to complete the task before being voted out of office.[71]

A founding member of the New Hampshire Historical Society, Bartlett served on two publication committees and the standing committee. He remained in Concord after losing the secretary of state office, publishing a newspaper and serving a term in the state legislature. He moved to New York City and met once with a New-York Historical Society officer but did not expect to be a part of New York historical society activities. Despite differences over slavery and racial equality with New Hampshire antiquarian John Farmer, Bartlett and Farmer corresponded, and Bartlett kept an interest in the New Hampshire society.[72]

One of Bartlett's main concerns was the loss of public records to fire. He encouraged Farmer to have the New Hampshire Historical Society ask the state erect a fireproof building and allow room for the historical society in it. Learning the prospects of New Hampshire doing so were slim, Bartlett predicted the eventual destruction of the State House and records in a fire. He wanted to impress the importance of fireproof archival buildings on the public and opted to publicize "the unsafe manner in which they [public records] are now kept in the several states & at Washington and the losses and destruction by fire which have already happened."[73]

Bartlett compiled his findings from his survey of public archives in 1836, less than a year before his death from cancer. The pamphlet, published the following year, contained an eight-page essay followed by sixty-two pages of responses to his survey and excerpts from related documents. Although he originally intended to omit correspondents' names, he included them so as to "add weight to the publication." Befitting concerns about fire, he stressed the importance of fireproof buildings first and foremost. He found "astonishing apathy" among "legislators, who would not sleep till their own title-deeds were on record and their buildings insured against fire" but did not extend the same consideration to public archives. He put his money behind his word, offering to contribute two hundred dollars to a subscription to raise a fireproof building for the New Hampshire society—conditional on nine other

Society members pledging the same or more. Although the Society relocated to a room over the Concord Bank, he was not called on to fulfill his promise, as the building was not fireproof.[74]

Despite awareness of the dangers, and numerous losses to fires, most of the officials who responded to Bartlett's survey admitted they kept records in buildings which were not fireproof. Amos Kendall, U.S. Postmaster General, either did not respond to the survey or his response did not reach Bartlett. Nevertheless, Bartlett noticed Kendall "neglected to answer my letter of inquiry . . . but immediately asked for a *fire-proof* building & made the Pres^t^ second him in his message." Ten days after Kendall's message, fire destroyed the building containing the general post office and patent office, prompting Bartlett to regret Kendall hadn't thought to ask for the fireproof building earlier.[75]

Bartlett's interest in archives extended beyond fire to modes of record-keeping. His approach to public records involved "Engrossing the Statutes & resolutions on vellum, or large, durable paper and binding them in volumes. . . . Arranging all other original papers in chronological order and binding them in volumes . . . [and] Copious Indexes, &c." While serving as New Hampshire secretary of state, he worked to organize the public records according to such guidelines, although the project was not completed. He endorsed the organization of Massachusetts's public archives, under the historian, Rev. Joseph B. Felt, as an example for other states to follow. Instead of files of papers which often wound up out of chronological order, or were even "abducted and never returned," Felt had documents bound into volumes based on subject, with tables of contents and indexes. At roughly the same time, Maryland embarked on an assessment of state records conducted by state librarian David Ridgely, a historian of Annapolis. While not directly connected to historical society activities, these actions reflected interest in improved preservation of and access to public records.[76]

The report on public records appeared as a pamphlet and as part of the New Hampshire Historical Society's fifth volume of *Collections*. The Society sent copies to state governors and legislators, the president of the United States, and the mayors of at least eight cities from Boston to New Orleans. Bartlett wanted it also distributed to United States senators, state secretaries of state, heads of departments, college presidents, and to a number of individuals, including Carrigain, who had first employed him as a clerk. At least one recipient, printer Charles W. Cady of Indiana, appreciated the work, although he wished it had included "some plans for small fire proof buildings, with estimates of cost, and particularly of construction."[77]

Bartlett did not restrict his comments to matters of fire and record-keeping—he also took an interest in state ownership and control over colonial papers. In 1836 he learned Farmer had successfully petitioned Governor Isaac Hill to appoint Farmer "to examine, arrange, index, prepare for & superintend the binding and otherwise preserving such of the public papers in the archives of this State, as may be deemed worthy of such cares," or, in short, to complete the organization of the archives which Bartlett had begun years earlier. Bartlett reminded Farmer that Rev. Jeremy Belknap had obtained many state papers while researching his *History of New Hampshire* during the American Revolution, documents which he carried with him to Massachusetts. Belknap's son had donated some of his father's New Hampshire papers to the New Hampshire society, but others likely existed in the Masschusetts Historical Society's collections. Bartlett advised Farmer to retrieve any Belknap papers which belonged to the state. If necessary, "they might be recovered by law." There is no indication Farmer made the attempt.[78]

Two other states did request the return of materials from the Massachusetts Historical Society, reflecting growing appreciation for public records' historical value and importance. Connecticut Secretary of State Daniel P. Tyler asked for the papers Belknap had acquired in 1794 from the son of Connecticut Governor Jonathan Trumbull. The request was partly due to the recently reorganized Connecticut Historical Society. Connecticut claimed the records on the grounds that the governor had collected them at the request of the state. The Massachusetts society asserted the documents were not state copies of documents but duplicates, gathered by Trumbull in his personal capacity. Moreover, it was a legal donation in keeping with the governor's desires. Physical possession helped the Massachusetts society carry the day. The Society eventually returned the papers in the 1920s.[79]

Similarly, Massachusetts secretary of the commonwealth and historical society member John G. Palfrey requested return of materials. Palfrey's predecessor, Alden Bradford, had conducted a survey of state public records at the request of the Massachusetts House of Representatives. Bradford discovered public and private documents colonial governor Thomas Hutchinson possibly collected while working on his *History of Massachusetts*, along with an unpublished volume of state papers. With the consent of the governor and council, Bradford decided these did not belong "to the government, or as any part of the records of the Commonwealth, or ancient colony or province." As some had value on the basis of antiquity, he placed them with the Massachusetts Historical Society, retaining a list of the documents among his official papers. Lest anyone perceive a conflict of interest, Bradford resigned his membership in the Society the same day. Palfrey was convinced the documents were state property and should remain under state control. The ensuing dispute between the Commonwealth and the Society stretched over several decades before the Society's own archival documents revealed the materials were deposited, not donated, and hence still belonged to the Commonwealth.[80]

"A Great Number Irretrievably Lost": States as Publishers

Along with fireproof buildings and public record organization, historical societies valued preserving American colonial records in print. Antiquaries in England had commenced published the parliamentary rolls and the Domesday Book beginning in the mid-eighteenth century. German antiquarians began to publish records in the early nineteenth century. The United States Congress followed suit, supporting historical publications despite declining to fund missions to Europe. Congress approved publication of Revolutionary records of the Continental Congress and diplomatic correspondence and later funded the *American State Papers* and *American Archives*.[81]

Historical society encouragement helped push states to also publish. Societies argued for state publication programs based on print as a preservative medium. "Fire or some other accident may in a moment destroy" any document for which only one copy existed, the American Philosophical Society and Historical Society of Pennsylvania advised the State of Pennsylvania in 1836. This would be a special loss because Pennsylvania's history "deserves and obtains a particular attention." Pennsylvania "alone" had a founder, William Penn, whose fame equaled "the most celebrated Legislators." Losses of Pennsylvania records to fire or misadventure might result in "false notions" of the state's history "by the ingenuity or perhaps design of future chroniclers." Moreover, while still a "poor infant colony," Pennsylvania legislators had financed publication of volumes of votes and proceedings, setting an example the societies argued the state would do well to emulate.[82]

The philosophical and historical societies developed a joint memorial to the state, highlighting the web of connections binding the societies. Each society appointed a two-man committee to the project. Peter Stephen Du

Ponceau, then president of the philosophical society and on the verge of becoming historical society president at the age of seventy-six, was on both. Hampton Carson, a twentieth-century historian of the Historical Society of Pennsylvania, suggested that the double appearance of Du Ponceau's name had an influence at the time. Du Ponceau had a reputation for scholarship and extensive circle of correspondents. The other philosophical society representative was J. Francis Fisher, an active member of the historical society, whom Carson believed wrote most of the memorial. The second signer for the historical society, lawyer Job R. Tyson, was elected to membership in the philosophical society that year.[83]

The Pennsylvania House selected J. Washington Tyson to chair a committee considering the memorial. Tyson's report reiterated the salient points from the memorial and added others. He reminded fellow legislators of the two societies' importance and contributions to the preservation of historical materials, and similarly of Du Ponceau's fame and reputation. Pennsylvania had published important documents as a colony and since the Revolution. In addition, governments in Europe and the national government of the United States published important early documents. Other states, "Maryland in particular," had recently begun gathering and publishing documents only to discover "a great number irretrievably lost."[84]

The Pennsylvania legislature passed a bill in the mid-1830s approving publication of the provincial council minutes. One thousand copies were to be printed, the cost not to exceed three thousand dollars. The historical society should receive at least twenty copies for "safe-keeping." The number of copies to be printed was eventually raised to 1,500, with many to be sold by subscription through the county treasurers. Only three volumes of the series, later known as *Colonial Records*, appeared before 1840, when the project went into abeyance. The remainder were not published until the second half of the nineteenth century, following encouragement from the historical society. By the early 1850s, the Commonwealth of Pennsylvania not only had funded completion of the *Colonial Records* but hired Historical Society of Pennsylvania member and editor Samuel Hazard to prepare the *Pennsylvania Archives*.[85]

About this time, the New-York Historical Society encouraged the State of New York to publish. After memorializing the state to fund Brodhead's mission to copy European documents, the Society helped convince the legislature to publish many of the copied records—in part based on the realization that otherwise society members, many based in New York City, would have to trek to Albany to view the transcripts. The result was the fifteen volume *Documents Relative to the Colonial History of the State of New-York.* The Society's efforts led to other documentary publications as well, including two volumes of the *Journals of the New York Provincial Congress.*[86]

Several states likewise embarked on publication projects around midcentury. Massachusetts and Rhode Island printed archives and colonial records beginning in the 1850s, as did Connecticut. The desire to publish and disseminate extended beyond the Northeast. The Louisiana Historical Society paired with B. F. French in producing five volumes of *Historical Collections of Louisiana.* The works featured lengthy translations of early Spanish and French explorers' accounts.[87]

While early historical societies focused on setting up collections and issuing publications, many turned their attention toward governments and government records after the Declaration Jubilee. Public documents and colonial records were critical materials for history—and these were clearly beyond historical society control. Joining with historians and sympathetic legislators, societies encouraged a variety of preservation initiatives, including copying European colonial records and organizing and publishing domestic state and colonial documents. Historical societies thus contributed in a significant way to shifts in government attitudes toward history and their records.

Inasmuch as historical societies looked outwards, their gaze fell first on governments, but they also paid attention to historic landmarks. The Rhode Island Historical Society heard a report in 1835 that Yale University was considering dismantling Whitehall, a building affiliated with noted philosopher Bishop George Berkeley. Writing to Yale, the Society requested repair and preservation of the building. Jeremiah Day, the president of Yale, affirmed that the university had no intention of taking down the building, which was on a ninety-nine-year lease, and promised to ensure it was properly maintained. At roughly the same time, the Rhode Island society attempted to save a separate building, then considered the oldest house in the state, but failed and received only a window for its collections.[88]

Officers reconciled preservation with progress, facilitating the building of modern cities. The Massachusetts Historical Society accepted a piece of the former home of colonial governor Thomas Hutchinson. The New York society received a piece of Captain Miles Standish's house. The Pennsylvania society accepted pieces of two churches. The New Hampshire society recorded donation of a window sash fragment. Similarly, in the 1840s several historically minded citizens of Deerfield, Massachusetts, protested the leveling of the Old Indian House, connected to and bearing scars of early eighteenth-century attacks; only the door survived, and was returned to the village after the Civil War. Scholars of historic preservation in the United States generally date the modern movement to the founding of the Mount Vernon Ladies' Association in the 1850s, with the Rhode Island society's earlier efforts in the 1830s as a prelude. These actions and gifts may also be considered examples of historical societies interpreting a broad mandate to avert danger to perceived historic resources.[89]

A New Model of Historical Societies: States as Sponsors

Shortly after midcentury, Wisconsin established a precedent for closer relations between a state government and state historical society. Organized in 1845, the Wisconsin Historical Society sputtered through two false starts before incorporating in 1853, after which members elected new arrival Lyman Copeland Draper as corresponding secretary. Sponsored by a wealthy relative, Draper had spent time roaming the nation in search of materials for a history of colonial frontier wars. He and other members lobbied the Wisconsin legislature for financial assistance—and became the first state society to receive an annual state appropriation. Shortly afterward, the Society became a trustee of the state. It received monetary subsidies, duplicate books forwarded from the state library, and postage and printing costs. The initial appropriation of two thousand dollars more than quadrupled within two years. The monies funded collection and publication activities, and garnered notice from other historical societies and states.[90]

Many later societies, particularly in the West, pursued similar state arrangements. By the end of the nineteenth century, all states boasted historical societies. In addition, the number of city and county historical societies multiplied, due in no small part to centennial celebrations of the Declaration of Independence. Citizens also founded societies to gather and protect the histories of racial and ethnic minorities and religious denominations—but historical organizations allied to local and state polities continued to predominate.[91]

Chapter Three

"Providing Materials for History"

Historical Collection Priorities

Historian Lemuel Shattuck sent the New Hampshire Historical Society a "Plan for Providing Materials for History" in 1832. Then working on a history of Concord, Massachusetts, Shattuck had a vested interest in how historical materials were preserved and made accessible for research. A member of both the American Antiquarian Society and Massachusetts Historical Society, he advocated asking "suitable individual[s]" to "anticipate the wants of future historians" and each year write up an account or chronicle of what had taken place. He provided a list of twenty-four subjects to address, including names of people holding public office (subject no. 1), fire prevention (no. 16), and weather observations (no. 22). His imagined chroniclers should take care to approach all subjects "with candor, faithfulness, and uncompromising impartiality, and adherence to truth." Preserved in a safe place, the accounts would offer interesting views at the time and "inestimable value" for future researchers.[1]

Shattuck's plan rested on a number of assumptions, including confidence chroniclers could guess what future historians would want. Many Early Republic historical society officers implicitly agreed with this assumption. Shortly after organization, the New Hampshire Historical Society announced an interest in collecting and preserving materials "for the future historian." Trustees of the Rhode Island Historical Society considered this to be their "sole object." They sought to serve not only contemporary historians but those of the future and evidently considered themselves able to anticipate future desiderata.[2]

Yet historical societies differed over the value of Shattuck's planned accounts. Rhode Island Historical Society officers did not want a historian in the future "to reproach us for having left him naught but arid chronicles of events." The Society hoped historians found instead "materials, not only for faithful narrative, but for philosophical exposition of the conduct, and principles, and institutions of our ancestors." Other societies and members repeated similar rhetoric. Alongside interest in facts, officers described their labors as identifying documents "now considered worthless, except by pastry cooks," which they "rescued from destruction and oblivion" so as to earn future generations' gratitude.[3]

Historical society officers grappled with how to describe what they sought so that individuals and groups possessing desired information or materials would contribute to society collections. The process of defining what to collect involved drawing distinctions. Collecting priorities elevated written materials over objects and emphasized particular formats, such as newspapers and sermons. Early collection rhetoric stressed historical facts and information. Officers valued newly created documents containing desired information alongside older works, often perceiving historical value as inherent in documents' contents rather than in documents as artifacts. In turn, emphasis on facts and information offered the potential for greater control over what entered society collections. Officers selected texts and, sparingly, objects that spoke to the people, places, and events most valued.

Society officers initially emphasized collection of information but over time prioritized materials based on connections to places, people, and events. In the process, they began to shift from fact- or content-based collecting to circumstances of creation. Some societies established comprehensive and expansive collection interests by defining materials in terms of connections to particular cities, counties, and states. Thus the process of setting collection priorities contributed to the modern emphasis on primary sources.

Wish Lists: Disseminating Ideas of History through Circulars

Historical societies could not simply open their doors and begin acquiring historical materials. Officers had to explain what they wanted to gather and help individuals possessing valuable materials realize these were of interest. The explanation process involved defining history and what was worth collecting for use in writing history, or rather attempting to define these concepts.

Society officers used a variety of techniques to collect historical materials. In the Massachusetts Historical Society's first decade, corresponding secretary Rev. Jeremy Belknap proposed individuals as resident and corresponding members based in part on their ability to contribute materials. Through correspondence and in-person encounters, he solicited collectors and families possessing important papers directly. On one occasion, he traveled to Connecticut to retrieve colonial records. Valuing federal documents, he petitioned the United States Congress and Society members in Congress for donations of government publications.[4]

Most significantly, Belknap adopted a tried and true technique of the time: circular letters. Directed to individuals, other societies, and newspapers, the circular letters detailed the kinds of information and documents the Massachusetts Historical Society wished to collect. Recipients were expected to pass the request along, sharing the letters with friends and acquaintances. The letters served as a "wish list" of Society desiderata, disseminating ideas of what had historical value. The circulars served as early incarnations of modern libraries and archives' collection development policies, practices largely dating to the late twentieth century. Other historical societies followed the Massachusetts society's example (see table 2) and their circulars collectively offer a means to explore ideas of history across the societies and over time.[5]

Jeremy Belknap and the Collection of "Historical Matter"

Belknap prioritized collecting historical information. He reviewed the newspapers sent to his son Joseph, a local printer, in 1793. These included *Dunlap's Daily Advertiser*, published six days a week in Philadelphia and comprised of four-to-six-pages of advertisements and legal proceedings with a few additional informative notices often copied from other newspapers. He considered the newspaper "the best collection of historical matter, in the *en passant* way, that is printed anywhere." Belknap esteemed the newspaper because it gathered the type of historical information he valued as it was put together—in passing—rather than as a document of a specific place and time.[6]

The Massachusetts Historical Society organized to collect "historical matter." Judge George Richards Minot and Attorney General James Sullivan

TABLE 2. Known Historical Society Circulars, 1791–1850

1791	Massachusetts Historical Society, Boston
1793	Massachusetts Historical Society, Boston (subtle differences)
1794	Massachusetts Historical Society, Boston (added of list of sources)
1800	Connecticut Academy of Arts and Sciences, New Haven
1805	New-York Historical Society, New York City
1815	Historical and Literary Committee, American Philosophical Society, Philadelphia
1817	New-York Historical Society
1819	American Antiquarian Society, Worcester, Massachusetts
1821	Essex Historical Society, Salem, Massachusetts
1822	Rhode Island Historical Society, Providence
1823	New Hampshire Historical Society, Concord
1823	Massachusetts Historical Society (reissue/adaptation of 1791)
1824	Maine Historical Society, Brunswick
1825	Connecticut Historical Society, Hartford
1825	Historical Society of Pennsylvania, Philadelphia
1830	New Hampshire Historical Society
1832	Indiana Historical Society, Indianapolis
1832	Virginia Historical and Philosophical Society, Richmond
1832? 1835?	Historical and Philosophical Society of Ohio, Columbus
1835	Universalist Historical Society, New York City
bet. 1835–1839	American Historical Society, Washington, District of Columbia
1837	New Hampshire Historical Society
1839	Georgia Historical Society, Savannah
1839	Western Methodist Historical Society, Cincinnati
1840	Connecticut Historical Society (2)
1841	Marietta Historical Society, Marietta, Ohio
1842	Kentucky Historical Society, Louisville
1843	Historical Society of Pennsylvania
1844	Maryland Historical Society, Baltimore
by 1845	Cincinnati Historical Society, Cincinnati (2)
by 1845	Louisiana Historical Society, New Orleans
1846	Dorchester Antiquarian and Historical Society, Dorchester, Massachusetts
1847	Maine Historical Society, Portland
1850	Minnesota Historical Society, Saint Paul
1850	Alabama Historical Society, Tuscaloosa

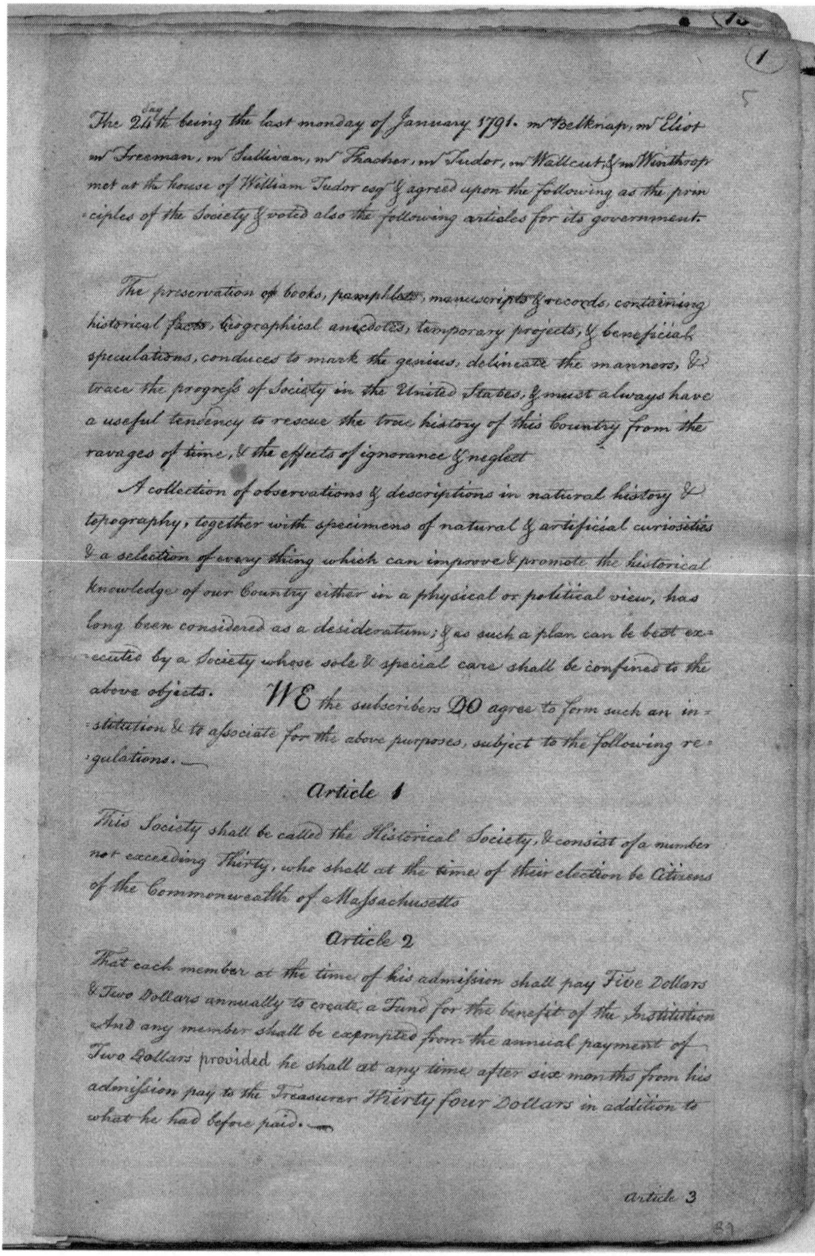

The 24th day being the last monday of January 1791. Mr Belknap, Mr Eliot Mr Freeman, Mr Sullivan, Mr Thacher, Mr Tudor, Mr Wallcut, & Mr Winthrop met at the house of William Tudor esqr & agreed upon the following as the principles of the Society & voted also the following articles for its government.

The preservation of books, pamphlets, manuscripts & records, containing historical facts, biographical anecdotes, temporary projects, & beneficial speculations, conduces to mark the genius, delineate the manners, & trace the progress of Society in the United States, & must always have a useful tendency to rescue the true history of this Country from the ravages of time, & the effects of ignorance & neglect

A collection of observations & descriptions in natural history & topography, together with specimens of natural & artificial curiosities & a selection of every thing which can improve & promote the historical knowledge of our Country either in a physical or political view, has long been considered as a desideratum; & as such a plan can be best executed by a Society whose sole & special care shall be confined to the above objects. WE the subscribers DO agree to form such an institution & to associate for the above purposes, subject to the following regulations.—

Article 1

This Society shall be called the Historical Society, & consist of a number not exceeding Thirty, who shall at the time of their election be Citizens of the Commonwealth of Massachusetts

Article 2

That each member at the time of his admission shall pay Five Dollars & Two Dollars annually to create a Fund for the benefit of the Institution And any member shall be exempted from the annual payment of Two Dollars provided he shall at any time after six months from his admission pay to the Treasurer Thirty four Dollars in addition to what he had before paid.—

article 3

FIGURE 1. "Minutes of the Massachusetts Historical Society meetings," vol. I (1791–1795), 9, Massachusetts Historical Society archives, Collection of the Massachusetts Historical Society.

drafted the Society's constitution. As shown in figure 1, they advocated "preservation of books, pamphlets, manuscripts, and records, *containing* historical facts, biographical anecdotes, temporary projects, and beneficial speculations." By implication, print and manuscript records' value lay in their contents: facts, anecdotes, and speculations. They described the Society's collecting objectives in terms of content and subject: "observations and descriptions in natural history and topography together with specimens of natural and artificial curiosities, and a selection of every thing which can improve and promote the historical knowledge of our country." The Society's collecting interests fell into two overarching categories: information and specimens.[7]

Within a year, the Massachusetts Historical Society emphasized collecting historical information alongside or even in place of documents and specimens. Officers, namely Belknap, identified fourteen different "articles on which the Society request[ed] information" in the first circular, issued in 1791. The Society reprinted its circular several times over the first three years. Newspaper practices of reprinting articles from other papers enabled the circular to reach as far as South Carolina. The Society included a revised version of the circular in the 1794 volume of their *Collections* and had an additional five hundred separate copies printed.[8]

Belknap did not create the first circular from scratch. He drew on his mentor, Boston historian Thomas Prince, who decades earlier had circulated a list of twelve subjects on which he desired information. The Society of Antiquaries in England tried a similar tactic in the mid-eighteenth century and failed, as did the Earl of Buchan's Scottish Society of Antiquaries. News of these earlier failures either did not reach Belknap or did not dissuade him. The Perth Literary and Antiquarian Society of Scotland issued a circular shortly before the Massachusetts society.[9]

The Massachusetts Historical Society's circulars reflected shifting priorities. The initial letter appeared in the *American Apollo* and contained an appeal from Belknap. The Society had already "amassed a large quantity of books, pamphlets, and manuscripts; and are still in search of more," in particular, any information correspondents possessed on fourteen articles. The number of articles grew to fifteen a few years later and was paired with a separate list of desired materials. The Society disseminated a circular recognizably based on the first version as late as 1823. The changes and additions to the original circular, as exhibited in the 1793, 1794, and 1823 versions, indicated the Society's increasing interest in historical materials and information relating to manufacturing, religious institutions, and improvements.[10]

From the outset, historical societies sought to document the past in service to the future. They did not conceive of their collections as shrines to the past or objects of homage or reverence, although local historians in New England used the materials to write works exalting their forebears. Rather, historical collecting activity reflected and responded to contemporary interests and concerns for further development and improvement. Belknap included a simple request for "accounts of manufactures and fisheries, and thoughts on the farther improvement of them" in the first circular, connecting documentation of the present with anticipation of "improvement." Interest in industry within two years prompted separation of that article into two separate queries that emphasized industry and manufacturing over fishing, as New Englanders began to industrialize and build factories.[11]

The Massachusetts society also broadened requests for religious material. The fourth item on the original 1791 circular reflected interest in the "time of gathering churches of every denomination; names of the several ministers; the times of their settlement, removal and death; and their ages at the time of their death." The point reappeared unaltered in 1793, 1794, and 1823. Officers added a list of printed materials the Society wished to collect, "for the civil and ecclesiastical history of this country" to the revised circular in 1794. First and foremost, the officers specified nineteen types of sermons of interest including century, election, anniversary and others connected with secular and political events (assizes, court days, town meetings, victories, defeats). Officers added new items to the circular by 1823, one each to the questionnaire and the list of sermons requested. The additions solicited information on religious improvement and sermons "on ordinations, installations, or removals of ministers, dedication of churches, &c." The changes reflected developing specificity as to the Society's interest in religion.[12]

Although the Massachusetts Historical Society included ecclesiastical history among its objectives, it focused on churches as civic institutions, and sermons as sources of historical information. Sermons commemorating centennial anniversaries, called "century sermons," were of particular interest, for they often reflected on the preceding hundred years. Non-member John Whiting gave the Society a century sermon in 1793, "a more minute account of the first settlement of the Town of Lancaster . . . than any publication extant." Other sermons contained less historical matter. Connecticut historian and corresponding member Benjamin Trumbull noticed the Society's interest in "election sermons" and gathered many from Connecticut. He read over them and did not find "any thing in them worthy of note." Based on this, he concluded that "in a historical view, [even] could a complete collection be obtained they would be of very little importance."[13]

The Massachusetts society sought to collect and preserve a history of improvement, reflecting the officers' views of American history as a tale of progress. The Society's mission involved documenting "all valuable efforts of human ingenuity and industry, from the beginning of its settlement." All versions of the questionnaire solicited information about the establishment and development of towns and cities along with "thoughts on farther improvements . . . to agriculture, roads, or canals" and manufacture. In addition to requesting information about religious associations, the 1823 version inquired about the existence of associations for "literary improvement, or the encouragement of the arts."[14]

Other societies exhibited similar interests in their circulars. Despite some doubt as to the tactic's efficacy, most early societies disseminated at least one circular, typically following establishment and sometimes combined with notice of a given society's formation and organizational documents. Historians took note, as several similarly crafted and disseminated circulars to gather desired information.[15]

Shortly after establishment, New-York Historical Society officers crafted a circular featuring a questionnaire and list of items solicited. They requested manuscripts and printed works, suggesting specific types of particular interest including orations and sermons; legal records; religious proceedings; and descriptions of towns, cities, educational institutions, manufacture, and commerce. A list of twenty-three queries followed, including several about the period of Dutch rule over the colony of New Amsterdam, about which relatively little was known. Other queries reflected interests in manufacture, commerce, and educational and religious institutions. On the whole, the Society was interested in information and material documenting public transactions, characters, events, and places—particularly those specific to New York.[16]

Circulars reflected hierarchical collecting objectives. On the one hand, societies included broad requests for historical materials such as books, pamphlets, manuscripts, and maps. Nevertheless, officers elevated particular kinds of information above others. This applied even to the circulars issued by the American Antiquarian Society and the American Philosophical Society's Historical and Literary Committee, whose officers used descriptive paragraphs rather than lists. One-quarter of the committee's circular requested memoirs, public documents, pamphlets, and eminent men's letters, either as gift or loan. The committee devoted an equal amount of space to addressing fellow Pennsylvanians, soliciting information about Pennsylvania, "particularly every thing relating to our venerable patriarch and founder William Penn, and his first associates." The American Antiquarian Society asked for materials generally while expressing especial interest in early documents published in the Western Hemisphere, natural specimens, and Native American antiquities.[17]

At least one individual expressed doubts about the usefulness of these circulars. Philadelphia lawyer William Tilghman, chairman of the committee, was disappointed in the results and publicly concluded direct solicitations were more successful. Nevertheless, most later historical societies issued at least one circulating letter.[18]

Historians assessing the value of these circulars ought to go beyond the immediate, direct response to consider them as part of a multifaceted education effort. Each stage in the process of solicitation, reception, and organization offered historical societies opportunities to emphasize and encourage certain types of materials over others. At a minimum, the circulars contributed to societies growing collections. The Massachusetts Historical Society reported many donations which collectively reflected an overview of the subjects on which the society collected information: public affairs, commerce, politics, and philosophy writ large. These gifts were also a mix of preexisting records and new articles describing the past and present. At the turn of the nineteenth century, the Society reported gifts from John Avery and ministers Thomas Hall, Abiel Holmes, and James Freeman. Resident members Holmes and Freeman's contributions appeared in the Society's *Collections* in short order. Hall, who had given several gifts of coins and medals, was elected a corresponding member the following year, and went on to give the Society European antiquities. Avery gave only a single gift and was never elected a member.[19]

Historical societies emphasized collection of targeted information throughout the first half of the nineteenth century. While officers included broad, all-encompassing mandates requesting anything considered historical, these were paired with and often subsumed within extensive lists suggesting specific types of facts and data. The newly established Alabama Historical Society disseminated a lengthy list at midcentury encompassing more than three pages of possible topics, from agriculture to geology, fisheries to livestock to Sunday schools. While determined donors focused on open solicitations, others responded to the requested subjects.[20]

"Reduced to Writing": Historical Biases for Textual Preservation

First and foremost, societies solicited written materials, due in no small part to the officers' pursuit of print as a means of preservation. Written documents could be replicated in printed form, increasing survival odds. In focusing on preservation through print, American historical societies drew on English precedents, as antiquaries in England in the late eighteenth and early nineteenth centuries undertook publication of parliamentary rolls and the Domesday Book. American focus on multiplication of copies dated to the start of the historical society movement in the Unites States. From the outset the Massachusetts Historical Society embraced three missions: "to *collect*, *preserve*, and *communicate*"; the last involved printing and publication, for "the surest way of preserving historical records and materials is, not to lock them up; but to *multiply the copies*." The Society set a pattern of early and frequent publication, averaging a volume of *Collections* every two years.[21]

No subsequent society matched the publication rate of the Massachusetts Historical Society, but most societies issued at least one volume or part of a volume, collectively publishing "about 184 major volumes . . . along with over 650 pamphlets" before 1860. Officers lacked the financial resources to publish all they received, which fueled the desire to collect all possible materials and to build fireproof buildings to house the collections, fire being a prime concern in the 1830s and 1840s in cities. Even when publication seemed unlikely, societies solicited written contributions. The Louisiana Historical Society acknowledged in its circular the unlikelihood it would publish a volume of *Collections*, but donations of articles would nevertheless furnish "subjects for the future historian."[22]

The historiographical considerations at the heart of societies' missions helped focus interest on written material. Founders asserted they were not in the business of producing historical works but collecting materials for others to use to write history. Officers of the New-York Historical Society claimed they "confine[d] the range of our exertions to the humble task of collecting and preserving whatever may be useful to others in the different branches of historical inquiry." Similarly, Historical Society of Pennsylvania officers averred the organization did not "undertake to compose a history; its desire is to collect materials for history." The disclaimer related in part to the miscellaneous chronological nature of the volume but also reflected the society's overarching interest in serving as a repository.[23]

Nineteenth-century historians increasingly attacked their eighteenth-century predecessors for insufficient regard for facts and use of supporting materials. Officers of the New-York Historical Society explained in their circular that "without the aid of original records and authentic documents, history will be nothing more than a well-combined series of ingenious conjectures and amusing fables." Increased mentions of existing documents in circulars (before queries rather than after) reflected recognition of primary materials as invaluable for historical writing, but interest remained in acquiring information not necessarily contained in existing documents.[24]

Historical societies issuing circulars after 1815 emphasized document formats of interest (journals, statutes, letters, diaries), but societies continued to solicit creation of new documents where existing ones did not contain the desired information. "It is not in printed books alone that history is to be found," the Cincinnati Historical Society declared in the early 1840s, requesting among other items "the stories of the pioneers *reduced to writing*."[25]

"Every Thing Printed and Written": Shifting Valuations and Priorities

By the 1820s, new historical societies shifted the balance in assigning historical value away from emphasizing information and toward circumstances of creation or non-topical connection to a person, place, or event. Inherently subjective, valuations based on content involved preferential treatment of particular topics and groups over others. Valuing an item because it was created in a particular place, by a person born there, or used by a person with such a connection, meant potential inclusion of materials within historical society collections regardless of contents. Opportunities for inclusion bias persisted, as society officers potentially excluded items deemed unimportant based on a person's gender, class, race, or place. Nevertheless, the shift to external circumstance versus content-based assessment was a step toward the modern elevation of primary sources as the building blocks of history, and part of the development of history as a specialized field.[26]

At first, historical societies used circulars to describe desired materials in terms of content. The New-York Historical Society encouraged donations "of rare and useful books and pamphlets" related to political and civil history. The Society affirmed interest in any American or foreign publications or manuscripts "which throw light on the history of our country." Such solicitations emphasized perceived connections to types of history (political, civil) or American history generally. By implication, publications or manuscripts that officers did not consider illustrative of history might be declined.[27]

Some officers began to locate historical value in the circumstances of production (who, when, where) rather than content. The Essex Historical Society issued a circular in 1821 requesting donations of items "printed in the commonwealth, and especially such as have been written by persons born or residing within the commonwealth." Any work printed in Massachusetts, or written by an individual born or resident at some point in Salem, held value for the Essex Historical Society because of the geographic connection, regardless of topic. The following year, the Rhode Island Historical Society used similar language to encourage donations of works "printed in this State—and manuscripts, especially those written by persons born or residing in this State."[28]

Philadelphian Peter Du Ponceau offers a clear example of the shift from topic-oriented collection to format. He served as corresponding secretary of the American Philosophical Society's Historical and Literary Committee and joined with other officers in 1815 to solicit "in short, every thing which may be considered as interesting to this country, in an historical, statistical, geographical, or topographical point of view." His inaugural address as president of the Historical Society of Pennsylvania, two decades later, encouraged collecting "in short, every thing printed and written that can throw light on our history."The later phrasing left the definition of history open to interpretation and shifted the emphasis from specific categories of topical information to print and manuscripts.[29]

Historical Value: Content, Place, Authorship, and Name-and-Date

Historical society officers utilized at least four valuation methods in determining what materials to solicit and accession. First and foremost, they focused on the documents' content—political, religious, military. Place offered a second means of valuation, wherein items were worth acquiring because they had a connection to a given location. Similarly, officers esteemed other materials based on authorship or who created materials, regardless of place. A fourth means of establishing value focused on the inclusion of identifiable names or dates and hence connections to people or events. These were applied in isolation or combination.[30]

Valuations based on content relied on ideas of what was history. Society officers and members might agree in the abstract, but assessing materials themselves was a different matter. Rev. Thaddeus Mason Harris, librarian of the Massachusetts Historical Society, drafted a letter in 1838 distinguishing between accepted and rejected items. The Society had received a collection of papers, and he explained his decision to keep certain materials that were connected "to facts or events of a general & public nature" and might be useful in writing history. Ample papers were not selected, including "the common files of a lawyer's office, such as Writs, Executions, depositions, letters from Clients . . . [and] letters of a merely personal concern." Such documents related to specific interactions between individuals and companies. By implication the rejected materials were not useful for historical writing. This opinion was not universal, and only private items may have been returned to the family. Twenty-five years later, another Society officer discovered a cache of rejected papers in the Society's attic and, considering their content historical, added them to the collection.[31]

Authorship as a mode of valuation existed alongside the focus on content. Author-based valuations underscored appeals for papers to the heirs of prominent political and military leaders. Historical societies shared their interest in materials connected to prominent national figures, such as George Washington, Benjamin Franklin, and the Marquis de Lafayette. Each society also had state, regional, and local notables and people of interest. Historians and historical societies seeking particular information or letters from specific individuals routinely accepted copies from trustworthy sources (other historians, government clerks) in place of originals. Printed texts also served as suitable substitutes for manuscripts.

Autograph collecting was one area where print or manuscript copies were not acceptable. Practiced far and wide over the nineteenth century, autograph collecting peaked in the 1830s and 1870s. Presbyterian minister William Buell Sprague was the "patriarch" of nineteenth-century autograph collecting and had more than seventy-five thousand autographs at his death. Sprague and other autograph collectors revered original signatures regardless of a documents' contents, although some collectors pruned or removed objectionable material. Late twentieth-century scholars noted autograph collections preserved items otherwise at risk of loss or destruction.[32]

For historical societies, autograph-based appraisals involved esteeming letters as non-substitutable artifacts. Some societies collected the autographs of elected officials and other notables. The Rhode Island society appointed a committee "to procure so far as practicable" signatures of all the state's governors. In a similar vein, the Connecticut society expressed a particular interest in the autographs of "gentlemen of distinction," such as state and federal government office-holders.[33]

Historians and societies frequently valued documents using multiple means. Historian and editor Jared Sparks visited state record offices in search of Revolution-era diplomatic correspondence. He also collected "revolutionary heroes and statesmen" signatures against the possibility of publishing a complete collection of facsimile autographs. For the first purpose, he paid clerks to make copies, but for the latter he needed originals. North Carolina Secretary of State William Hill allowed Sparks to take a number of originals, including letters from Revolution-era notables Thomas Jefferson, Patrick Henry, John Jay, and Henry Laurens. The copies made by the clerks were "deposited in the files" in place of the originals. An official in charge of the Maryland state archives made a similar offer to allow Sparks to take originals instead of copies, on condition of approval by the governor and council. State officials focused on continuity of the contents within the archival files. Government record-making practices often involved the creation and circulation of multiple instances of documents; thus, copies could satisfy archival purposes.[34]

A third valuation means, particularly prevalent among state and local historical societies, involved esteeming materials based on connections to specific places. The Alabama Historical Society asked for materials created by people who were physically present in Alabama (residence, pass-through) apart from people with explicit connection to the state's history. Other historical societies organized around geographic identities did not emphasize physical presence in-and-of-itself to the extent that Alabama did, but most focused on gathering materials related to their particular city, county, state, or region.[35]

Valuations based on the inclusion of names-and-dates had the potential to encompass far more diverse materials than content, author, or place. Rhode Island Historical Society member Rev. Edwin M. Stone donated to the Society 225 documents he had saved from deliberate destruction out of "a conviction that not a scrap bearing a name & date, should be destroyed." Under this rationale, the critical elements for preservation were the ability to connect a given document with a specific person and time. Content, author, and place mattered less. The items Stone saved bore this out, including materials connected to the abduction and sale of enslaved people. Many historical society officers favored ending slavery, but their members and potential donors included ardent defenders of slavery. Amid rising tensions over slavery, historical societies focused on past practices rather than present conflicts. Based on analysis of historical society records for the first half of the nineteenth century, few donated manuscripts were specifically described as documenting slavery and enslaved peoples. What materials the societies did accession were generally print rather than manuscript, such as pamphlets issued by abolition and colonization societies. Stone's donation, justified on the basis of names-and-dates, was an exception.[36]

While name-and-date was Stone's primary mode of valuation, he used other modes to distinguish between the items. In describing 177 letters, broken into 5 lots, he noted authors and, for the most part, subjects. More than 70 letters related to customs and or maritime history. One lot of 58 "brief" letters, dating from Albert Gallatin's term as secretary of the Treasury, Stone considered "chiefly valuable for their autographs, & for the dates of decisions to which they refer." In a related vein, he noted a letter in another lot contained a valuable Jefferson autograph. Thus Stone divided his finds into documents worth preserving as artifacts due to autographs or as reservoirs of information (dates) on the one hand and items with valuable historical content on the other.[37]

People selecting material to preserve in historical society collections or publications used a variety of valuation modes including content, author, place, autograph, and name-and-date. These were not exclusive, and appraisals might invoke multiple modes. Content was perhaps the most prevalent and the most open to interpretation; value based on content varied dependent on any given individual's ideas of history.

"Any Remarkable Persons": Political, Civic, Religious History—and Institutions

Historical societies solicited conversion of the unwritten past into the written past, but the shared interests of historical societies' memberships constrained and constricted the pasts they sought to preserve. The member rolls drew heavily from the ranks of gentleman of property and standing, particularly lawyers and politicians. Efforts to define historical boundaries took place within the broader political climate. Collection of particular subjects and time periods reflected local and national preoccupations, and the act of including and excluding subjects took on greater importance, particularly when controversial. The circulars delineated the particular pasts members sought to preserve, emphasizing a history of European-American control over the land, past and present, and drawing boundaries based on race, wealth, and shared or communal experiences.

Most society officers requested information on politics, economics, and religious institutions, while a few asked for social and cultural information. A circular issued by the New-York Historical Society soon after the famous duel between Aaron Burr and Alexander Hamilton left Hamilton dead included a request for information on "the state of *morals* in our country, at different periods, such as the comparative frequency of *drunkenness, gaming, duelling, suicide, conjugal infidelity, prostitution,* &c. &c.?" The Historical Society of Pennsylvania's 1845 circular incorporated an enquiry about "any peculiar notion, custom, or superstition," reflecting the influence of romanticism. Apart from individual society idiosyncrasies, circulars contained a basic litany of subjects relating to the establishment and maintenance of the United States.[38]

The most common subjects in circulars included topographical descriptions, sketches of local towns and first settlements, biographical notices of prominent men and original settlers, sketches of churches and religious institutions, and indigenous peoples. Historical societies also solicited information on development and improvements in education, manufacture, commerce, and the spread of religion. These subjects reflected control of the land, from mapping the grounds itself (topography) to the establishment of European presence (local towns, first settlements) to improvement and progress (biography, religion, education, and commerce) and the fading presence of the original peoples (narratives of Native Americans). The topics sought would have been familiar to the general public. Many appeared regularly in the newspapers, which featured official documents, price lists, ship arrivals, and extensive advertisements, rather than independent reporting.[39]

One reason historical societies sought to collect complete files of newspapers printed within their respective states or the nation as a whole was the subjects of interest listed in the circulars. Officers asked publishers to contribute volumes, given the limitations of their coffers. At least one resented the "call for a gratuitous file." Within a week of the Connecticut Historical Society vote to request periodicals from state publishers, the New Haven *Daily Herald* noted that only printers and publishers received such requests, not other tradesmen or professionals, so it qualified as an unjustified levy on them. Fortunately for the societies, many other printers and publishers proved less resistant.[40]

Societies' focus on the common world at the expense of private realms extended into the world of business. The society members requested information, such as economic data (accounts of exports, imports and prices), about charitable institutions or voluntary organizations, but not records of private businesses, even those whose proprietors were long dead. Business records were private papers and the societies did not solicit blanket donations of private materials.

Some societies expressed interest in the personal history of individuals, but such references were few and usually buried in long lists. The Alabama Historical Society solicited "Memoirs, correspondence, anecdotes, &c., of any remarkable persons, *male or female*, residing in or passing through the State; or in any way connected with its history;—together with all letters, documents and papers illustrative of *public or private history*." This was a highly unusual acknowledgment of the existence of remarkable women. Other societies requested information on remarkable, distinguished, or eminent people, either using explicitly male terms or generic plurals that left interpretation to the discretion of the reader and by default requested information about men. The societies sought to preserve personal information about persons who qualified as public figures by virtue of their professions "as ministers of the Gospel, politicians, lawyers, physicians, or mechanics" or by their actions on local, regional, or national stages (Roger Williams, William Penn, George Washington).[41]

Historical society officers sought to document and preserve the public world shared by wealthy and eminent men of predominantly British descent. The language used in circulars generally presumed British ancestry. Few requested non-British information on topics such as Spanish, French, and Dutch encounters or settlements. The poor, other than as the implicit recipients of charity, were largely missing. Native American peoples appeared on nearly every circular, but Americans of African descent, whether free or enslaved, did not.

Societies emphasized Anglo-American connections by excluding references to countries other than Great Britain. Few historical societies named countries outside of Great Britain in their circulars, or even mentioned generic "Europeans" in the context of interactions with Native American peoples. The New-York Historical Society' queries about Dutch settlement referred to Dutch control in the distant past. The Alabama Historical Society's circular placed Spanish and French presence in the land as part of the transition from Native Americans to the United States. Other society officers used discrete references seeking information on unnamed countries to which colonies were "first annexed." A rare explicit invocation of England in the Essex Historical Society circular connected American ancestors with distinguished persons in England. The references reflected and reinforced progression of control from non-British nations to England and the United States.[42]

While stressing British roots, historical societies minimized African presences in the Americas, although a few circulars mentioned African Americans, slavery, and abolition. Both slavery and abolition appeared in the New-York Historical Society circular, where officers sought "Minutes and Proceedings of Societies for Abolition of Slavery" along with other documents. The Louisiana Historical Society asked in its 1846 circular about the "increase and progress of population in your parish, distinguishing blacks and whites; advantages of schools and libraries enjoyed; proportion educated?" The invocation of "progress" was ambiguous as to the intentions of the circular's authors with respect to slavery and racial inequality; perhaps the Society's New England-born members sought information to advocate for reconsidering slavery.[43]

The earliest historical society publications focused on governments and places with people often reduced to aggregate numbers (such as morbidity statistics). An anonymous contributor to the *Virginia Historical Register*, "L.M.," encouraged the Virginia Historical Society to rethink collection priorities in the 1840s. L.M. reminded the Society that history should include "not merely, or mainly, the transactions of the *government* of a country, but the doings, the progress, the character of its *people*," and suggested ways to carry this out through compiling data. The author may have had additional motives for the contribution, given references to the adoption of progressive institutions and means of medical treatment, and the prevalence and disappearance of "certain demi-savage passtimes" including "cock-fighting" and "gander-pulling."[44]

In response, society officers began to question collection priorities. Historical Society of Pennsylvania officers published a circular shortly after its organization. Most historical societies continued to use circulars for decades, but the Pennsylvania society published a very different one two decades later. The individuals behind both circulars set forth "to collect all the documents and written or printed evidence, and all the traditionary information that may still be attainable" and suggested topics of interest. The drafters of the earlier version featured subjects focused around public places and eminent or distinguished persons. In contrast, the later circular spanned three times as many pages and solicited descriptions of present and past landscapes, peoples, and activities, and advised readers not to leave out anything "because it may seem trivial or unworthy of notice. . . . *Collect all you can;* whatever it may be, it will be clear gain."[45]

Two other historical societies, founded at midcentury, took different approaches to accomplish the same goal of gathering anything relating to their respective locales. The Alabama Historical Society followed the examples of Massachusetts, Pennsylvania, and others and filled several pages with suggested topics before expressing a desire for "not only what is of local interest . . . but whatever relates to any part of our whole country—whether book document, manuscript, or natural object." Farther to the north, citizens in the territory of Minnesota formed a historical society and immediately published a small pamphlet of *Annals* to "forward . . . to Historical Societies and individuals in order to produce an interchange of reciprocities." Rather than consuming pages specifying the types of information they wished to collect, the organizers satisfied themselves with requesting anything that might "illustrate and perpetuate the history and settlement of our Territory." Content still mattered, but the societies had begun to expand their collections.[46]

"Different Branches of Historical Inquiry": Specimens and Antiquities in Historical Collections

Historical society officers placed high importance on collecting materials for their libraries and paid less attention to specimens or artifacts, presaging the establishment of separate natural and historical museums later in the nineteenth century. In practice, most societies accepted some non-textual items: primarily art, medals, coins, natural history specimens, Native American antiquities, and other items with a connection, real or perceived, to notable historical figures such as John Smith (Virginia), William Penn (Pennsylvania), and Captain John Cook (Rhode Island).[47]

Officers came from the ranks of elite white men, and the very proliferation of commodities made them seem common. Most historical societies overlooked the flourishing market in consumables when accumulating materials. Officers collected some types of artifacts, such as currency specimens, avidly but disdained the vast majority. Medals, coins, and portraits were the most commonly solicited items. The former included written characters and were produced through a process related to printing. As for portraits, Christopher Columbus Baldwin, librarian of the American Antiquarian Society, averred that "the true history" of material objects was "handed down by painting." Baldwin expressed prevailing ideas about historical society collecting after visiting the New-York Historical Society in 1833. "They have many medals and coins, and several interesting old pictures were shown to me," he reported, but "they collect nothing but books, mss, coins, medals & pictures." He approved the New York society's decision to "reject all curiosities excepting they have historical virtue." For his part, he personally discouraged donations to the American Antiquarian Society of artifacts, particularly "old coats and hats and high heeled shoes!"[48]

Even as officers added new areas of textual interests, they narrowed their collecting with respect to non-textual materials with two primary exceptions: natural history specimens and Native American artifacts. Most societies collected antiquities, which they dissociated from contemporary tribes. In contrast, historical societies largely ceased collecting many specimens over the decades.

"With Written Accounts Respecting Them": Specialization between History and Natural History

Historical societies participated in the specialization of learned culture during the late eighteenth and nineteenth centuries, both as specialized organizations differentiated from general learned societies and subject to the further specialization of natural history from history. From the first, historical society founders recognized their narrowed focus distinguished them. "To pursue one particular subject is the only way of succeeding," Massachusetts Historical Society founder John Eliot noted, arguing the Society differed from extant Boston learned organizations because he and other historical society founders "mean to confine our attention to this business of collecting things which will illustrate the history of our country."[49]

For the earliest historical societies, collecting history included establishing cabinets or museums housing coins, curiosities, and natural specimens. The Massachusetts and New York historical societies originally featured natural history among their objectives. The Massachusetts society solicited "natural or artificial productions, which may enlarge the Museum." Officers published a pamphlet including organizational documents and eight appendices with instructions for the preservation of animals, skins, vegetables, "Marine Productions," and "Mineral and Fossil substances." The New York society expressed an interest in natural specimens from the start. After moving into the former city Alms House in 1816, Society officers sent out several circulars requesting mineral, zoological, and botanical specimens for the cabinet, and they also approved the formation of an herbarium.[50]

By and large, officers requested donation of written descriptions and physical specimens. When drafting the American Antiquarian Society's circular, officers restricted interest in specimens to those "*with written accounts respecting them*," effectively making written documentation key to a specimen's value. The creation of new written material containing desired information served as an acceptable substitute for specimens, particularly those difficult or impossible to transport across distances.[51]

Proximity to learned societies focusing on natural history contributed to the uneven decline of historical society interest in natural history. The American Philosophical Society's Historical and Literary Committee did not make natural history a priority. The area was the purview of a different committee of its parent society. Moreover, Philadelphians had recently founded the first separate natural history society, the Academy of Natural Sciences. Cincinnati, the nation's sixth largest city, hosted an active local natural history community, and as a result the Cincinnati Historical Society, established in 1844, had no reason to request natural specimens.[52]

Geography and city size contributed to disassociation of natural history from history. Of societies founded in the 1820s, Essex County (Massachusetts), Rhode Island, and Pennsylvania did not include natural history while Maine, New Hampshire, Indiana, and Virginia did. By the 1830s, societies founded in or near large cities did not request physical specimens in general. Younger historical societies, particularly in the South and West, did continue to solicit natural history donations. The Dorchester Antiquarian and Historical Society asked for "any natural or artificial curiosities" relating to New England's history shortly after establishment in the 1840s, although located near Boston.[53]

The establishment of separate natural history societies led historical societies to reconsider the place of natural specimens in their collections. In Europe scientists began to separate natural history from theology and history by the early nineteenth century although the number of dedicated European naturalists and museums did not swell until the 1830s to 1850s, roughly contemporaneous with similar developments in the United States. Gentlemen in New York City established the Lyceum of Natural History, and Bostonians organized the Society of Natural History. In the 1830s, the Massachusetts and New York historical societies quietly transferred their specimen collections to these nearby natural history societies. The specimen collections were not outright gifts, for the Massachusetts society, at least, specifically chose to "deposit" natural history items, "taking a receipt for the safe-keeping and a list of the same."[54]

"The Few Fragments": Native American Pasts versus Presents

With respect to documenting Native American history, historical society officers projected assumptions onto the historical landscape in three key areas: recognition (or lack thereof) of contemporaneous local presences, collection of the history of white interactions with Native American tribes, and preservation of indigenous histories. Most historical societies, from the longer-settled eastern states to the younger states in the Northwest Ordinance, sought information about Native Americans. Basically, the societies solicited artifacts and histories of indigenous peoples because it was safe—the Indian wars had moved beyond the Mississippi by midcentury. Native nations no longer exerted local political or military power, nor did the collection and preservation of their history threaten national unity, unlike the case with slavery and abolition.

Geography contributed to the non-recognition of natives in the contemporary landscape. The historical society movement originated and flourished in the Northeast. As it spread to the South and West, it followed the paths of settlement. The societies came into existence contemporaneous with marginalization of tribal nations. At least one territory hosted a historical society before achieving statehood, but most citizens did not establish historical societies until lands were firmly under European American control.

Georgians founded a society in 1839, after the expulsion of Cherokee and Creek people was underway. Officers of the American Historical Society did not refer to current Native American presences or activities in their circular. The omission likely reflected the influence of the society's second president, Lewis Cass, who was primarily responsible for carrying out President Andrew Jackson's policies of relocation.[55]

The societies collectively projected and reaffirmed notions of Native Americans as vanishing peoples. Few historical societies were organized close to the Mississippi River, but exceptions included the Missouri Historical and Philosophical Society, established in Jefferson in 1844, the Minnesota Historical Society, established in 1850 in Saint Paul, on the eastern side of the river, and the New Orleans–based Louisiana Historical Society, established in 1835. The Louisiana society asked in its circular "if Indians still [are present], in what condition?" This, along with a query about the presence of Americans of African descent, reflected Louisiana's complex racial history, continuing French and Spanish influences, and the geographical proximity to the trans-Mississippi tribal lands. The Cincinnati Historical Society circular, issued contemporaneously with the Louisiana society's, "endeavor[ed] to snatch the few fragments concerning [Native American peoples], still in existence among the whites, before they are irretrievably lost."[56]

Historical society members conceptualized Native American peoples as geographical ancestors or "our predecessors." Such views were not unique to America. Early modern German accounts of America featured notions of indigenous peoples as non-progressive and vanishing, whose remnants turned the United States "into a historical rather than a natural landscape" for European visitors. Only a few historical societies admitted the possibility of Native Americans' contemporaneous presence among European Americans in their circulars. Belknap's original language for the Massachusetts Historical Society circular, reused as late as the 1820s, included a request for the "number and present state of any remaining Indians among you." The New-York Historical Society enquired after "the Indian tribes which formerly inhabited your district, or which may now occupy any portion of it." Even as these societies allowed for current coexistence, they emphasized past possession.[57]

In collecting and preserving Native American history, most societies favored materials documenting the history of white experiences versus indigenous ones. Officers asked about place names derived from Native American words and their meanings. Although the names survived to become part of the map of the United States, the request reflected interest in documenting European control over the land. Societies also sought treaties and accounts of negotiations between Native American nations and Europeans. While many officers acknowledged imbalances in the treaties, preservation of the documents affirmed white legal control of the land. Furthermore, societies requested narratives of wars, particularly with European settlers, and "the adventures and sufferings of Captives, Voyagers, and Travellers." Such accounts stressed justifications for the transition of legal control to whites through battles and ill treatment of captives and helped perpetuate identification of them as other than and unequal to the Europeans.[58]

Textual preferences worked against efforts to document the history of Native American peoples. Some societies solicited translation and conversion of oral tradition into new written documents, but the desire to capture in paper and ink contributed to cultural reappropriation of indigenous oral traditions as myths rather than history. Several Native American peoples, particularly the Cherokee, began to endorse and facilitate the efforts of some whites to document their history and to write their own histories by the 1830s, but historical societies' emphasis on writing privileged European American accounts of indigenous peoples. Further, much of historical societies' early interest in Native American history focused on languages versus lives and lived experience. The Historical and Literary Committee of the American Philosophical Society studied Native American languages, such as that of the Lenni Lenape in the late 1810s. John Farmer of the New Hampshire Historical Society argued two decades later that Massachusetts Historical Society publications "should exclude all Indian Grammar, Indian Vocabularies," which he considered more appropriate "place[d] in the Amer[ican] Acad[emy] or Philosophical Transactions," presaging the development of ethnology and anthropology separate from history and historical societies.[59]

Inasmuch as society officers solicited historical artifacts other than medals, coins, and portraits, they sought Native American antiquities. Collection of artifacts relied heavily on found items and extraction from the ground, either in the process of digging building foundations or through funded excavations. The American Antiquarian Society supported excavations in the Mississippi Valley to literally dig history out of the ground. At the time, Society officers considered the mound-builders an extinct people, more advanced than living Native American peoples and unconnected to them. In the Northeast, this contributed to continuation of whites' overlooking contemporaneous indigenous presences in settled New England villages in favor of a reimagined, storied past. Such attitudes extended elsewhere as well. Officers of the Historical Society of Pennsylvania asked about "Indian graves, mounds, or battle-grounds" or "those who recollect when Indians lived in your vicinity," implying all Native Americans within the state were dead or removed to other places.[60]

At the same time, historical society officers delineated the temporal boundaries of American history as starting with discovery and settlement. Through interest in the arrival of whites, they affirmed existing American historians' focus on European presences as the starting point of American history—Columbus, Jamestown, and Plymouth. Native artifacts, particularly those predating European arrival, potentially complicated the linear narrative of American progress. As one scholar noted, the swiftness with which American scholars adopted the term "prehistoric" to apply to Native American peoples, following its coinage by a Scottish archaeologist in 1851, suggested investment in conceptualization of a past before the start of American history.[61]

Historical societies' interests in Native American peoples included controversy. An early conflict within the American Antiquarian Society was about focusing on digging up ancient American history versus preserving Anglo-American printed materials. Despite divisions over the subject, historical societies solicited written and material culture artifacts documenting Native American presences in the past and, to a lesser extent, present. The conversion of Native American traditions from oral to written contributed to contests over tribal histories taking place within European-dominated venues as individuals involved in disputes could point to written, published accounts as authoritative sources. Collection and preservation of materials removed from the earth or found on property in the control of individuals of European descent emphasized the perceived disappearance of Native American tribes from the historical landscape and affirmed European possession and control of the land.[62]

"The Things of Today": Revising Collecting Priorities

By and large, historical societies understood their mission as gathering historical information for use in the writing of history. The emphasis on facts and information prompted members and correspondents to create new documents—chronicles, local histories—addressing the types of information the societies requested. Officers valued documents as much or more based on content than circumstances of creation, although they gathered documents as sources of information rather than as artifacts in and of themselves. The New England Historic Genealogical Society went further near midcentury, advocating preservation of manuscripts whether or not they had been printed. It reminded readers that future historians might wish to view originals to resolve contradictory passages. The publication of document extracts often inspired the desire to review the omitted passages. The Society was horrified that many people permitted destruction of manuscripts "*because they had been printed from*, and hence *could be of no further use!*"[63]

Some historical society members recognized the extent to which past and present actions constricted future writing of history. New Hampshire historian John Kelly asked fellow antiquarian John Farmer, then putting together a New Hampshire *Gazetteer*, "Will it not be worth while for you to *preserve* the manuscripts which have assisted you . . . ? It would, I think, be a *treat* to you, I am sure it would to me, to have the rummaging of those which were once in the possession of the [eighteenth-century New England] Annalist [Thomas] Prince." Kelly's query positioned the manuscripts Farmer utilized as valuable in relation to the end product, with curiosity as a rationale for the manuscripts' preservation. Comparing Farmer's manuscripts to those used nearly a century earlier by Prince implied future historians would find them of interest. Perhaps Farmer agreed with Kelly as to the potential value of the documents, for he owned several manuscript versions of his publications when he died.[64]

In the process of collecting materials for future historians, societies effectively focused primarily on the past. Lemuel Shattuck had suggested the solicitation of town chroniclers to record events for future historians. While officers largely agreed on their duties in service to future generations, differences over how to carry these out extended to overlooking active documentation of their own times. A few individuals were perturbed that their fellows focused on older documents versus contemporary ones. An officer of the Rhode Island Historical Society encouraged preservation of ephemeral materials, for "the things of today will be history tomorrow." Similarly, Pennsylvania historian Edward Armstrong warned fellow historians that, even as they regretted their ancestors' lack of action in many instances, "we are indifferent . . . to the familiar present, and any neglect to preserve what now can be perpetuated, may, one hundred years hence, become in turn, to our successors, a subject of equally unavailing regret."[65]

While most historical societies considered collecting and preserving historical materials a rationale for existence and action, there was an exception. Twenty subscribers in Hadley, Massachusetts, organized a society named for their neighborhood: the Plainville Historical Society. Rather than amassing and protecting materials documenting their history, the members purchased works of history and biography for circulation. The organization began as a social library with the choice of name reflecting a particular interest in historical writing. The Plainville Historical Society exemplified the coexistence of different understandings of historical societies in the early Republic. The multiplication of societies during the second quarter of the nineteenth century included not only geography and religion but approach and purpose. Other historical societies sought to ensure ample documentation for future historical writing. The Plainville members wanted to read history.[66]

Chapter Four

"Disjointed Fragments"

Materials as History versus Materials for History

THE EARLY UNITED STATES HELD dangers for vulnerable documents. An accidental flame, a blocked chimney, or a lightning strike could easily set structures afire, destroying homes, lives, and records. War was another menace. The Revolution and the War of 1812 wrought havoc on documents, including the books in the early Library of Congress. Water threatened written materials through dramatic floods or the slow growth of mold. Against these perils, people had at least one recourse: the printing press. Since the fifteenth century, printers in Europe had promoted the idea of printing as the art that preserved all other arts, and settlers carried the message to the North American colonies.[1]

Early historical society officers embraced publication as a part of their preservation mission, so they did more than collect and keep documents, they made, produced, and compiled them. As part of doing business, officers generated internal records: constitutions, bylaws, rules, meeting minutes, correspondence, financial accounts, library catalogs, and more. Of equal importance, the societies produced publications intended to be disseminated, read, and used to write history. Learned societies on both sides of the North Atlantic printed circulars, pamphlets, and volumes. By the end of the eighteenth century, historical and antiquarian societies preserved valuable documents and disseminated multiple copies through publication even as they accumulated book, manuscript, and artifact collections.[2]

Historical societies actively participated in the production of printed works. A scholar identified Rev. Jeremy Belknap, founder of the Massachusetts Historical Society, and pioneering historical editor Ebenezer Hazard as the originators of complementary but separate traditions of historical repositories and documentary publications, yet many historical societies actively produced printed collections. The Massachusetts society was responsible for nearly a hundred items and averaged a volume of *Collections* every two years, while the New-York Historical Society had produced eighty-five publications by 1850. These societies were exceptions, as most produced at best a few pamphlets or a volume. Some did not print at all. Society publications have received little scholarly examination. Most scholarship has focused on the period before 1820 or historical societies as nurturing the development of the local history genre.[3]

Volumes produced by historical societies reveal an increased focus on providing the raw materials of history versus organizing the materials into connected, documentary histories. Officers viewed their responsibility as accumulating historical facts and materials for others to use in producing future historical works. Thus they drew distinctions between preserving history and writing it. Publication committees worked to avoid controversy and selected materials aimed at members' interests and ideas of history. At the same time, society officers supported or sponsored the production of historical treatises by others, giving them access to collections or contributing financial assistance toward publication costs.

Publication and Precedents

When officers of the Massachusetts Historical Society decided to publish, they had European and American precedents on which to draw. England's Royal Society began producing *Philosophical Transactions* in the mid-seventeenth century, shortly after the restoration of Charles II. Closer to Boston, the Philadelphia-based American Philosophical Society published a volume of *Transactions* in 1769, a second in 1785, and two in the 1790s. These works featured member-provided papers, an early form of peer review as inclusion in society publications was a mark of distinction. The American Philosophical Society *Transactions* for 1785 filled four hundred pages and included forty-five communications, three from Jeremy Belknap.[4]

The London-based Society of Antiquaries published several installments of *Archaeologia* in the late eighteenth century. Whereas philosophical society publications emphasized member-authored works, *Archaeologia* volumes presented a mix of original articles and historical documents covering a wide range of dates and interests. Fellows of the Society were expected to subscribe to the publications but were not prompt at providing payment. They owed the Society nearly one thousand pounds by 1807, even after a round of letters sent to individuals in arrears.[5]

It is unclear if members of the Massachusetts Historical Society involved in early publications were aware of the example of the *Archaeologia*, since it was mentioned in neither the Harvard College's 1790s library catalogue nor that of the Massachusetts society. The American Antiquarian Society consciously followed in the Society of Antiquaries' footsteps, naming its major publication the *Archaeologia Americana*. Institutional documents and two early accounts of exploration filled the first pages of the *Archaeologia Americana*, but the rest of the volume was member-authored letters and descriptions of Native American peoples and the mound-builders, considered a separate race at the time. The work thus mirrored the Society of Antiquaries' preferences for member contributions about more distant pasts. The American society's volume also included costly engraved maps and illustrations of mounds in imitation of the London publications, possible because founder Isaiah Thomas subsidized the publication. The volume sold slowly.[6]

Historical society publications implicitly affirmed and promoted specific ideas of historical value. The act of creating historical societies launched a process wherein every step justified and legitimized the next. Societies sought to gather authoritative collections of materials documenting the history of specific places, events, or peoples. Officers selected materials, which were used to publish volumes. In turn, the volumes supported the society's legitimacy and authority. Success encouraged imitation. Through exchanges and complimentary copies, societies asserted local identities and histories and affirmed, reaffirmed, and disseminated ideas about their importance and how to carry out their missions.[7]

Publishing a volume of several hundred pages required sizable commitment on the part of an historical society. Most had few funding sources other than member dues. Officers relied on the volunteer labor of publications committees, typically two to five members. Societies usually assumed the costs and risks of publication. They donated complimentary copies to notable benefactors or other learned institutions. The Historical Society of Pennsylvania gave or exchanged publications with more than thirty learned societies from South America and Europe over its first quarter century (see table 3).

TABLE 3. Learned Society Publication Gifts to and from the Historical Society of Pennsylvania, 1825–1850

	Voted to Distribute To	**Received From**
Pennsylvania	Academy of Natural Sciences American Philosophical Society Apprentices Library (Philadelphia) Athenæum of Philadelphia Athenæum of Westchester City Library (Philadelphia) Dickinson College Library of the Legislature of Pennsylvania (Harrisburg) Library Company of Philadelphia Mercantile Library (Philadelphia) Southwark Library (Philadelphia)	Academy of Natural Sciences American Philosophical Society Mercantile Library (Philadelphia)
Northeast	Albany Institute (New York) American Antiquarian Society (Massachusetts) Connecticut Academy of Arts and Sciences Harvard University (Massachusetts) Massachusetts Historical Society New Hampshire Historical Society New-York Historical Society Rhode Island Historical Society	American Antiquarian Society Brown University (Rhode Island) Maine Historical Society Massachusetts Historical Society New Hampshire Historical Society New-York Historical Society New England Historic Genealogical Society (Massachusetts) Regents of the University of New York Rhode Island Historical Society
South and West	Georgia Historical Society Indiana Historical Society Library of Congress (Washington, D.C.) Literary and Philosophical Society of New Jersey Michigan Historical Society Transylvania University (Kentucky) University of Virginia	Historical Society of the University of North Carolina Indiana Historical Society Kentucky Historical Society Maryland Historical Society Michigan Historical Society New Jersey Historical Society Smithsonian Institute (Washington, D.C.) Virginia Historical Society

TABLE 3. Learned Society Publication Gifts to and from the Historical Society of Pennsylvania, 1825–1850 (*continued*)

	Voted to Distribute To	**Received From**
Outside the United States	Academy of Sciences (Guatemala) Bibliothèque Royale (France) Historical and Geographical Society of Brazil Library of the British Museum (England) Library of the University of Leyden (Holland) Royal Library at Göttingen (Hanover) Royal Library at Stockholm (Sweden) Royal Society of Northern Antiquaries (Denmark)	Cambridge University (England) Geological Society of London (England) Literary and Historical Society of Quebec (Canada) Royal Society of Northern Antiquaries (Denmark)

Data from "Board Minutes, 1825–1844," [24, 54]; "Society Minutes, 1824–1843," [111–13]; and "Library Accession Book I, 1825–1862," Historical Society of Pennsylvania Archives, Historical Society of Pennsylvania, Philadelphia.

Problems of Format, Content, and Arrangement

Producing publications required reconciliation of differing philosophies of historical society publication. Societies appointed publication committees of two to four members, usually drawn from the officers and board. The committee members often lived in close proximity and could conduct business face to face, thus relatively little documentation of their labors and decisions exists in institutional records. Fortunately, correspondence concerning the 1824 installment of the *Collections of the New Hampshire Historical Society* (henceforth *NHHS Collections*) survived, showcasing the types of negotiations and decisions involved in producing printed works.

Concord historian and author John Farmer and New Hampshire Historical Society president and former governor William Plumer Sr. both conceived of Society publications as vehicles for preserving materials relating to New Hampshire history. Farmer focused on preservation, preferring to prioritize printing materials not readily available. Plumer emphasized the state as an organizing theme and imagined the *NHHS Collections* as a central resource containing all relevant materials documenting New Hampshire's history.

Based on their letters and the elements of the final volume for which they were responsible, they represented competing views of historical societies as producers versus selectors and interpreters.

Although William Plumer Jr. served on the publication committee, his father was more involved in the project. Born in Newburyport, Massachusetts, Plumer Sr.'s family moved to New Hampshire when he was young. He became a Baptist preacher, then a lawyer and politician in the legislature of New Hampshire and Congress. He was twice elected governor of New Hampshire, then retired to focus on writing projects, including a history of North America and an autobiography, neither of which he finished. Months before the establishment of the New Hampshire Historical Society, future founder John Kelly noted Plumer Sr. "would make a good President of an Antiquarian or Historical Society in this State."[8]

Ill health and the difficulties of travel prevented Farmer from attending the meeting to organize the New Hampshire Historical Society, but he was one of the forces behind its creation and early successes. Farmer grew up in Amherst, New Hampshire, and published his first historical work at the age of twenty-four. Although not a member of the Massachusetts Historical Society at the time, he contributed historical sketches of two New Hampshire towns to the *Collections of the Massachusetts Historical Society* (henceforth *MHS Collections*). He moved to Concord in 1821 to become an apothecary but became involved in antiquarian, historical, and genealogical publishing ventures. He was elected a member of the American Antiquarian Society in 1820 and a corresponding member of the historical societies of Massachusetts in 1822 and New York in 1819. Along with Concord printer Jacob B. Moore, Farmer produced the annual *New England Register* (1822–38), the short-lived periodical *Collections Historical and Miscellaneous* (1822–23), and a *Gazetteer* of the state (1823). His historical labors made him a natural choice for the publication committee.[9]

Geographic distance and business distractions combined to make Farmer the pivotal individual involved in producing the first volume of *NHHS Collections*. Lawyer and fellow committee member Parker Noyes of Salisbury was preoccupied with court business. The other member, William Plumer Jr. of Epping, spent much of his time in Washington, where he represented New Hampshire in Congress. Plumer Jr. "refers the business of print to Mr. Noyes and myself," Farmer noted, "and I suppose Mr. Noyes will refer it to Mr. Plumer and myself" then "perhaps between us all, we shall do nothing."[10]

The committee accomplished rather more than nothing, mostly due to Farmer. Distance between the committee members necessitated use of correspondence to conduct most of their business. Many letters survive as part of the papers of Plumer and Farmer. The collection of Farmer's correspondence includes exchanges with New Hampshire Historical Society Recording Secretary John Kelly, whom Farmer had wanted appointed to the committee.[11]

Periodicals or Volumes?: The Matter of Format

The initial decision facing the committee involved determining format: a volume or periodical numbers. Kelly approved of the latter as more cost effective than "launching out in a big book at once," an important consideration, as the New Hampshire Historical Society had little money. Farmer discussed the matter with librarian Jacob Moore, who later contracted to print the volume. Moore believed that "proper attention on the part of the members of the Society" could result in sufficient subscribers to cover publication costs and evidently convinced Farmer of the same. Plumer Jr. likewise preferred a single work, calculating that "a volume of 400 pages, costing $0.75, would sell of $1.50 at least, so that a hundred & fifty subscribers would pay for our 300 copies." His father also favored a volume, offering the optimistic view that "every member of course would take one, & other gentlemen would subscribe or purchase." At length, the committee collectively concluded the Society had enough funds to cover publication of a volume, and the format would be better received by members and the public.[12]

The New Hampshire society made publication decisions following in the footsteps of other historical societies in general and Massachusetts in particular. Both Farmer and Plumer Sr. were corresponding members of the Massachusetts Historical Society and familiar with the Massachusetts society's publications. Farmer and Moore owned the *MHS Collections* and loaned them on occasion. Kelly admired the publications overall and "hope[d] ours will equal theirs," while Plumer explicitly encouraged the committee to produce a substantial volume "similar to those of the first volumes of the Massachusetts Historical collections."[13]

In actuality, the New Hampshire society followed the Massachusetts society's second publication model. The Massachusetts Historical Society's first publishing initiative was not volumes but inserts in the *American Apollo*, a local periodical. Two young Boston printers, including Belknap's son Joseph, started it less than a year after the Massachusetts society's foundation. Society officers agreed to provide sufficient content to fill four or eight pages for each issue. These would be separately paginated, and the Society would receive fifty copies. Publishing in the *American Apollo* offered officers a chance to preserve materials, disseminate them widely, educate readers about the Society and its objectives, and solicit donations.[14]

The *American Apollo* became a short-lived effort by the Massachusetts Historical Society to engage popular interest and financial support. Belknap and Young directed their proposal to "Friends of Science, Arts, Agriculture, Manufactures, and Commerce." The publication offered a variety of political, business, and entertaining content. The intended audience represented a small portion of the general populace but far more than the young Society's membership rolls. The publishers aimed to reach an audience of professional men and political, commercial, and literary leaders plus their wives and daughters, as women were encouraged to study history. The Society's first supplement contained documents with a general theme and appeal: Massachusetts's 1745 capture of Louisbourg in French Canada during the French and Indian War. Primarily letters, the documents formed an epistolary history of the expedition interspersed with reports and the occasional anecdote.[15]

The first issue also included a prefatory introduction from the elder Belknap appealing to national pride and challenging citizens to ensure they preserved the nation's history. Regional pride also warranted support, as settlers and colonists of early New England "were early attentive" to the matter of history. Interest in preserving through publication did not appear until halfway through the three-page essay.[16]

The manner in which the Massachusetts Historical Society's contributions appeared undercut their potential for appeal beyond the membership. The items in the first issue were related, but later contributions had a miscellaneous character. Belknap foresaw the potential for problems and advised readers in the first issue that documents arrived unpredictably, therefore time might not allow sufficient "opportunity to digest them in the best order." Officers would print them in whatever order seemed appropriate and provide a yearly index. The documents varied widely in length, date, form, and content. They included acknowledgments of donations, descriptions of Worcester and Dorchester, letters between colonial leaders, brief anecdotes, and a memoir of Daniel Gookin with the first installment of his *Historical Collections of the Indians in New England*, which may have been serialized over several issues.[17]

Ultimately, the published materials provided by the Massachusetts Historical Society did not meet the subscribing public's expectations. Belknap attributed the venture's failure to subscribers looking for "a regular" (narrative) history and finding instead the miscellaneous items the Society provided. The number of subscribers, originally more than a thousand, declined dramatically within six months. This was typical of eighteenth-century magazines, a large proportion of which failed within a year. The *American Apollo* did well to last as long as it did. Joseph Belknap and his partners had assumed the risk of the project in hopes of reaping financial rewards but lost money even after renegotiating terms with the Society. The arrangement was dissolved in 1794.[18]

In face of the *American Apollo*'s failure, Jeremy Belknap appealed to the public to provide popular financing for the *MHS Collections*. He requested "a generous subscription and an extensive circulation" to encourage the Massachusetts society's publications. The Society would share everything it received, he assured the public, not merely history but also biography, topography, travel accounts, and information on manufacture and commerce so as "to do real service to the community." He invoked national pride again, this time as a threat. If the Society did not receive enough support, it would "record this as one of the characteristics of the American people, that they are backward to encourage the publication of materials for the history of their own country." The appeal failed. The Society published annual volumes of *MHS Collections* from 1791 to 1795, thanks to the supplements for the *American Apollo*, but did not issue volumes for two years.[19]

Following the failure of the *American Apollo*, the Massachusetts Historical Society assumed financial risks for future publications. The Society focused on its members as sources of money and subscription agents to continue publishing. As a sign of the magnitude of the problem, the Society appointed a six-person committee to investigate whether to continue publishing. At a special meeting, the committee recommended continuing the *MHS Collections*. The Society voted to publish four hundred or more copies of volumes in quarterly numbers of seventy-two pages, priced at twenty-five cents per number. Competition among publishers was high, and the developing nation lacked a book distribution system until into the 1820s. Faced with the challenge of selling the volumes, the committee opted for a subscription mode. Success at subscription-based publication was a mark of prestige within learned society circles. Society officers asked resident members to solicit subscriptions from others and subscribe for two copies themselves. The *MHS Collections*' success thus rested on volumes that appealed to members[20]

Old Documents and New Essays: Prioritizing Content

Shifting to produce member-subscribed volumes instead of a periodical supplement did not require changing volume content for the Massachusetts Historical Society. The Society had rarely considered popular appeal, and the *MHS Collections* contained little of a personal nature. Publication committees chose excerpts from private and personal sources for relevance to public events and persons. Thus, volumes featured official reports, correspondence, and documents alongside articles describing public places, institutions, and knowledge (churches, schools). The description of Wellfleet, Massachusetts, written by local minister Levi Whitman for the Society (see figure 2), appeared in the 1794 volume and included the kind of information the Society had requested in its circular: topography, climate, town incorporation, schools, and oldest residents, as local historians often took gazetteers as a model for organizing information. Whitman also provided a five-page bill of mortality covering the preceding decade. Such entries pleased scholars. German professor Christoph Daniel Ebeling described the volumes he received that year "without flattery" as "the only source wherein one *may drink deep*, as Pope says." The information, while valuable, hardly made for scintillating reading.[21]

The *MHS Collections* contained a sizable miscellany of older documents and newer accounts, addressing a variety of subjects. The table of contents for the twelfth volume, published in 1814, featured forty-four articles. The articles ranged in date from 1626 (one item) to 1814 (six items), with a disproportionate number documenting the early nineteenth century. They were not organized chronologically or geographically within the volume. Many items provided historical, topographical, or statistical information connected to specific places, including a 1626 list of items needed to venture to Virginia, vital statistics for two Massachusetts towns, and a "Letter on the Condition of Georgia, 1735." One described a natural history topic (a fossil tooth). Another offered a recent summary of the state of Native American peoples, including the Wyandots, Shawnees, Miamis, and Cherokees.[22]

Consistent with learned culture practices, historical societies encouraged scholarship by their members. Officers expected to receive copies for physical or printed collections. Members regularly read papers at quarterly meetings

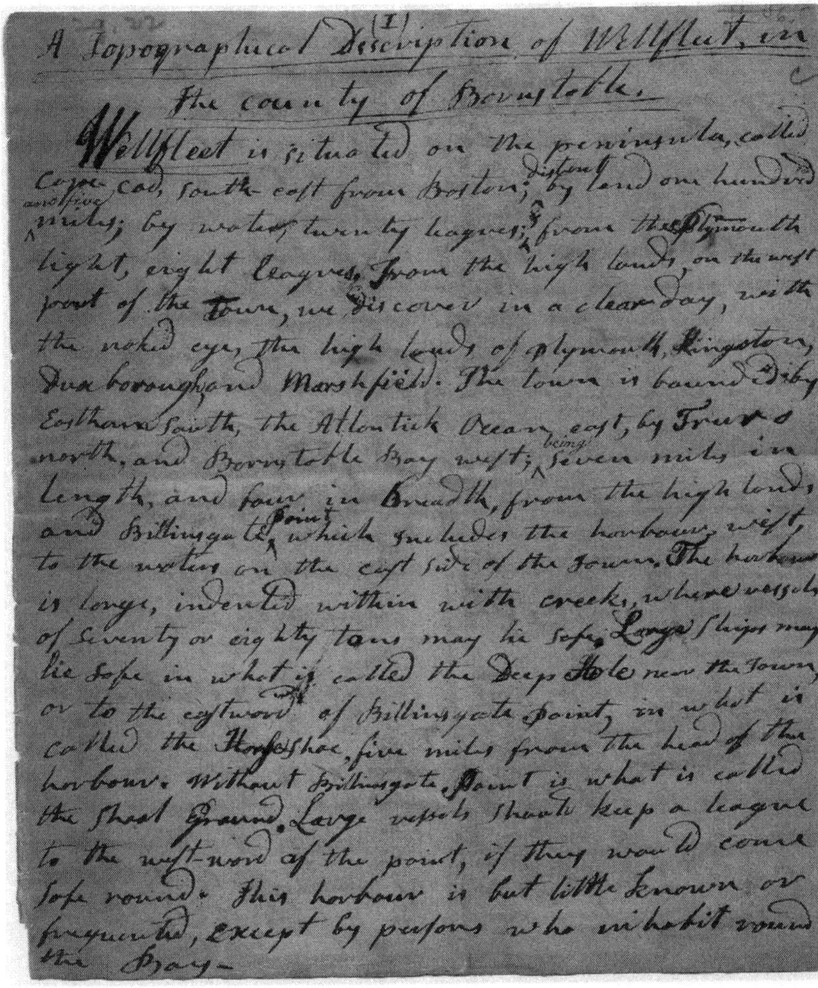

A Topographical Description of Wellfleet, in the county of Barnstable.

Wellfleet is situated on the peninsula, called Cape Cod, south east from Boston; distant by land one hundred and five miles; by water, twenty leagues; & from the Plymouth light, eight leagues. From the high lands, on the west part of the Town, we discover in a clear day, with the naked eye, the high lands of Plymouth, Kingston, Duxborough and Marshfield. The town is bounded by Eastham south, the Atlantick Ocean east, by Truro north, and Barnstable Bay west; being seven miles in length, and four in breadth, from the high lands and Billingsgate Point, which includes the harbour, west, to the waters on the east side of the Town. The harbour is large, indented within with creeks, where vessels of seventy or eighty tons may lie safe. Large ships may lie safe in what is called the Deep Hole near the Town, or to the eastward of Billingsgate point, in what is called the Horseshoe, five miles from the head of the harbour. Without Billingsgate Point is what is called the Shoal Ground. Large vessels should keep a league to the westward of the point, if they would come safe round. This harbour is but little known or frequented, except by persons who inhabit round the Bay.

FIGURE 2. Levi Whitman, "Topographical description of Wellfleet (Mass.)," Collection of the Massachusetts Historical Society.

that later appeared in print. On one occasion, Philadelphia gentleman Joshua Francis Fisher brought what was to become an article on early Pennsylvanian poets and poetry, as well as items related to William Penn. These subsequently appeared in print. Samuel W. Eager of New York attributed publication of his 1846 *Outline History of Orange County* to the encouragement of the Historical Association of Newburgh, New York. Historical societies did not select all materials for publication. Casper Morris's paper on Robin Hood for the Pennsylvania society did not make it into print, probably because the topic was irrelevant to American history.[23]

The Massachusetts Historical Society produced volume after volume featuring miscellaneous old and new works. On one occasion officers deviated from their usual presentation of miscellanies to print a single work long enough to fill two volumes: William Hubbard's seventeenth-century manuscript *History of New England*. Rather than undertake the financial risk of printing the work on its own, the Society petitioned the Massachusetts legislature for support. After all, in 1682 the Massachusetts General Court had given Hubbard fifty pounds for his historical work. In the interim, other historians had made use of the volume, including Thomas Prince and Thomas Hutchinson, each of whom considered it of great value. The legislature promptly passed a resolution agreeing to purchase six hundred copies. This enabled the Society to publish Hubbard's *History* as two volumes of its *Collections* in 1815.[24]

In contrast to Massachusetts, the New-York Historical Society initially offered a publication with popular appeal and a unified subject: foundational documents establishing what became New York. Although organized in 1804, the Society produced a first volume seven years later. Its work celebrated the centennial of Henry Hudson's navigation of the river named for him and featured content included his journals. The work also incorporated an anniversary discourse by Society member Rev. Samuel Miller placing Hudson's voyages in the context of other explorers and explaining why Hudson deserved recognition for discovering New York and not Florentine Guivanni da Verrazzano, whose account of his discovery in the name of France was also included in the volume.[25]

The first volume of the New-York Historical Society thus formed the type of historical arrangement that Belknap thought the public expected of the *American Apollo*, and the Massachusetts society had not delivered after the first issue. The contents traced an arc from discovery and navigation of the Hudson River through the settlement of New Netherlands, its interactions with New England, and the eventual establishment of New York under English laws. In addition to Hudson's journals, the work included extracts from Ebenezer Hazard's collections, specifically records documenting New York's early history. The Society justified republishing them because they were otherwise scattered throughout the records and "have not been so extensively read as they deserve to be." The items consisted of official correspondence between the New England commissioners and Dutch governors Willem Kieft and Peter Stuyvesant. The volume ended with the 1656 conditions set for settlers in the New Netherlands, the 1650 act delineating the border between New Netherlands and New England, and laws for New York following England's assumption of control. In toto, the work affirmed state pride and New York's Dutch antecedents.[26]

The New York society's publication committee perceived the potential for public disappointment with the next volume but focused on the issue of chronology alone rather than combination of chronology and subject. The committee included a preface notifying readers that the chronological arrangement in the first volume was "convenient, and deemed expedient," but the Society considered itself "at perfect liberty" to provide materials in non-chronological order in the future. In point of fact, two of the Society's next volumes (III and IV, 1821–26) presented a chronological history of New York from the pen of a former chief justice.[27]

Historical societies shared interests in descriptive material particularly of political, civil, and indigenous matters, but many chose to print comparatively recent documents rather than older works. The topics often had a narrow appeal and sometimes the volumes resembled gazetteers, as local historians in particular found in the form a model for treating their subjects. French-born Peter Du Ponceau shaped the idiosyncratic publication of the Historical and Literary Committee of the American Philosophical Society. The work resembled the parent society's *Transactions*, favoring member-authored articles and correspondence. Du Ponceau's interest in Native American languages developed through correspondence on behalf of the committee, and as a result the volume featured four items discussing languages. Similarly, the American Antiquarian Society's second volume of *Archaeologia Americana* (1836) featured member Albert Gallatin's lengthy description of Native American peoples and languages, which filled more than four hundred pages and dwarfed the remaining materials. Other historical societies also published works containing predominantly new material—addresses, topographical sketches, local histories, and compiled data.[28]

When the New Hampshire Historical Society publication committee decided to follow the Massachusetts Historical Society's miscellany approach, it turned its attention to content. Appealing to members meant providing the kind of materials they valued. Even more fraught than the format of the volume was the question of what to publish. Plumer Jr. off in Washington, recommended an article on the 1775 census and an eye witness account of Bacon's Rebellion in Virginia, which he had found in the Library of Congress in Jefferson's handwriting. He had "seldom read a more curious document," although he admitted that there was "matter enough in New Hampshire," so the New Hampshire society should probably not "go to Virginia for materials." Farmer concurred that the volume should focus on New Hampshire materials and declined to include the Virginian document. He did include the census. Locale was a continuing theme: the *NHHS Collections* should center on New Hampshire.[29]

The first volume of *NHHS Collections* closely resembled the Massachusetts society volumes. New articles filled much of the publication, including historical and topographical sketches of Concord, Bedford, and Enfield, New Hampshire, a list of Hillsborough County Congregational ministers, and mortality statistics for Rochester (1776–1822) and Fitzwilliam (1802–22). Some articles were unsolicited, but Farmer took an active role in arranging content. He asked Kelly to encourage submission of materials among his connections and also provide the introductory sketch about the Society. When the first version did not meet Farmer's expectations, he pushed Kelly to lengthen it.[30]

Chronological, Topical, or Miscellaneous Arrangement?

The New Hampshire society's imitation of the *MHS Collections* extended to the volume's physical appearance, replicating and reinforcing assumptions that its primary audience was scholars. The work included a table of contents, but no index or list of articles by author and no chronology. Many entries in the table of contents were simple descriptions encompassing the type of document, author or origin, and date. The contents listed "Deposition of Elizabeth Miles" without any indication that the item contained a discussion of relations between settlers and Native Americans and the latter making away with enslaved people. Volume presentation rested on assumptions that readers were either sufficiently familiar with peoples, places, and events to identify articles from the descriptions or would read the whole of the work.[31]

Overall, historical society publications lacked coherent organization, lessening their appeal. The New-York Historical Society's first publication committee stressed that chronological arrangement was "by no means considered essential, or even important in a compilation, professing to furnish *materials* for historical composition, rather than connected history."

Similarly, the Historical Society of Pennsylvania admitted in the preface to its first volume that the contents were so disparate that arranging them in "historical order is impossible." The publishing committee hoped the lack of chronological order "will not impair the interest which such collections usually excite; and the variety of the facts may compensate for the irregularity of the arrangement." Other historical societies followed similar practices, but by midcentury the reorganized Virginia Historical Society complained about the lack of chronological order and inclusion of "disjointed fragments." These practices might reduce publication committees' labors, "but the result has been that comparatively few have read the volumes thus prepared." The Virginia officers vowed to be different by selecting materials on related topics and organizing volumes chronologically. The reports laying out the Virginia society's complaints and plans appeared in the quarterly *Virginia Historical Register*. Ironically, William Maxwell, Society recording secretary, corresponding secretary, and librarian, produced the *Register*, which also featured disjointed content and a lack of chronological arrangement.[32]

Society volumes were intended to form series, even when issued irregularly with large gaps between installments. Most societies did not reach the point of producing navigation aids to locate materials in the series as a whole. The Massachusetts Historical Society, on the other hand, produced thirty volumes by 1850, and expected subscribers to buy all installments. Therefore, the Society offered aids in every tenth volume. The first, printed in 1809, included an "accurate and elaborate" index to the contents first ten volumes, an index of authors, a general table of contents, and a chronological table listing the "most remarkable events recorded in the ten volumes." These emphasized division of the contents by author, topic or content, date, and geography. The general table of contents listed 381 items overall and was separated into seven categories proceeding from history through biography to local history sequentially. The sections relating to Native Americans and topography or local history were further subdivided by state or colony and region. The categories repeated in the subsequent general tables of contents published in the tenth volumes of the second and third series (1823 and 1849).[33]

At least one Massachusetts Historical Society member had issues with miscellaneous arrangement. Although the volume printed in 1814 (second series II) had the same table of contents as preceding installments, the verso of the table of contents featured two aids to navigating the work: an alphabetical list of authors and a table arranging the articles by chronology. Three of the following volumes, printed in 1815, 1816, and 1818, were not miscellaneously organized. Instead, the contents were divided into categories, drawing on those created for the general table of contents. Each volume also contained a chronological table of articles. Some publication committee member invested time and energy into the categorical arrangement and provision of volume-specific navigational aids. After 1818 the publications largely returned to their former miscellaneous arrangement.[34]

Collectively, the Massachusetts Historical Society's volumes affirmed pride in place through materials centered around Massachusetts, then New England, and at length the United States and Western Hemisphere. The classification scheme used in the indices reflected the Society's interests in official materials. Two categories together comprised more than 60 percent of the articles: "History" and "Topography, Statistics, and Local History." Chronologically organized, history entries included all documents relating to wars and colonist-indigenous conflicts, accounts of the Salem witch trials of 1692, and articles on the American Revolution. The local history category contained almost exclusively newer articles and descriptions, such as that of Wellfleet, and was subdivided geographically. Massachusetts-related articles dominated indices, but where the first index included twenty-five describing places outside New England, the second index had only three. "Biography and Characterizing Papers" was the third-largest category, a mixture of older letters combined with memoirs and accounts of men such as deceased Society officers. A separate section on Native Americans did not include cross-references to articles documenting conflicts with colonists; instead, it featured Anglo-American descriptions of Native American tribes and languages. Native American authored documents did appear in the *Collections*, but most were brief letters or accounts dating to before the American Revolution such as a letter from Wampanoag leader Metacomet, also known as King Philip, written in the mid- to late seventeenth century. Categories of religious and natural history contained few items, these included a mid-seventeenth century ecclesiastical history of Massachusetts and accounts of earthquakes.[35]

The presentation decisions of the publications committees of the Massachusetts society assumed its readers had some degree of historical knowledge or the persistence to review materials thoroughly. The same volume that contained the article on Wellfleet also had historical documents capable of exciting popular interest. Between descriptions of Wellfleet and Wells, Massachusetts, lay a series of early eighteenth-century letters from Puritan ministers Increase and Cotton Mather to Massachusetts Governor Joseph Dudley, and an excerpt from Cotton Mather's private diary. These appeared in the table of contents with the names of senders and recipients and the dates, with nothing to indicate their content. Only individuals familiar with the reputations of the Mathers or Dudley might guess the letters contained livelier language than the topographical descriptions to either side. In one, Increase Mather informed Dudley "that since your arrival to the government, my charitable expectations have been greatly disappointed." He proceeded to itemize his suspicions that the governor was guilty of bribery, unrighteousness, hypocrisy, falseness, disloyalty to his country, and complicity in murder, plus absence from church on the Sabbath.[36]

Other historical societies followed models stressing the exchange of member-produced content and presentation and likewise made publication choices aimed at members. The New-York Historical Society produced one volume with a coherent theme, two containing a chronological history, and others featuring speeches given before the membership. The Historical and Literary Committee of the American Philosophical Society and the American Antiquarian Society each selected member-produced writings for their volumes. The majority of these works thus favored the models set by the Royal Society and American Philosophical Society, disseminating contemporary peer-approved discourses, memoirs, and other treatises, in contrast to the Massachusetts society's mix of old documents and more recent member writings.[37]

"Very Judiciously Republished": The Matter of Reprinting

Historical society publication committees drew a sizable number of items from works that were printed in early newspapers, periodicals, and volumes because reprinting was a common practice in the nation at the time. Copyright lasted at best twenty-eight years, contingent on the author being alive at the fourteen-year mark to renew the copyright. When the New Hampshire Historical Society began work on its first volume of *NHHS Collections*, anything printed before 1795 was available for use, as were many more recent works since authors, publishers, and printers rarely copyrighted ephemeral productions such as newspapers and broadsides).[38]

The act of reprinting within historical society publications implicitly presented earlier materials as important for use in writing new histories. State historical societies understood their mission as providing materials to undergird writing a history of a given place since its settlement or colonization. The historical societies of Rhode Island, Massachusetts, and Georgia, along with the American Historical Society, choose to reprint old pamphlets. In many respects, these resembled the modern materials other societies printed, as they centered on colonial and local identities and situations and offered detailed discussions of historical conditions. Whether or not materials documented political or civil history was a primary consideration in determining what to publish.[39]

Farmer and Plumer Sr. agreed on the importance of including reprinted materials. One of the committee's first substantive decisions was to republish early historian Samuel Penhallow's *History of the Wars of New-England, with the Eastern Indians* (1726). Plumer Jr. described it as "a New Hampshire book (one of the very few published here before the Revolution)," which made it of particular relevance. Its rarity offered a strong justification for republication as the work "had become so exceedingly scarce, that it was with some trouble a complete copy could be found." At Farmer's request, Cambridge minister Abiel Holmes looked through the Harvard College Library and consulted the American Academy of Arts and Sciences without luck. At length, he located a copy with "to my great joy, the *title page* entire, though in great jeopardy, the two next leaves, containing the *Preface* . . . being entirely loosened from the book" in the Massachusetts Historical Society. Reviewers for the *North American Review* and the *American Monthly Review* praised the inclusion of Penhallow, the former describing it as "very judiciously republished."[40]

Yet reprinting served as the ostensible point of disagreement between Farmer and Plumer Sr. with respect to the first volume of *NHHS Collections*. Plumer Sr. approached the prospect of publication from a nation- and state-oriented perspective. His interests centered on the state's legislative and judicial history. He saw no problem in publishing items available in other printed works. Early in December of 1823, he sent Farmer a view of the possible volume. His suggestions traced an arc from the organizational documents of the New Hampshire Historical Society, to Penhallow's *Indian Wars*, and then to topographical descriptions of New Hampshire towns and documents related to the various professions (ministry, medicine, and the law, including the legislature and judiciary). He wanted "every thing . . . that is really valuable, embodied in our Collections." Indeed, he suggested including several recently printed items, including Farmer's article on Amherst, New Hampshire, and Moore's on Andover. While Plumer Sr. acknowledged the importance of printing as a means of preserving documents through multiplication, he emphasized content over rarity in choosing documents for inclusion.[41]

For Farmer, rarity mattered more. He did not approve of reprinting in the *NHHS Collections* anything that had appeared in print within the preceding decade. As far as Farmer was concerned "the object . . . is to *preserve* and multiply copies of what has become scarce, or that does not exist in duplication." The article on Amherst should not appear again in print unless thoroughly revised. Plumer also suggested including in the volume a work on the ecclesiastical history of New Hampshire. This had appeared as parts in separate periodical issues, and Farmer allowed that consolidating the parts into a single whole was a worthwhile proposition, although he was not convinced the work warranted inclusion in the New Hampshire society's first volume.[42]

The majority of the publication resembled Farmer's vision. Plumer Sr. recognized the potential for meddling in the project. As president, he had chosen the members of the publication committee. He asked Farmer to "*not* consider me as *dictating* what course you ought to pursue, but simply *suggesting* a few things that have occurred to me on the subject, & which, perhaps, may be worthy of your consideration." The final volume did not include the sketches of Amherst or Andover or the ecclesiastical work. It did feature Moore's Historical Sketch of Concord, which had not yet appeared in print.[43]

The clash over including reprinted works repeated the following March, this time regarding Plumer Sr.'s contribution for the volume. He hoped to create a collection of related documents—a condensed version of his historical journals, similar to the New-York Historical Society's first volume which he had much admired. He had copied documents into eighteen manuscript volumes over the years. Reviewing these, he selected documents for the *NHHS Collections*, specifically "a copy of royal grants & instructions, messages of governors, answers of the legislature, the substance of some votes of the house & council (for the senate did not then exist)" along with letters. The whole he intended to "form materials for a legislative history, & furnish some facts for the general history of New Hampshire." Plumer's compilation included documents printed in Jeremy Belknap's *History of New Hampshire* (1784–92), Ebenezer Hazard's *Historical Collections* (1792–94), and William Hubbard's *History* (1815). After laying out these plans, Plumer Sr. began copying, and delivered the result a few months later.[44]

The already printed works did not fit Farmer's conception of the volume. He preferred to direct his attention toward materials not yet sufficiently protected against loss. "Have I misapprehended the objects of the publications of the [New Hampshire Historical] Society," he asked Kelly in confidence, "or are we to republish what is already well preserved against the ravages of time"? Moreover, Farmer suspected one of the documents Plumer Sr. had provided, a deed between four Native Americans and a party of settlers including minister John Wheelwright dated 1629, was a forgery. The deed's authenticity was a subject of open discussion, and two of his Society correspondents were convinced it was a forgery.[45]

The resultant volume represented a compromise between the two positions. Farmer was not willing to reject Plumer Sr.'s contribution altogether. He may have feared angering father and son. Instead, he included many official documents, particularly those originally printed in Hazard's *Historical Collections* and Hubbard's *History*. For others, he merely listed the document title and a citation for where the item could be found. The latter category included items taken from New England sources: Jeremy Belknap's *History of New Hampshire*, Benjamin Trumbull's *History of Connecticut* (1797), and the *MHS Collections*. By implication, he assumed interested readers would be able to access copies of these works, suggesting a narrow, learned society-oriented idea of the volume's readership. With respect to the potential forgery, he did not include the deed itself in the volume. Instead, he offered a citation to where it might be found in Belknap's *History*. Immediately afterward, he inserted a five-page essay by Plumer explaining why he believed the deed was authentic; a subsequent volume contained further documentation of the forgery. Plumer accepted the compromises and declared himself "satisfied" with Farmer's treatment of his documents. Nevertheless, it discouraged him from subsequent contributions. Farmer acknowledged this impact but remained certain he had "acted in accordance with the wishes of the members."[46]

Ironically, the two-page table of contents reflected Farmer and Plumer Sr.'s different visions of historical society publications. The first page featured thirty-eight articles Farmer selected. The second boasted article 39 and itemized the twenty-nine governmental "Ancient Documents" Plumer contributed. The former were miscellaneous and presented in no particular order, while the latter shared a common theme and were arranged largely in chronological order.[47]

Plumer Sr.'s interests providing connected documents was not motivated by a desire to appeal to the public as a whole. Early in the process of compiling the volume, he described one of the goals as "to invite the attention of the public" to the New Hampshire society's work. His concept of the public focused on a specific subset: the same scholarly, political, and commercial leaders other societies courted. Indeed, after the work's appearance, he noted with approval that the volume was "well received by literary men." This was the public whose opinions he valued.[48]

"The Most Ready Sale": Alternative Historical Society Publication Models

Historical societies did not unilaterally adopt the miscellany approach. Publications varied in a number of respects. Some societies emphasized newer, member-generated content where others preferred older works. Although many favored volumes, a few attempted to sustain periodicals. The Rhode Island Historical Society favored subsidizing single titles over outright financing of miscellanies, while the Georgia Historical Society commissioned a history of the state.

The Rhode Island Historical Society opted for a different course due to awareness of audience limitations. The Society publication committee originally planned to publish documents addressing the history of Rhode Island in chronological order, but members were "conscious that neither the resources of the Society nor the limited degree of interest evinced by the Public in the Subject, would warrant that course." Similarly, the Society avidly collected materials related to founder Roger Williams but opted not to print everything. Instead, officers published a single work from his pen.[49]

The Rhode Island society made single items the focus of each publication. The selections included early tracts (Roger Williams's seventeenth-century *Key to Indian Languages*) and a recently authored history (Elisha R. Potter Jr.'s *Early History of the Narragansett*). Other societies typically assumed the responsibilities and risk of publication. In contrast, the Rhode Island society brought forth several volumes under financial arrangements whereby the author or editor assumed the risks of publication and received any profits. For its part, the Society permitted volumes to be published as part of the *Collections of the Rhode Island Historical Society* and subscribed one hundred dollars. In return, the Society received eighty to one hundred copies. This reduced publishing expenses for the Society and freed up funds to purchase materials for their collections. The arrangement required no lessening of quality because publication committees reviewed works before granting final approval. Although the volumes were essentially the product of the editors and authors, they appeared under the auspices of the Society.[50]

The officers of the Rhode Island society officers preferred materials that would "meet with the most ready sale." They were interested in the *Historical Discourse* by John Callender, a Harvard-educated Baptist minister in colonial Rhode Island. The book was first printed in 1739. Concerned about potential sales, they asked honorary member Robert Walsh of Pennsylvania whether anyone in Philadelphia, a major center of publication at the time, planned to republish the work. Assured this was not the case, the Rhode Island society reprinted it in 1838.[51]

Callender had written the *Historical Discourse*, also known as the *Century Sermon*, to commemorate a hundred years of Anglo-American settlement in the colony of Rhode Island. Brown University professor Romeo Elton, who prepared the republication, considered the discourse "the only history of the Colony or State of Rhode Island, which has been written." Educated at Brown, Elton served as a pastor in two Baptist churches before retiring due to ill health. Accepting an appointment from Brown to teach Latin and Greek, he first traveled to Europe for study and to prepare to teach. Later, while living in Providence, he became an active member of the Rhode Island Historical Society and published memoirs of Roger Williams and Rev. Jonathan Maxcy, first president of Brown, as well as Callender.[52]

No standard of ethics existed for documentary publication at the time. Peter Du Ponceau of Philadelphia laid out a philosophy of editing, explaining that as a translator and editor, he took "no liberty with the Author's work which I was not sure he would have approved of if he had been living." When preparing George Washington's writings for publication, editor Jared Sparks used a similar approach and treated the papers as he thought Washington would have wanted him to. As a result, Sparks silently omitted materials he did not consider appropriate for publication, substituted terms such as changing Washington's references to "Old Put" to the more respectful "General Putnam," and altered grammar and spelling to conform to nineteenth-century standards. Sometimes editors advised readers of changes they had made, but this was by no means required or even expected.[53]

In the absence of standard documentary ethics, historical society members utilized a variety of strategies to affirm the authenticity of materials. These included the use of introductions and prefaces to assure readers the contents were unchanged or barely altered and, in particular, to ward off concerns of fraud. Historical Society of Pennsylvania member Joshua Francis Fisher provided letters by William Penn for several of the Society's *Memoirs*. In one volume, Fisher described the letters as "inedited" and explained in a preface that he had copied them from papers in the possession of Penn's family. Supplying an additional installment of letters for the fourth volume, Fisher took care to explain that "all I am responsible for, is the genuineness of the paper, which is altogether in the hand-writing" of Pennsylvania proprietor James Logan, "who endorsed it as presented by William Penn." Member Benjamin Chew did not include a similar introduction to the letter he provided but took care to note it was in Penn's hand and bore seals with the Penn family arms.[54]

The Rhode Island society publication committee and Elton went to lengths to produce an editorial work which placed author and discourse in their historical context. The two members on the publication committee, lawyer Albert G. Greene and Brown University professor William G. Goddard, assured readers that all of the documents in the volume were "carefully compared with the originals, and no pains have been spared to ensure their correctness." Although Elton did not prepare an index, he provided an introductory memoir on Callender and an appendix of relevant documents. He specified the extent to which he "substitute[d]" contemporary orthography and punctuation. These references were offered for the sake of clarity and to reassure readers of the authenticity of the content.[55]

No other historical society duplicated the Rhode Island society's model, but the Georgia Historical Society undertook a related action in commissioning a history of the state. Shortly after its establishment, members of the Georgia society decided a new state history was required. The Society praised the "persevering zeal" of Major Hugh McCall, author of a previous state history, who wrote while confined to bed and was "unused to literary efforts." Yet the work was deficient and imperfect, leaving Georgia's history "untrodden ground." Given the Society's establishment and the state's recent acquisition of copies of British records documenting the state's colonial history, officers decided the time was ripe for a new history and asked founding member Rev. William Bacon Stevens to undertake the labor. He gave a course of popular lectures on the subject while at work on the project. Following publication of the first volume, *Southern Quarterly Review* proclaimed "no disposition to deny the general excellence of the work."[56]

At least one critic considered the Georgia society's support of commissioned history premature. An anonymous essay argued the Society ought to have collected manuscripts, published them, reprinted rare and choice tracts in chronological order, and produced essays on aspects of Georgia history. After that, with citizens' interest piqued and the library of materials complete, "some one should have *then* been appointed to digest these copious materials in one historical work." The Georgia society, in contrast, saw no problem with collecting, publishing, and supporting historical writing at the same time. The Society subsequently subsidized publication of Stevens's second volume.[57]

While the Rhode Island Historical Society partnered with members to subsidize their scholarship, the Georgia Historical Society effectively commissioned a completely new history of the state. Together, these represented movement toward societies taking an active role in providing monetary support for historical scholarship. Few societies had much in the way of funds to disburse, but these actions pointed to officers expanding their roles in assisting historians write histories.

Of Readers and Audiences

Society publications emphasized the labors of their members. This in and of itself was not problematic, as officers considered the documents valuable and worth printing. However, the heavy use of member-authored materials contributed to topical and chronological disconnects between items within any given volume. The publication committees' labors matched the circular letters the societies sent out to encourage contributions. They emphasized applied history, materials for use in establishing present conditions in comparison with the past and development of the future.

By and large, officers understood society goals as preserving materials *for* history. By electing not to provide materials *as* history or documentary collections organized around subjects calculated to arouse popular interest, officers affirmed distinctions between scholarly and popular circles. This was not a uniform preference; several societies invested some degree of effort to attract readers from the public, albeit based on narrow constructions of the public in terms of men of station. In addition, society memberships included individuals interested in providing compilations of documents on related topics. Nevertheless, the root focus of the societies was on preservation.

As a result, historical society publications involved a narrow focus on the interests of a core audience consisting of society members and scholarly circles. The societies protected a valuable array of documents, distributing copies far and wide. Published materials emphasized topics in general discourse: political and legal events, military actions, and commercial information. Assumptions about readers' knowledge and access to scholarly resources thus contributed to a general absence of navigational aids other than tables of contents, discouraging popular audiences. This reduced officers' ability to raise money through sales of their publications and also limited the public exposure of their labors, further focusing attention on their members.

While cultural literati recognized historical society publications as valuable, they viewed these publications as primarily of interest to antiquarian circles. The *Monthly Anthology and Boston Review* described the first volume of *MHS Collections* as "contain[ing] a copious fund of information, and abound[ing] with matter profitable and delightful." Nevertheless, reviewers warned readers that "whoever expects to find in these volumes a well digested relation of facts, or even a series of original papers, ranged in chronological order, must be disappointed." By the time reviewers reached volume VI, they had "stated so fully the importance and the dryness of the documents in general, their value to the regular annalist, and their indifference to the ordinary reader, we shall spend no further time on these or collateral topicks."[58]

Historians and other society members formed any given publication's primary audience. The societies supported the creation of national histories through printed works more than libraries and manuscript collections. George Bancroft, a resident member of the Massachusetts Historical Society, referenced publications associated with historical societies from Michigan to Virginia in the first six volumes of his *History of the United States of America* (1834–74), although unfortunately he omitted footnotes from volumes 7 to 10. However, he publicly thanked only the Connecticut Historical Society, whose officers had allowed him to borrow and remove manuscripts from their collections. Richard Hildreth, one of Bancroft's contemporaries, wrote a history of the United States drawing on the publications of the American Antiquarian Society, American Philosophical Society's Historical and Literary Committee, and ten historical societies: Cincinnati, Georgia, Maine, Massachusetts, New Hampshire, New Jersey, New York, Ohio, Pennsylvania, and Rhode Island.[59]

By the 1830s some officers admitted their publications lacked popular appeal. While delivering his inaugural address as president of the Historical Society of Pennsylvania, Peter Du Ponceau complimented Society members on collecting and preserving valuable historical materials but encouraged them to print more, specifically popular publications, so "they will be more generally read, and more extensively diffused." The Executive Council of the Virginia Historical Society offered a blunter condemnation, pledging to try "to make the [Society's] volumes less repulsive to the general reader, than collections of historical societies usually are."[60]

Repulsiveness, like beauty, lies in the eye of the beholder. Nevertheless, the Executive Council's use of such a descriptor highlights tensions about the role and use of historical society publications. Likewise, contemporaneous critiques of the volumes raises questions as to the historical societies' intended audiences and purposes. A scholar of the New-York Historical Society suggested elitism explained the Society's failure to appeal to the common reader, which effectively affirmed members' standing as true scholars. In either case, the societies' collective publication choices reflected schisms between academic and popular history.[61]

Chapter Five

"Less Repulsive to the General Reader"

Popular History and Historical Societies

On New Year's Day 1850, Hartford resident Mary Jane Hale Welles, wife of Connecticut public servant Gideon Welles, took her thirteen-year-old daughter Anna Jane and sons Edgar Thaddeus and Thomas Glastonbury, six and three respectively, to visit the Connecticut Historical Society rooms. Other Society visitors that day included painter William Hays Pierson of Morristown, New Jersey; Trinity College student Charles J. Hoadley; joiner William Blatchley of Hartford; and nineteen-year-old Delia C. Wilson of Windsor, Connecticut. Over the course of the year, more than 3,700 people stopped by the rooms long enough to sign the visitor logs.[1]

The Connecticut Historical Society appealed to the public as a popular place to visit. The equivalent of nearly one-quarter of Hartford's thirteen thousand residents stopped by the Society rooms that year. Most historical societies' rooms did not serve as public attractions, and at best societies allowed their members' guests to make arrangements to view their collections. The New-York Historical Society had more than ten thousand visitors in 1869. If it had had a similar number in 1850, this represented only 2 percent of the total population of New York City. The Massachusetts Historical Society's earliest visitor register accumulated a mere 6,400 signatures over a half-century (1858–1913).[2]

Historical societies' lack of engagement with broader publics contrasted with the rise of popular history in the same era. Individuals throughout the nation exhibited interest in history over the course of the nineteenth century. Writers and publishers developed and distributed historical works intended to appeal to the growing middle classes. Popular history writers utilized a number of techniques to engage readers, including "patterns of causal sequencing, historical explanation, and character assessment." Of equal importance, publishers packaged histories with ample illustrations to catch potential purchasers' attention and hired salesmen to sell the works door-to-door to reach broader audiences.[3]

Critical elements included content, presentation, and availability. The public embraced narratives and illustrations. The door-to-door sales of popular histories reached audiences where they lived. In contrast, an individual interested in purchasing historical society publications had to know a historical society member or someone who knew one and was willing to make an introduction. The Connecticut Historical Society had unusually diverse collections along with ample open hours, making visiting on impulse possible, whereas visiting comparable societies required familiarity with society members and plenty of advance notice.

Historical societies were not popular, and this was not by accident. Despite opportunities to reach broader audiences, most society officers made decisions limiting their reach, except in allowing women of their own class expanded access. Events held in public, including services, processions, and lectures, attracted some degree of attention. The Massachusetts Historical Society achieved a degree of popularity among Boston literati with their lecture series, but most societies failed to match this level of activity. The attraction of the Connecticut Historical Society's rooms for a diverse array of visitors in terms of age, gender, and class was an exception.

"The Manners of the Times": Differing Approaches to Publication

Historical society officers rhetorically endorsed producing publications with popular appeal, but their actions focused on narrower constituencies. The Executive Council of the Virginia Historical Society attributed the lack in part to arrangement and presentation decisions. This also derived from historical societies' emphasis on facts versus stories.

Each society which produced publications had to decide how to organize materials within volumes or periodical issues. Jeremy Belknap of the Massachusetts Historical Society initially advised the public that materials would not necessarily be arranged by subject or chronology. The New-York Historical Society also warned readers not to expect chronological arrangement. Likewise, the Historical Society of Pennsylvania admitted in the preface to its first volume that the contents were so disparate that arranging them in "historical order is impossible." The publishing committee hoped the lack of chronological order "will not impair the interest which such collections usually excite; and the variety of the facts may compensate for the irregularity of the arrangement." Other historical societies followed similar practices.[4]

By the age of Jackson, historical society leaders recognized that their publications failed to engage popular interest in history. Historical Society of Pennsylvania President Peter Du Ponceau addressed the issue in his inaugural address in 1837, encouraging production of more appealing materials to engage a broader readership. Officers of the Virginia Historical Society went further, promising to do their best to ensure their publications were "less repulsive to the general reader, than collections of historical societies usually are." The phrase "general reader" did not encompass the whole of society or even all of the free portions. Historical societies focused attention on educated, professional classes possessing influence, power, and wealth. Women of station counted as general readers, but not men or women of the laboring classes, racial minorities, or most non-English ethnicities. Yet historical societies did not achieve popular appeal even among professional classes.[5]

Society publications emphasized facts rather than stories or narrative. The rise of popular histories over the nineteenth century involved deliberate use of sequencing and narrative explanation. The society officers' endorsement of facts undercut the potential for their publications to attract wide audiences. Officers understood their missions as preserving materials for the writing of history rather than writing history per se and wanted to avoid controversy. Samuel Hazard, a Historical Society of Pennsylvania member and son of historical editor Ebenezer Hazard, published the *Register of Pennsylvania* in the 1830s, a periodical "devoted to the preservation of every kind of useful information." Hazard notified readers that "on the subject of Politics, only such facts will be given as are necessary to a complete History of the

State—entirely avoiding controversy, which may be offensive to any party." The attempt at neutrality lowered his odds of offending subscribers and contributed to the periodical's dryness. The phrasing implied that controversy was not part of history; rather, he believed, history was rooted in objective facts. Du Ponceau held similar sentiments and advised Historical Society of Pennsylvania members that "facts, and not party opinions are what history demands of us." Historical societies generally avoided taking sides on contentious matters. Du Ponceau's comment about party opinions followed directly on a discussion of slavery and abolition in Pennsylvania, delicate issues he considered too contemporary for historians to address.[6]

Both the Pennsylvania society and Hazard understood their primary purpose was providing access to valuable political and civil information to present and future generations, with popular appeal a secondary consideration. They shared ideas of what types of information needed preservation, and their respective publications balanced each other. The Society favored member-authored papers on historical subjects, while Hazard featured a mix of recent and historical documents. A mid-twentieth-century historian of the Pennsylvania society argued that competition from Hazard depressed the Historical Society of Pennsylvania's ability to sell its own volumes during the 1830s and 1840s. Instead, choice of content and presentation told against both. At the time, the Society did not appear concerned about Hazard as competition, for members supported his periodicals as important in and of themselves. After the *Register* ceased publication, Du Ponceau expressed a hope that state assistance would enable Hazard to resume publication.[7]

Several historical society members prepared external publications featuring different types of content than their own societies favored. Massachusetts Historical Society member Jared Sparks achieved a high degree of popularity in no small part due to publications of American Revolution correspondence, biographies, and collected writings of nationally notable figures. Between 1828 and 1854, he assembled a biographical volume featuring the writings of early Connecticut traveler John Ledyard, twelve volumes of the *Diplomatic Correspondence of the American Revolution*, and six documentary series, filling thirty volumes, of the papers of American Revolutionary leaders Benjamin Franklin, Gouverneur Morris, and George Washington. These were works focused on individuals, differing in style and arrangement from societal publications, and invoked popular appeal through their subjects.[8]

Philadelphia editor William Duane Jr. produced a work that highlighted this historical society emphasis on collective materials over individual and pointed to a growing divide between the interests of historical societies and those of the common people. While a member of the Historical Society of Pennsylvania, Duane published excerpts from the diary of Revolution-era politician Christopher Marshall at his own expense. His rationale for deciding which excerpts to include involved subject and manners. While his first priority was documenting the Revolution, he also sought to illustrate "the manners of the time," albeit without including material of a "merely private nature." Manners was "a species of information which historians in general mistakingly think beneath their notice," implicit commentary on his contemporaries' research and writing. Duane distinguished between public affairs, manners, and private affairs; the latter included things "uninteresting" or improper to publish so as to protect "the feelings of the living" such as events and comments they might consider libelous. Manners occupied a middle ground, including evidence of daily life.[9]

"Something Adapted to All Ages, Classes, and Tastes": Historical Societies and John Warner Barber's Historical Collections

Massachusetts offers a clear illustration of these differences between popular history compilers and historical society publications. Editors and authors of popular historical works stressed narrative and illustrative elements while societies preferred factual documents. The Massachusetts Historical Society's *Collections* and the competing *Historical Collections* of popular editor John Warner Barber differed in numerous respects from content to arrangement to intended audience. Nevertheless, possible confusion between the works troubled an officer of the well-established Massachusetts society.

Historical compiler John Warner Barber posed a challenge to the Massachusetts society. He valued social history and focused on sources for insight into the lives and times of earlier inhabitants. Society officers preferred to transcribe documents and memorialize members through posthumous memoirs. Both relied on manuscript and printed sources. For the Society, these filled their publications, arranged in no particular order. The Society's volumes contained a higher proportion of original and unpublished sources compared with similar societies, which favored reprints and member-authored papers. In contrast, Barber integrated quotes from sources into a coherent narrative with illustrations and paratextual tools (such as indexes) to help readers locate specific people, places, or events.

Barber grew up on a farm in Windsor, Connecticut. Discovering a talent for drawing, he won an apprenticeship as an engraver at age fifteen, and later set up his own engraving business in New Haven. He eventually bought a horse and wagon and traveled the country sketching, collecting stories, and preparing publications of historical materials. People perusing books in the mid- to late nineteenth century could spot popular histories by the extensive use of illustrations—and Barber did not stint in this regard. The product of an era of village enlightenment, wherein villages throughout New England established libraries, literary societies, debate clubs, and other organizations, he set to work producing works of popular history. By the mid-1830s, he had published a volume of historical sketches and incidents documenting the colony of New Haven and a second work on the whole of Connecticut.[10]

In the process, Barber established a style of presentation pairing engraved sketches with geographically organized anecdotes and an emphasis on social history. He consulted written works, conducted oral interviews inasmuch as he spoke with older settlers and took down their stories, and made drawings. His approach to preparing historical miscellanies involved topics "generally passed over by those who write regular histories" as "too trivial to be inserted in historical works." He considered worth preserving "any facts or traditions which can hereafter be cited to throw light on the history of the times, manners and opinions of our forefathers," whether or not in agreement with prevailing ideas about how the world worked. For instance, he described an incident wherein witnesses saw "a ship in the air." Although usually written off as a delusion, "modern science" offered the explanation that viewers at the time had perceived a ship at sea reflected on the clouds, and he believed "other occurrences related by our forefathers as facts, but which are now deemed by us as fabulous, will be found upon investigation equally worthy of credit" and therefore worth noting down for posterity.[11]

This philosophy helped Barber enliven his texts with anecdotes and images, contributing to the works' popularity. His books sold well enough to attract imitators. Merchant and surveyor Sherman Day composed a similar volume for Pennsylvania. Henry Howe, son of a New Haven bookseller, left a job on Wall Street to join with Barber and produce state-oriented publications for New Jersey and New York. Howe later compiled additional volumes in Barber's style on his own. He described Barber and himself as historical compilers "an humble class—mere Camp followers of the great army of Authors," rather than authors of historical works in their own right. The gendered language acknowledged the split between scholarly and popular history, with a degree of bitterness over their place vis-à-vis other historians and authors, as the most infamous category of camp followers were prostitutes. Yet at the same time Howe affirmed satisfaction so long as they were able to "amuse and instruct."[12]

Barber set his sights on Massachusetts in 1837. He journeyed throughout the state, making drawings for most of the engravings "on the spot" and taking down stories for inclusion in his work. The preface to his Massachusetts volume acknowledged research assistance from the librarians of the Massachusetts Historical Society and the American Antiquarian Society. He would later write to Massachusetts society librarian Rev. Thaddeus Mason Harris noting his debts.[13]

Despite helping Barber, the Massachusetts Historical Society objected to the title of his forthcoming volume. The Society considered *Historical Collections, . . . Relating to the History and Antiquities of Every Town in Massachusetts, with Geographical Descriptions* too close to the title of their regular series, *Collections of the Massachusetts Historical Society*. Moreover, the labels on the backs of both volumes would read "Massachusetts Historical Collections." Harris suggested Barber retitle his work *Massachusetts Topographical Collections*, as it included history, statistics, and geography.[14]

Barber's publishers, Dorr and Howland, rejected the suggestion. The potential for problems had occurred to them, but they decided the chosen wording would cause no injury. For one, as Dorr and Howland pointed out to the Massachusetts society, Barber's volume would be sold in a very different manner than the Society's *Collections*: not in bookstores or by historical society members but by paid subscription agents, as with many other popular history publications. The agents traveled throughout the Commonwealth identifying individuals willing to subscribe to the book, later delivering the final product and collecting monies. Barber's books sold by the thousands, dwarfing the Society's print runs. Barber did not become rich because payments to the subscription agents reduced the works' profits. By the time the Society protested the title, Dorr and Howland also argued it was too late to change, as they were in the middle of printing and binding. They did agree to alter the back cover label to read "Barber's Historical Collections," a compromise the Society accepted.[15]

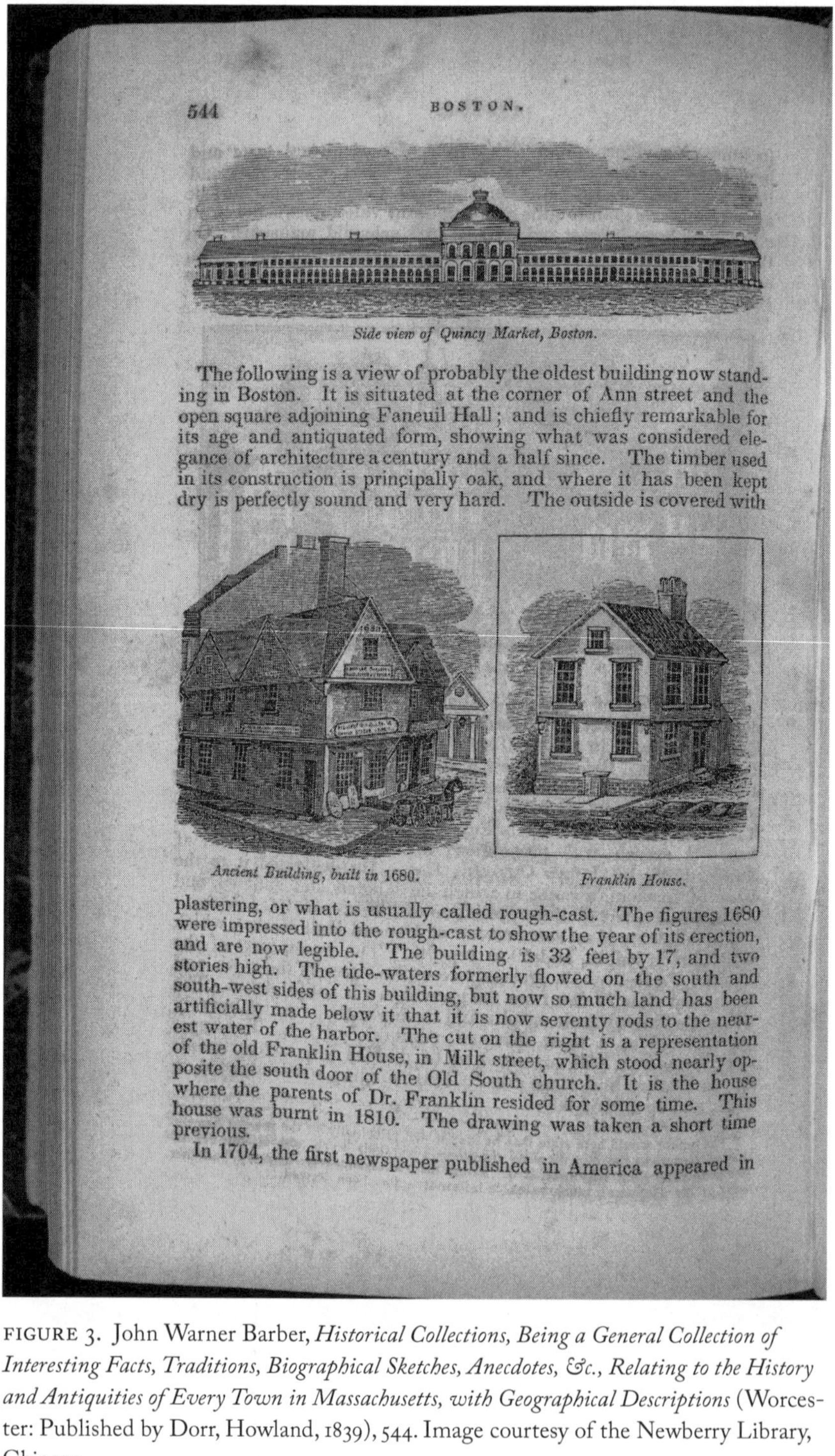

544 BOSTON.

Side view of Quincy Market, Boston.

The following is a view of probably the oldest building now standing in Boston. It is situated at the corner of Ann street and the open square adjoining Faneuil Hall; and is chiefly remarkable for its age and antiquated form, showing what was considered elegance of architecture a century and a half since. The timber used in its construction is principally oak, and where it has been kept dry is perfectly sound and very hard. The outside is covered with

Ancient Building, built in 1680. *Franklin House.*

plastering, or what is usually called rough-cast. The figures 1680 were impressed into the rough-cast to show the year of its erection, and are now legible. The building is 32 feet by 17, and two stories high. The tide-waters formerly flowed on the south and south-west sides of this building, but now so much land has been artificially made below it that it is now seventy rods to the nearest water of the harbor. The cut on the right is a representation of the old Franklin House, in Milk street, which stood nearly opposite the south door of the Old South church. It is the house where the parents of Dr. Franklin resided for some time. This house was burnt in 1810. The drawing was taken a short time previous.

In 1704, the first newspaper published in America appeared in

FIGURE 3. John Warner Barber, *Historical Collections, Being a General Collection of Interesting Facts, Traditions, Biographical Sketches, Anecdotes, &c., Relating to the History and Antiquities of Every Town in Massachusetts, with Geographical Descriptions* (Worcester: Published by Dorr, Howland, 1839), 544. Image courtesy of the Newberry Library, Chicago.

Barber's volume differed notably from the Massachusetts society's *Collections* in presentation as well as method of sale. He organized material geographically—by county and town—prefaced by an overview of the state's history. At the front of the work, he included a table of contents listing the towns in alphabetical order, and provided an index to people and events. These suggest that he presumed his readers might want to go directly to materials on specific places, people, or topics rather than read cover-to-cover. His volumes featured extensive illustrations of contemporary places (see figure 3). Howe explained the appeal of Barber's work in terms of a simple style paired with extensive detail. Instead of aiming for "high literary merit:—the dignified style,—the generalization of facts,—the philosophical deductions of regular history," he and Barber favored "minor, but interesting incidents." As a result, the variety offered "something adapted to all ages, classes and tastes." Barber and Howe emphasized that the decision to favor a popular style over scholarly meant their volumes "reached MORE MINDS, and ha[ve] been more extensively read."[16]

Most of the Massachusetts society's publications matched Howe's description of "regular" historical works. The Society published extensive contemporaneous materials earlier in the century, but by the 1830s primary source materials predominated. Instead of anecdotes, the publication committees of the Society selected manuscripts documenting politics and government and rarely, if ever, included illustrations, although an 1840 volume contained a catalog of portraits then in the Society's possession. The same volume featured the whimsical "Forefather's Song," reputedly composed in the first years of the settlement at Plymouth. The song warned new arrivals "The place where we live is a wilderness wood" where "We have pumpkins at morning and pumpkins at noon; If it was not for pumpkins we should be undone." While not the first poem or song printed in the *Collections*, this was an exception rather than the rule and perhaps was inspired in part by Barber's work, published earlier.[17]

The Historical Society of Pennsylvania expanded its collection of historical information following publication of a Barber imitator. Artist and engineer Sherman Day published the *Historical Collections of Pennsylvania* in the style of Barber in 1843, with plenty of illustrations and stories collected from around the state. Within two years, officers of the Pennsylvania society drafted a new circular. An earlier 1825 version had filled three pages requesting documents related to early settlers and "distinguished persons" but was largely focused on political, civil, religious, and literary information.

In contrast, the 1845 call required three times as much space. In addition to the usual queries for information about civil and political topics, the new circular solicited books, records, drawings, "revolutionary songs, ancient ballads, letters, papers, narratives, orderly books," and even "peculiar notion[s], custom[s], or superstition[s]." The circular advised readers not to exclude anything "because it may seem trivial or unworthy of notice." Perhaps Du Ponceau's request for popular publications inspired the request, but the timing suggests a connection to Day's volume. The Society's next publication contained several responses to the circular.[18]

"To Feast the Eye and the Imagination": Historical Lectures, Celebrations, and Commemorations

Beyond publications, several societies held events and celebrations open to the public, including women. Class and race barriers remained, although some events took place partly in public spaces open to any and all watchers. While society meetings were generally restricted to members and guests, by the 1830s some societies began hosting lectures open to anyone who could afford the entrance fee. Societies also commemorated historic events with special festivities. These offered opportunities for performance, ritual, and exchange.

Historical society lectures reflected the overlap between historical and literary organizations. The Massachusetts Historical Society successfully held its first lecture series in 1833, an expression of Boston literary culture and the lyceum and lecture movement. The Society's rooms were inadequate, so officers hired facilities (Boston Athenæum, Masonic Temple). Historical talks could be quite popular. An attendee arriving a half hour before the start of a lecture by historian Jared Sparks had to sit at the back of the hall. The Massachusetts society relied heavily on its membership for lecturers. Officers charged one dollar for a series of lectures on a variety of subjects from fall 1841 to spring 1842. The proceeds more than covered expenses, which ranged from rent for the lecture room and an attendant at $13 a night to an honorarium of $15 for a nonmember speaker, with lesser expenses for printing, tickets, and publicity in newspapers. Overall, the Society realized nearly $650, although other years were less remunerative. The Connecticut Historical Society also offered lecture series at a charge of twenty-five cents at the door, which proved popular with middle and upper class gentlemen and ladies, as did the New-York Historical Society. The Rhode Island Historical Society, after being initially successful, was unable to find enough speakers and abandoned the idea of further lecture series.[19]

Joseph B. Felt and the Massachusetts Historical Society demonstrate the connections between collecting, publication, and public events. A Congregational minister, Felt was a member of the Massachusetts society and served as its librarian. He gave a number of lectures including one on colonial governor Sir Edmund Andros's time in New England and another on rivalries between French officers in seventeenth-century Nova Scotia. The Society's *Collections* subsequently printed documents on these subjects. Growing physical collections, in short, provided material for lectures which helped prioritize items for inclusion in the Society's publications. Historian and editor Charles Francis Adams, a distant relative of Felt, considered him an uninspiring preacher but found one of Felt's lectures "a more fruitful one of romantic incident than I expected," which, even in the hands of Felt, "was far from dull." Adams himself lectured on his grandparents, John and Abigail Adams, and was pleased with the results. His lecture became the basis of his preface to a volume of her letters to her husband.[20]

Lectures served as an extension of society practices. Annual meetings constituted a core function of learned society, including the election of officers and an address from a respected historian or society member, which non-members might attend, combined with socializing at meals. By mid-century, women had been active in antislavery circles and on lecture circuits. A gathering of women demanded the vote at the Seneca Falls Convention in 1848, and within a year, the Connecticut Historical Society voted to allow members to bring women to hear the addresses and the New York society decided to allow women to remain for receptions following lectures. Officers solicited many addresses for publication.[21]

Women and other general publics could also observe historical society celebrations, which included street processions, open to all to view, and services in churches with public addresses. While parts of festivities were restricted to members and invited guests, in particular dinners, the rest took place in the open. Local newspapers reported on commemorative events, alongside lectures and annual meetings, further disseminating information to interested publics.

Historical societies hosted anniversary celebrations to stimulate public awareness of and interest in history—and as opportunities for attendees to socialize. The Massachusetts society helped commemorate the bicentennial of Boston's settlement. The Historical and Philosophical Society of Ohio celebrated the forty-eighth anniversary of Ohio Territory settlement. The New-York Historical Society honored the semicentennial of George Washington's inauguration as president, as well as its own fortieth anniversary, the latter particularly sweet as the Society was finally debt free. Although the Connecticut Historical Society missed Hartford's bicentennial, members celebrated the bicentennial of the colony's first civil constitution, albeit in 1840, a year late.[22]

Commemorations combined religion, public display, serious discourse, and social festivities, affirming and disseminating state and regional identities and encouraging historical consciousness. The Connecticut society's bicentennial of the colony's first civil constitution began with members and notables gathering in the state senate chamber at ten o'clock. After mingling for an hour, they processed through public streets to Centre Church. Dignitaries sat on the platform, others ranged in the pews. The program included prayers and a benediction by local ministers, four hymns, and a psalm, giving it a solidly Protestant character. State notable Noah Webster delivered an historical discourse, and the Constitution of 1639 was read, the whole service lasting two hours. Ladies attended the services, and authored two hymns.[23]

Inherently backward-looking, commemorations celebrated past successes measured against the present. The societies were reactive in choosing events. Participants and orators often romanticized aspects of the past. Conservative Federalist Noah Webster, speaking before the crowd in Connecticut, rejected innovation and advocated a proper respect for the past. Connecticut society president Thomas Day incorporated related sentiments when honoring Webster with a toast later in the day. Musing on "this age of locomotion, when every one is looking and going ahead—(except those who miss their foot-hold and fall back)," Day argued "it is refreshing to look out, through an opening at the half-way resting-place, and view the plains and fields and streams [i.e. the past] below." The past offered an example of progress through the settlers' and colonists' labors, which present attendees were encouraged to use as examples.[24]

The Connecticut Historical Society invoked the past physically as well as through words. The event involved celebratory trappings common to other voluntary associations: processions, services, addresses, banquets. Immediately following the service, attendees visited the graves of Hartford's first settlers and the 1639 Constitution framers, places open for public visitation. Thus attendees ventured out of the immediate present into a melding of present and past complete with the physical markers of the dead and their buried remains. At dinner, the walls were hung with many early settlers' portraits on which "to feast the eye and the imagination," inherently bringing the past into the present with the dead watching the living celebrate. Other historical commemorations likewise mingled past and present. Virginians organized day trips to visit Jamestown, setting services and addresses amid the settlement's ruins.[25]

Historical societies often restricted attendance at the festive banquets to men. Philip Hone, a former New York City mayor and New-York Historical Society vice president, was unconcerned over attendance at the New York society's service celebrating the anniversary of Washington's inaugural, for it was free and he expected a good turnout to hear former president John Quincy Adams's oration. The dinner cost money, and while most attendees paid, societies covered the costs for dignitaries and invited guests. Hone worked to avoid empty seats, despite there being nearly three hundred places, and achieved "an assemblage of first-rate men, large as the saloon of the City Hotel could conveniently accommodate." The Connecticut society commemoration included a festive dinner, ample toasts, and a reading of letters from the Society's original founders. These were reported extensively in the Hartford *Daily Courant*, stretching over several days and numerous columns.[26]

The Connecticut Historical Society commemoration reflected the intersection of two different visions for the Society. Even as the ceremony and celebrations helped reinvigorate the Society, they had an impact on collections. The Society's membership rolls resembled those of other state historical societies. With few exceptions, members—officers in particular—were professional men of wealth, education, and standing, born within the boundaries of the nation, and descended from Anglo-American settlers. Most Connecticut society leaders envisioned the society as an enclave of learned men exchanging ideas and publications and collecting materials for scholars to consult. They had a parochial, Hartford-focused understanding of the Society as a private, nonprofit association of gentlemen with common historical interests providing public service.[27]

In contrast, Connecticut society officer Henry Barnard II imagined an expansive and populace-focused future. An idealist committed to merit over birth, he had just begun to take up the cause of public education at the same time he participated in reorganizing the Society. He wanted to elect active members in every part of Connecticut, publish a popular historical and genealogical periodical, and develop a cadre of speakers to give lectures to local groups and represent the Society throughout the state. While Barnard failed to convince the Society to adopt all his initiatives, his influence was central in the encouragement of statewide contributions. During the Society's early years, he served on several committees including those charged with drafting bylaws and creating a circular.[28]

Barnard chaired the Connecticut Historical Society's bicentennial committee and thus contributed to the Society's diverse material collections. The evening before the event, Society president Thomas Day and wife Sarah Coit Day welcomed historical society members and their guests to a masque or dance at which four men and twelve women wore old clothing on loan from local families. Colonel James Ward dressed "in full white wig" as "an old clergyman of Wethersfield." Miss Louisa Barnard wore items once the property of a niece of Lord Baltimore, Miss Mary Ely a black gauze mantle connected to the Thomas Hooker family, and Miss Harriet Day a yellow brocade dress from the family of Connecticut Secretary of State Royal R. Hinman.[29]

One masque participant, Miss Elizabeth Day, sported "white apron-shoes [once] worn by the mother of John Ledyard the traveler" (figure 4). A month before the bicentennial, Dr. John L. Comstock donated to the Connecticut Historical Society shoes described as having belonged to Mary Young Ledyard, mother of Revolutionary War hero Colonel William Ledyard and grandmother of the noted traveler John Ledyard. Comstock included provenance tracing the shoes' connection to their original owner, his wife's ancestor. The shoes were the first unusual artifacts recorded in the Society accession records.[30]

The commemoration and masque materially affected the Connecticut society's collections. It's unclear which came first, Comstock's donation or planning for the masque. In either case, a short time after the gift the Hartford *Daily Courant* printed a notice, likely authored by Barnard, of the upcoming celebration along with a request for people with printed materials, manuscripts, "portraits, *dresses*, &c. which show 'the form and *fashions*' of other days, [to] bring them up with them to add interest to this occasion," and preferably "deposite them for safe keeping and consultation" with the Society. Within a month the request bore fruit. Miss Hannah Whittelsey, a

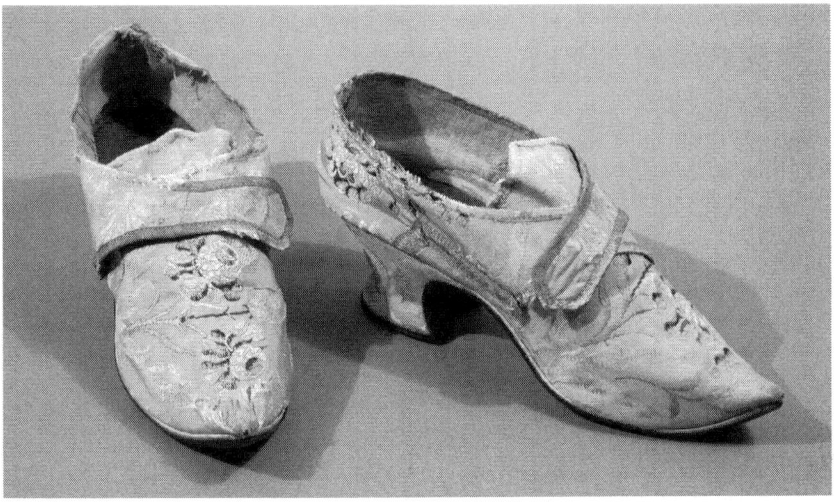

FIGURE 4. Woman's Shoes, originally owned by Mary Ledyard, made by Jonathan Hose and Son, about 1750–60, handstitched leather, silk brocade, and linen, with silk-covered wooden heel; gift of Dr. John L. Comstock, 1840.3.2ab, The Connecticut Historical Society.

descendant of the storied Edwards family, heard "a wish had been express'd" for donations "that would show the Costume and throw light on the early history of the Colony." She gave a pair of embroidered ladies' shoes, a piece of needlework, and a silk painting, "which labelled historically may illustrate the character of the times."[31]

"Throw Light on the Early History of the Colony": Connecticut Historical Society Collections and Visitors

In addition to collecting shoes, the Connecticut Historical Society accumulated materials that proved popular to a comparatively wide swathe of the population. The Society differed from others in key respects: varied collections from a large number of donors, a paid librarian, extensive open hours, and a large number of visitors. Those who stopped by the Society rooms came largely from the same ranks as the members, that is, well-off Anglo-American, Protestant families. Yet the visitors included a contingent of laborers and craftsmen who may have used it as one means toward achieving upward mobility.[32]

"The Gov. Trumbull's Hat Committee": Accumulating Varied Collections

First and foremost, the Connecticut society differed from others in the size and scope of its artifact collection. The majority of historical societies did not make artifacts a high priority. They had cabinets or museums, but officers focused on libraries. Most societies accepted non-textual items, primarily art, medals, coins, natural history specimens, Native American artifacts, and other items with a connection, real or perceived, to notable historical figures. The Rhode Island society twice attempted to locate a piece of Captain John Cook's ship *Endeavour* for deposit in the society's cabinets. Inasmuch as historical societies drew their officers from the ranks of professional men of station, the very proliferation of commodities made them more common and material artifacts of less interest. Christopher Columbus Baldwin, librarian of the American Antiquarian Society, endorsed historical societies "collect[ing] nothing but books, mss, coins, medals & pictures." Curiosities should be rejected unless they possessed "historical virtue," and Baldwin discouraged donations to the American Antiquarian Society of such artifacts as "old coats and hats and high heeled shoes!"[33]

In contrast, the Connecticut Historical Society acquired hats, high-heeled shoes, and much more. People gave books and manuscripts, as well as fragments of famous trees, pewter plates, iron tongs, a flat iron, military memorabilia (cannon balls, bullets, swords), and specimens of manufacturing (cotton thread). Many items documented early luxuries. Nearly all the shoes were intended to be worn by women on special occasions, several described as wedding shoes. These were mementos, items valued as physical connections or symbols of past people, places, and events. The Society held an "exhibition of ancient dresses and occurrences" in 1845, further showcasing these artifacts alongside books, manuscripts, and art.[34]

Recording Secretary Charles Hosmer accepted artifact donations, laying the groundwork for the growing collection of non-literary items. A merchant, printer, and publisher, Hosmer himself gave artifacts, including specimens of fireplace tiles and several wooden artifacts connected to historical trees. By all indications, he recorded every gift, including Harriet Johnson of Alabama's donation of a Comanche horn spoon and a sword (i.e., very large) bean pod. An 1845 visitor described the collection at length, taking particular note of everyday items associated with noted early colonial and revolutionary figures from a dinner pot once the property of Captain Miles Standish to a tavern sign once the property of General Israel Putnam. Barnard's interest in wider membership rolls and general activity intersected with Hosmer's willingness to accept and record artifacts, resulting in a collection with a degree of popular appeal.[35]

The Connecticut society accumulated not only rooms filled with more varied materials for visitors to examine than its peers but a larger and more varied pool of donors. Connecticut donation records document gifts from nearly a thousand donors during the 1840s. Other societies boasted less than half as many, with only the New-York Historical Society exceeding five hundred known donors over the decade. Sixty percent of Connecticut donors were men who were not members of the Society, less than 20 percent were members, and just under 10 percent were women. By and large, donors came from Connecticut, with 40 percent from Hartford County alone. Moreover, many Connecticut society donors understood artifacts to have historical significance, as numerous people outside the ranks of historical society members interacted with history through ceremonies and objects. A third of Connecticut society donors gave at least one artifact, where similar societies received artifacts from less than 20 percent of their smaller pools of donors.[36]

On at least one occasion, an item was removed from the collections. Mr. or Mrs. W. Radcliff Hudson took a hat of the late Governor Jonathan Trumbull and sent it out of state to New York, arguing it rightfully belonged to J. Trumbull Hudson. The Society appointed a committee "to regain possession of Gov. Trumbull's Hat." Members negotiated its return on the condition that the Society "would do justice to any claim J. Trumbull Hudson might make." The collection today includes a brown wool tricorne recorded as once the property of Governor Trumbull. The incident demonstrated the lengths the membership would go to in order to maintain possession of a material artifact and the value members placed on the hat.[37]

Historical artifacts valued as relics of men bore testimony to the complex place of women and women's work with respect to preservation. Consider the Connecticut Historical Society's accession and treatment of the shirt and waistcoat of Lieutenant Colonel William Ledyard. A tragic hero of the American Revolution, the tale of Ledyard's death—supposedly attempting to surrender to save his men from slaughter by a much larger British force—imbued his relics with a romantic aura and consequent historical value. On learning of the existence of Ledyard's clothes in 1841, Society member and schoolmaster Simeon Hart succeeded in procuring the waistcoat from Ledyard's daughter-in-law and arranged to present it in a glass case.[38]

Society president Thomas Day promptly mentioned the waistcoat in a letter to the governor discussing the Society's progress. He described how it still had "the holes in it made by the sword, where it entered his body and where it came out on the other side" but made no mention of blood or stains. The family assigned sentimental, perhaps historical, value to the clothes from the first as the holes show no sign of mending. On the other hand, the waistcoat was laundered sufficiently to remove viscera and make any remaining blood stains negligible. An 1845 visitor considered the Ledyard relics a forcible reminder of patriotism in the face of oppression, describing everything from the glass case to the cuts in the waistcoat. It was available for viewing when historian and editor Jared Sparks visited two years later.[39]

When contacted about donating Ledyard's waistcoat, his daughter-in-law, Maria Van Tuyl Ledyard, also mentioned she had his shirt. She had married into the Ledyard family after the Colonel's death and inherited them from her mother-in-law, Anne Williams Ledyard. Both women came of an age that valued clean linen. Despite the hardships of the Revolutionary War, officers were instructed to ensure enlisted soldiers kept their linens as clean as possible. Yet both wife and daughter-in-law preserved the shirt with noticeable bloodstains intact for more than sixty years. *Not* washing the shirt, beyond removal of viscera so as to prevent mold or foul odors, suggests they considered it a familial memorial of his life and manner of death. Van Tuyl Ledyard refused to part with the shirt during her life but left it to the Connecticut Historical Society on her death in 1844.[40]

Librarian Thomas Robbins objected to displaying Ledyard's shirt because it might offend ladies visiting the historical society's rooms. He had the shirt washed to remove or reduce the bloodstains (figure 5), although it remains noticeably more stained than the waistcoat. He thus fundamentally altered the artifact Ledyard's wife and daughter-in-law cherished. A bachelor, he drew a distinction between the delicate females of station who visited the Society rooms and women of lesser status such as the laundress who likely washed the shirt. Robbins's concern over offending female sensibilities overrode considerations of the blood stains' historical and sentimental value and recreated the shirt as a relic of the nineteenth century's increasing obsession with cleanliness.[41]

"Sweeping and Brushing": Putting Collections on Display

The Connecticut Historical Society made its collections readily accessible for visitors. As librarian, Robbins opened the Society rooms six days a week,

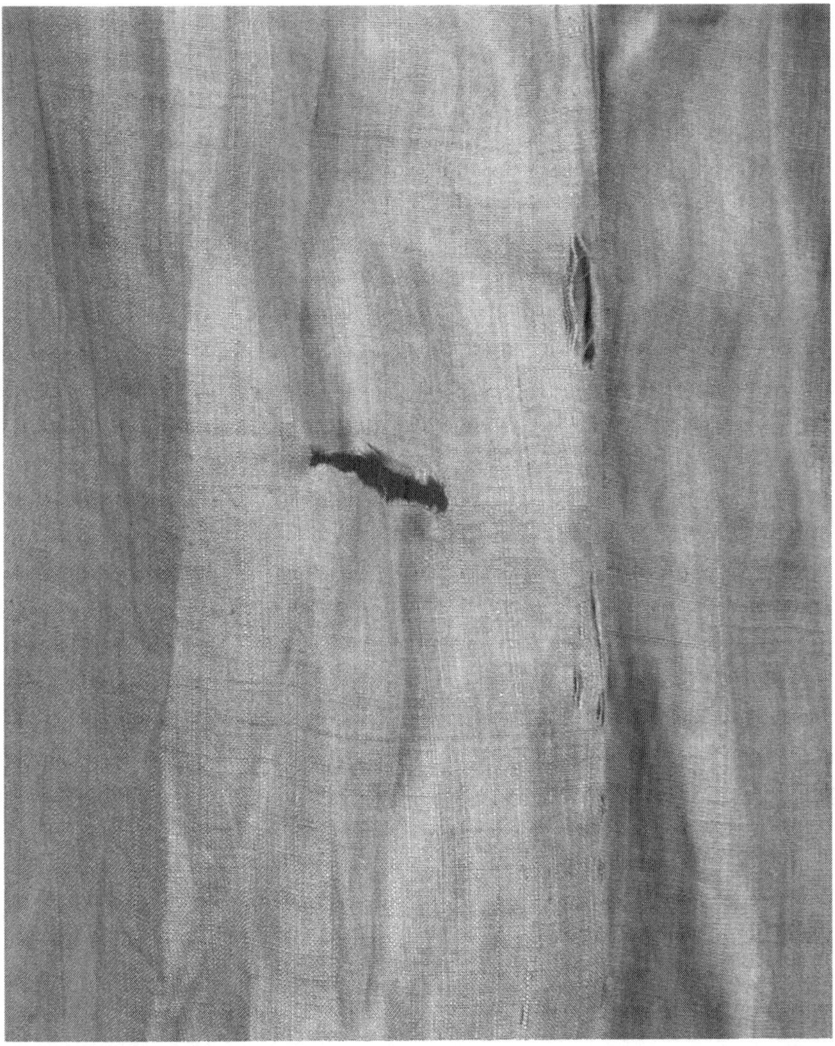

FIGURE 5. Man's shirt, originally owned by Colonel William Ledyard, about 1781, handstitched linen; gift of Mr. and Mrs. Daniel Ledyard from the estate of Mrs. Maria Ledyard, 1844.48.0, The Connecticut Historical Society.

typically from 10 a.m. to 12 p.m. and 2 p.m. to 6 p.m., arranging for substitutes when traveling. His position involved assisting researchers and organizing and caring for collections. The latter occupied a great deal of time. His diary entries noted days spent "sweeping and brushing" and working on the books or library.[42]

Robbins's labors to keep the collections open were key to the Connecticut society's popularity. He devoted less space in his diary to visitors than to weather, politics, and other matters. Many references to visitors were either passing comments about having had "company" or complaints about the many visitors impeding his ability to work on his library. He decided not to allow unaccompanied minor boys in his rooms after he "had losses, a considerable number, and some valuable."[43]

Daily entries in Robbins's diary affirm the collections rooms of the Connecticut Historical Society were popular. In August "twenty young women" visited his room before "going to the West as teachers." The following month "a large number of mutes from various parts of the country" visited his rooms, undoubtedly attending the first meeting of the New England Gallaudet Association of the Deaf. At other points in the year at least two Sabbath schools stopped by, as well as "visitors from all parts of the land not excepting Minnesota."[44]

The Connecticut Historical Society's location within the Wadsworth Athenaeum contributed to the influx of visitors. When wealthy art patron Daniel Wadsworth decided to erect a gallery of fine arts in Hartford, Barnard helped persuade Wadsworth to add space for the Society. The Athenaeum featured historical paintings and landscapes, and visitors may have wandered into the historical society rooms. In fact, Robbins mentioned the picture gallery as a draw for visitors. One visitor considered the gallery had "nothing very valuable in it yet" as of July 1845, but a few months later another visitor described the walls as hung with "valuable portraits" and busts of notables including Massachusetts minister Increase Mather, Pennsylvania founder William Penn, and Connecticut author Lydia Sigourney. The building also housed the Hartford Young Men's Institute (which became the Hartford Public Library) and the Natural History Society.[45]

In addition to the collection being housed in a popular Hartford cultural building, it was located in an optimal site, namely the state capital of Connecticut. Although the second-largest city in the state at the time, it sat in the center of the state rather than close to the border. In addition, the Society hosted numerous well-attended lectures and events—and went to lengths to hold some meetings in the largest city in the state, New Haven, to expand their reach. Significantly, Hartford was a convenient stopping point on land-based travel routes between New York City and Boston. Many out-of-Connecticut visitors may have been traveling elsewhere than Hartford but happened to stop in the city for some period of time.[46]

"From All Parts of the Land": Connecticut Historical Society Visitors in 1850

All too often scholarly analysis highlights those who produced materials and events rather than the masses who attended, purchased, read, or in the modern parlance consumed historical products. Many societies, museums, and libraries offered guests large volumes in which to inscribe their names and the dates of their visits. Scholars often ignore these books. The volumes contain a wide variety of handwriting specimens, some hard to decipher. On occasion autograph hunters removed evidence of notable visitors, resulting in gaps for historical researchers. Some books contain few signatures, leaving open to question whether there were only a small number of visitors or, for whatever reason, visitors didn't sign in. Even scholars examining museum attendance in modern times face difficulties identifying visitors and deciphering visitor logs.[47]

Yet the information in visitor logs is historically valuable: so-and-so was *here*. The Connecticut Historical Society logs document the Society's popularity. The number of known visitors per month in 1850 ranged from 131 to 670. Of equal import, the Society asked visitors to provide names, places of residence, and birthplaces, and many obliged. As a result, the logs connect visitors to three places: birth, residence, and Hartford as of the visit. Using the U.S. Census for 1850, the logs connect Society members, collections, and neighboring institutions with citizens of the city, state, nation, and world.[48]

The logs were large bound volumes which originally contained blank pages. The pages for 1850 show little evidence of autograph hunters abstracting valued signatures. At the top of most pages, Robbins or another member identified the information requested (see figure 6). Most visitors signed for themselves, so the process of transcribing the logs and matching visitors against the census involved numerous decisions mediating data.[49]

Bear in mind the volumes document only those individuals who entered their names. Unknown numbers did not sign. Robbins described two Sabbath school visits (Norwich and Willimantic) as each numbering more than a hundred. Twenty-eight visitors from Norwich signed the register during the Sabbath school visit, and only nine from Willimantic. The log thus documented at best thirty-seven out of more than two hundred visitors.[50]

The Connecticut Historical Society rooms were undoubtedly popular, but with whom? Given the culture of the times and the makeup of early historical society membership visitors were, unsurprisingly, born or resided in Connecticut, of European (primarily British) descent, and many men were merchants or in the professions. The number of women visitors was sizable

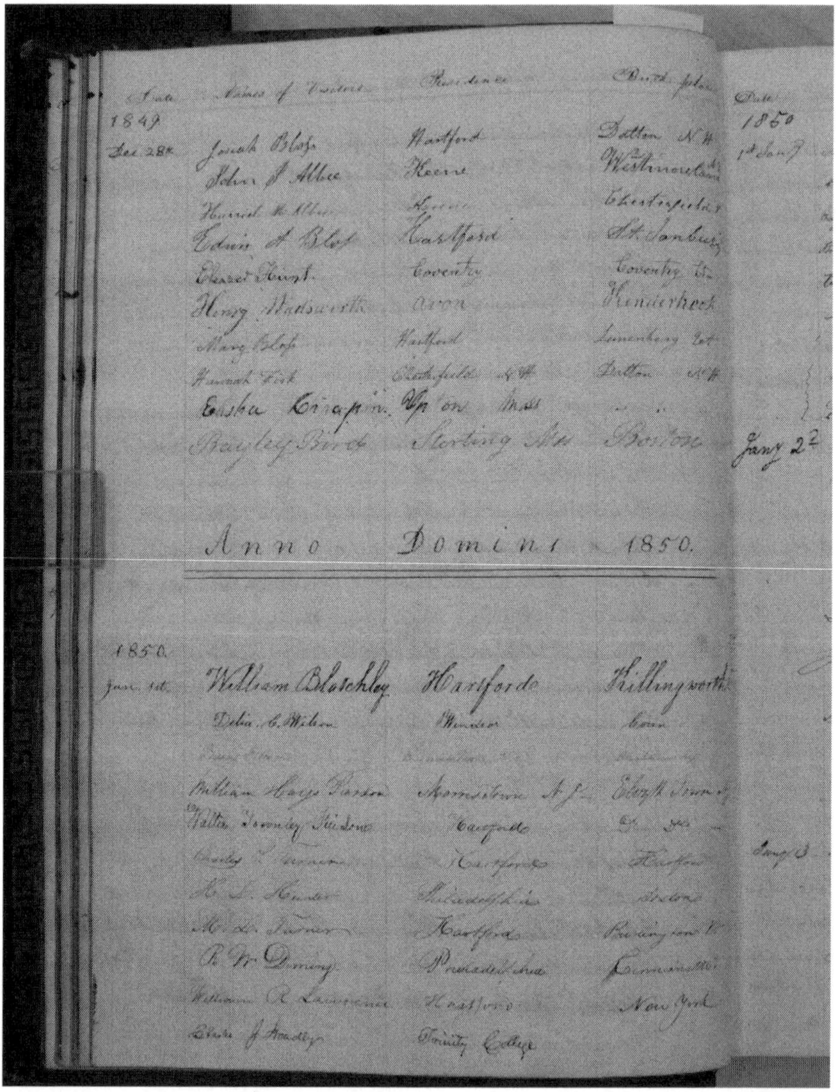

FIGURE 6. Sample page, library visitors' logs, 1850, CHS Institutional Archives, The Connecticut Historical Society.

despite the lack of women as members. Nevertheless, closer analysis shows the historical society rooms were also involved in upward mobility.[51]

A number of notables signed the visitors log in 1850, including abolitionist Sarah M. Grimke and educator and author Almira Lincoln Phelps. A

Clement C. Moore of New York visited, the acknowledged author of *The Night before Christmas*, as did at least five members of the Gallaudet family. The volumes document a few groups someone considered worthy of additional note, such as the "Committee on Public Charitable Institutions of Mass." Members of other historical societies also visited, including Edward C. Marshall and George H. Moore of the New-York Historical Society, the latter the librarian. So too did historian and minister William Bacon Stevens. One visitor became notable long after visiting the society: twelve-year-old J. Pierpont Morgan signed the register twice.[52]

The Connecticut society's collections constituted a regional point of interest. Half the visitors lived in Connecticut, two-fifths were born in the state, and a third were both born in and lived in Connecticut. Another third came from neighboring states (Massachusetts, New York, and Rhode Island) and more than a quarter listed those states as birthplaces. All told, three-quarters came from the Northeast. Slightly less than one-third of the Connecticut signers listed Hartford as their place of residence, although many recorded living in nearby towns and villages. Of the Hartford residents, less than one-quarter were also Hartford born, attesting to the mobility of the city's population.

Visitors of European descent dominated to the extent the rooms were a de facto white-only space, as no visitors found in the census were recorded there as non-white. Europe, mainly Great Britain, provided a small but significant contingent of visitors. Some were European or Americans living abroad. The visitors who gave India as their residence listed their occupations as missionaries. Ireland ranked second to England as place of birth. A mass emigration from Ireland was underway, escaping the potato famine. Yet many of the Irish-born historical society visitors were Anglo-Protestants rather than Catholics.[53]

Women accounted for more than a third of known guests. Many daughters and wives of upper and middle class white men—professionals, merchants, wealthy farmers, and skilled artisans—formed literary societies, voluntary associations organized to encourage mutual improvement. The Connecticut Historical Society drew its visitors from among these same circles and the rooms formed a site of civil society accessible to multiple constituencies. Prescriptive writers endorsing particular curricula considered history a suitable subject of study for women. The twenty "Young Ladies going to the West as Teachers" who viewed the collections affirmed connections to the State of Connecticut and its history. They entered their names as a group across the lines soliciting places of birth and residence, suggesting the visit formed part of a transitional phase between place of birth and previous residence and the westward locations to which they headed. Perhaps the high number of women visitors contributed to the number of women donors.[54]

Many visitors were young, although not necessarily younger than the population as a whole; the median age for the country at the time was roughly nineteen. The wide range in age of visitors indicates the collections' appeal extended beyond the young. Robbins noted the presence of both young and old more than once, albeit in conjunction with Sabbath schools, but older individuals also visited on their own or as part of smaller groups. Connecticut residents Sarah Francis and H. S. White, both octogenarians, signed the register, as did fellow octogenarian Sylvester Bliss of New York.[55]

Whether young or old, a sizable number visited in groups. Adult Sunday schools stopped by, and so did deaf individuals in town for the New England Gallaudet Association and female teachers headed west. Mary Jane Welles of Hartford brought three children in January. Abigail H. Frost of Springfield, Massachusetts, likewise was accompanied by ten-year-old Charles P., seven-year-old Emily A., and four-year-old Elizabeth on her visit in September. A group of Danbury citizens visited two days later, including wealthy farmer Frederick Wildman with his wife, Julia, and seventeen-year-old daughter, Lucy, along with two more Wildmans (merchant David D. and wife, Fanny) and Lucius Hoyt, possibly a neighbor or other connection.[56]

Over ninety Norwich residents left signatures on thirty-eight days that year, a testament to the Connecticut society's attractions as Hartford lay over forty miles away. Visitors may have taken the train through Willimantic and Manchester to reach Hartford. Most signatures appeared alone or in small groups. Only twice out of thirty-eight days did the number of signatures indicating Norwich residence top four. Thirteen signed on August 7 and twenty-eight on September 5, the day of the Sabbath school visitation. The Sabbath school probably came from Central Baptist Church of Norwich, as Baptist clergyman William P. Palmer and his wife, Sarah Bennett Palmer, were among the visitors. He had retired from leading the First Baptist Church of Norwich but remained in the town affiliated with the Central Baptist Church. More than a third of the Norwich signers were women, and at least six couples visited the rooms together.[57]

Of particular note, some families visited on multiple days. Connecticut-born Ephraim Kirby Chamberlain stopped by on October 16 with his niece, twenty-three-year-old Sarah M. Kendrick. Earlier in the year both resided in the Cincinnati household of Sarah's father, Elijah Kendrick. Two days later, thirteen-year-old Kendrick H. Chamberlain signed the register. Perhaps reports from his father and cousin motivated the visit, or his father ordered it to further his education. Similarly, boatman Henry Starr of Medford, New Jersey, visited in April. Four months later, his sons, John H. (12), L. Jacob (10), and Mulford (7) signed the register. Georgiana and Caroline Nock of Windsor Locks, Connecticut, aged twenty and seventeen, visited in September and a month later, their father George, a foreman at the Iron Works, brought their younger sister Harriet A. (7). The fifteen- and sixteen-year-old sons of state legislator and education committee chairman John Denison Baldwin of Hartford visited on July 29. Less than two weeks later, their fourteen-year-old sister visited, and their seventeen-year-old sister followed in September.[58]

Forty-seven individuals made repeat visits in 1850, including Alfred Driggs, a farmer born and resident in Vernon, Connecticut. Driggs signed the register in August, only to return six weeks later with his fifty-year-old mother, Martha. Two individuals visited four times: sixteen-year-old Miss Anne Lyman of Hartford, accompanied on her first visit by her fourteen-year-old sister Susan, and Williams College student Oliver B. Hayes of Hartford. Lyman's visits were spread over the course of seven months while Hayes's took place within the span of forty days.[59]

Hartford's Trinity College supplied a large cohort of visitors scattered across the year. Charles J. Hoadley visited on New Year's Day and went on to become a lawyer, librarian, and historian, holding the offices of state librarian from 1855 to 1900 and president of the Connecticut Historical Society 1894 to 1900. A flurry of visits in February—seven students visited on five separate days within a two-week timeframe—perhaps arose in conjunction with schoolwork. Other students stopped by later in the year.[60]

Visitors included a range of occupations and professions. Their occupations mirrored historical society membership rolls to a degree, rarely among the first ranks of the political, social, or cultural elites. Nevertheless, the number and variety of higher level professions (law, medicine, ministry) and higher-status occupations (merchants, banking), affirm the collections' draw for the educated and financially well off. Farmers were the largest contingent, at 129, in an era when the primary occupation was farmer. More than 60 merchants signed the logs as did more than 50 clergymen, all from Protestant denominations.

Several wealthy landowning individuals visited. The 1850 census reported only real property or land ownership, omitting personal property. Of 753 men over the age of twenty matched with the census, 280 reported owning real property. The wealthiest was Pennsylvania-born John Davies Jones of Cincinnati, with $150,000, who visited on September 21. A dry goods merchant and head of Jones Brothers and Company, Jones may have stopped by after visiting his son, a Yale student in nearby New Haven. The richest Connecticut visitor was Hartford attorney William D. Ely ($75,000), who practiced railroad law and later moved to Providence, Rhode Island. Twenty-one women owned land, with the wealthiest being Eliza Lydia Royce Sheldon Butler of Hartford, whose property was valued at $15,000. A widow, she may have controlled the estate bequeathed to her then-ten-year-old daughter Eliza Sheldon Butler, worth over $100,000. Twenty-one year-old Trinity College student Charles Hoadley was the youngest landowner ($300).[61]

The number and variety of occupations among visitors attested to the collections' appeal to the developing middle classes. The 814 visitors for whom occupations are known included two hundred craftsmen. Many worked with metal or wood, such as armorers, smiths, and a wire drawer on the one hand and cabinetmakers, carpenters, and joiners on the other. The ranks also included three butchers, two cigar makers, and twelve painters.

The carpenters and joiners were part of the local visitors. The thirteen carpenters were born and resided in southern New England (Connecticut, Massachusetts, and Rhode Island) with two exceptions: Daniel Cooke resided in Vernon, Connecticut, but was born in Kingston, Canada, while Horace Childs came from Henniker, New Hampshire. Another Henniker resident, farmer Benjamin Colby, visited the same day as Childs. Both claimed sizable real property, Childs worth $5,000 and Colby $3,500. Two carpenters, Amos Allan and David L. Maples, owned real estate (worth $3,000 and $2,000, respectively) and came from Norwich with the Sabbath school. Maples's wife Lucinda C. also accompanied the school group. Of the seventeen joiners, only three were born outside Connecticut (one in Rhode Island, two in Massachusetts) and only one lived outside of Connecticut, in Massachusetts. Two owned land: Orrin M. Rising of Suffield, Connecticut ($500) and William Palmer of Hartford, Connecticut ($2,500).[62]

Men described as laborers or involved in semi-skilled occupations (bartender, carder, peddlers, factory operators) also visited the Connecticut society. Census occupations alone may be deceiving. The laborers included Eleazer R. Crane of Mansfield, Connecticut. Sixteen years old at the time of his visit, he worked on his father's farm and attended school. In 1860 he still worked on his father's farm but was described as a farmer and held personal property worth $500; his father was worth $4,500 in real property and $2,000 in personal. On the other hand, the laboring ranks included Charles Tudor of East Granby. In 1850, at the age of twenty-three, he lived on a farm owned by Watson Thompson. Ten years later Tudor was still a laborer with no declared real or personal property, residing on the farm of Edward Thompson in East Granby.[63]

Visiting the Connecticut Historical Society arguably formed part of an overall course of improvement for some individuals. Several listed under semi-skilled and labor occupations in 1850 matched with the 1860 Census under different occupations. Irish-born Nicholas Killam was a porter in Hartford in 1850 but by 1860 moved to New York City and became a grocer. Listed as a peddler in 1850, Samuel Fitch traded merchandise up into Canada before renting a factory in Rockville and producing knit goods; by 1860 he was a manufacturer. Joseph Metcalf, involved in factory operations in 1850, visited the Society on August 12 with his nineteen-year-old son Charles. Over the following decade he became a carpenter. Hatfield Soule of Massachusetts went from being a carder in Chicopee Falls to a book agent in Lowell. Laborers in 1850, David Northway (34), James C. Taylor (22), and George P. Bradley (19) of Massachusetts, and James E. Woodbridge (19) of Connecticut all turned to different occupations by 1860: whipmaker, tanner, boarding school teacher, and accountant, respectively. Woodbridge, who visited the Society on June 27 with his forty-year-old mother Sophrona Barber Woodbridge, later dealt in lumber in New York.[64]

An Accidental Harbinger

The Connecticut Historical Society's diverse collections, donor base, and visitors highlight the contingent nature of historical society activities. Interesting items for viewing surely attracted many of the visitors, some of whom in turn became donors. The whole hinged in part on the confluence of connecting the Society's centennial celebration with desire to showcase material artifacts, and an officer who valued and donated non-textual works. It raises questions as to what other societies could have collected had their officers held artifacts in greater esteem. Further, the variety of visitors, particularly with respect to gender and class, speak to historical interest outside the ranks of the elites. The visitors resembled the middle class membership of later local historical societies. Whether or not the members intended as much, the Connecticut Historical Society was a harbinger in the collection of historical material artifacts and offered a partial model for engagement with broader publics.

Yet the comparative popularity of the Connecticut society's collections likewise reveals how little historical societies engaged with popular history and the general public. Societies drew on a small cadre of professional men, few to none of whom ranked among the highest business or government circles, and who primarily interacted with each other. Despite rhetoric endorsing appeals to popularity and the occasional public performative activity, their choices undermined any outreach efforts.

Officers repeatedly opted to limit their spheres of action. Broad general publics expressed interest in stories and anecdotes, but societies offered dry facts and information. Popular histories featured extensive illustrations; society volumes included few to none. Authors and publishers of popular works invested time and money in crafting navigational aids to allow readers to easily locate discussions on particular places, people, and events. Cash-strapped societies were either unwilling or unable to lean on members to provide similar labor for their volumes. Artifacts attracted visitors, but most societies did not actively collect them. Lack of money contributed to these differences, as officers faced fiscal limitations associated with operating quasi-public, member-supported organizations. Nevertheless, the contrast emphasizes the extent to which historical society officers chose to narrow their visions.

Chapter Six

"An Oblivious Society"

Inclusion, Exclusion, and Omission in Historical Collections

"THEY OUGHT TO ABOLISH THEIR *Historical* Society at once and form an *Oblivious* Society," New Hampshire historian and lawyer John Kelly suggested in 1825, on learning the New-York Historical Society might sell its library. Historical societies labored to preserve information for future generations, while an oblivious society would "devise ways & means to prevent the knowledge of their Vandalism & ignominy reaching posterity." Although a member of his state's historical society and vested in its success, Kelly recognized historical societies affected what was preserved for future generations.[1]

In particular, society officers exerted control through what they collected. Officers or designated members reviewed proffered materials. References to selection appear in historical society correspondence without any indications the practice was an unusual occurrence. The societies did not have stated accession policies; members reviewing materials possessed discretion as to what to accept or return. Rhode Island Historical Society officer John Howland reviewed a collection of manuscripts in 1822, all seventy or more years old, of which "many [had been] partly destroyed by mice." He chose an assortment and returned the rest. A quarter century later, fellow officer William R. Staples reported receiving "a large mass of old papers" from which he "selected" those he considered appropriate. In a similar manner, Rev.

Edwin C. Stone, who later became an active officer, presented the Society with a variety of materials with the caveat that "should they, on examination, be deemed too unimportant for your Archives, you will make such disposition of them as your judgment shall dictate."[2]

Donors' deferral to historical society's judgment were not rhetorical, for officers could reject proffered items. Shortly after the death of American Antiquarian Society founder Isaiah Thomas, Christopher Columbus Baldwin was appointed librarian. Baldwin proved an indefatigable collector, adding nearly five thousand publications to the Society's collections. After visiting the New York society and viewing the collections, he wrote approvingly, "they reject all curiosities excepting they have historical virtue" and, by implication, other items as well. Then as now, if an influential donor was disposed to make a sizable contribution, officers might accept it in toto, rather than risk antagonizing the giver and losing the gift. Nevertheless, language reflective of choice recurred throughout the early nineteenth century.[3]

Decisions of selection and rejection reflected notions of historical value. An important element in choices was whether a given document or collection's *content* was considered historical. Early officers relied on ideas of history (military, political, religious) that focused on events, progress (settlement, government, churches, schools), and iconic individuals. Other valuation means took into account author or creator(s), privileging inclusion of items connected to notable persons, or connections to specific places or events.[4]

What did early historical societies *not* collect? Officers focused on materials documenting the public worlds they shared. In short, they overlooked laboring classes, women, and racial and ethnic minorities. Upper class women enjoyed comparatively greater access to historical society members, nevertheless they used a variety of tactics to contribute materials documenting women's lives and labors. Anxious to not antagonize portions of their membership, officers generally avoided addressing the issue of peoples of African descent and the practice of slavery. In a similar vein, they constructed chronologies that reduced Native American nations' presences and land claims. These choices, exclusions, and omissions did not go unnoticed. Other historical society members, women, and individuals of African and Native American descent challenged exclusions at the time, primarily through external publications. Individuals with sufficient means or support from patrons produced histories and documentary editions affirming the historical importance of a far more diverse array of peoples.[5]

"Any Remarkable Persons, Male or Female": Gender and Class in Collecting

Society officers paid little attention to ethnic and racial minorities, women, and the laboring classes. Consider collection of personal papers or family holdings, where in rhetoric officers expressed broad interest in gathering documents, inviting readers and listeners to consider themselves and their families' papers solicited for collection. In practice, officers assigned historical value to everything connected to a small coterie of iconic individuals. A larger, middle group included men of lesser or more local renown: their papers were desirable, but not to the degree of the top echelon. Most people fell into the last category, where connection to pivotal events was key to assignments of historical value.

Shortly after establishment in the early 1840s, the Cincinnati Historical Society reminded potential donors "it is not in printed books alone that history is to be found" and solicited, among other items, "the stories of the pioneers reduced to writing." The Missouri Historical and Philosophical Society regretted the loss of papers in individual hands, when the items could be placed with the Society. Other society officers also mourned losses and encouraged donations.[6]

Collecting papers from individuals and families offered societies multiple benefits. Officers recognized collecting caches of documents containing facts as an efficient way to preserve historical information. Widespread record-making practices blurred lines between public and official correspondence with personal. As a consequence, family collections often included valuable official materials or other historical materials alongside family-oriented documents. The rise of romanticism contributed to growing interest in biographies and popular historical works, further encouraging historical societies to gather people's papers.[7]

Officers rarely named specific individuals when circulating general requests for materials. Instead, they used collective descriptors such as "remarkable" or "distinguished." The Alabama Historical Society established separate categories of people and documentation in 1850. Officers asked for "Memoirs, correspondence, anecdotes, &c., of any remarkable persons, male or female, residing in or passing through the State; or in any way connected with its history." Separately, the officers wanted materials "written by, or at the suggestion of" state citizens. Other societies specified who qualified as "remarkable" or "distinguished" either by virtue of their professions "as ministers of the Gospel, politicians, lawyers, physicians, or mechanics," or notable roles in city, state, region, or national history. The Virginia society's executive committee solicited information on "all who have been distinguished in the annals of Virginia, or connected with its history, whether particularly named in the [Society's] resolutions or not."[8]

With very few exceptions, "remarkable" persons were presumed male. A few circulars specifically referred to men in soliciting papers and biographies. Others used generic plurals ("persons," "pioneers") and left interpretation to the discretion of the reader. An overwhelming majority of donors giving private manuscripts opted to contribute men's writings. The 1850 Alabama society offered a rare explicit acknowledgment of remarkable women whose lives and papers warranted preservation. The reason behind the use of "male or female" is unknown. Perhaps the officers had in mind women such as socialite and writer Octavia Walton Le Vert, the "Pride of Mobile" and friend to literary and political figures from Washington Irving to Henry Clay. The women's movement was in its early stages, and women were not seen as a major part of the political landscape. The Rhode Island Historical Society mentioned only one woman when officers drafted a list of fifty-two general subjects for investigation: seventeenth-century Quaker leader Mary Dyer, whose posthumous fame focused on her trial and execution by the colonial Massachusetts government for violating banishment and advocating the Quaker faith.[9]

When push came to shove, officers pursued papers documenting the lives of a small cadre of individuals including nationally recognizable names (e.g., George Washington and Benjamin Franklin). Each historical society also had local or regional notables. The Historical Society of Pennsylvania pursued documents and memorabilia of colony founder William Penn and the Rhode Island society likewise valued connections to Roger Williams. Such notables' letters, documents, and artifacts had historical value as artifacts of their lives, apart from any appraisal based on content. When gathering Benjamin Franklin's letters, early historical editor Jared Sparks came across a cache of Franklin's correspondence with his London landlady, Mary Stevenson, and her daughter, Mary Stevenson Hewson. Sparks described the letters as "wholly of a private & domestic character, but . . . marked with all the peculiarity of Dr. Franklin's style and manner" and thus worthy of publication. Despite a general reluctance to appropriate funds for books, Congress placed a high value on presidential papers. Over the second quarter of the nineteenth century, the government purchased papers of George Washington (1834 and 1849), Thomas Jefferson (1829 and 1848), and James Madison (1837); these are now part of the Library of Congress. Washington's papers alone cost Congress forty-five thousand dollars.[10]

The example of military personages offers a clear demonstration of perceived relationships between rank and historical value. Historical societies collected officers and enlisted men's papers in inverse proportions. Nearly all recorded donations of veterans' papers came from the officer corps, disproportionately reflecting the service and experience of higher ranking officers. The higher a person's rank, the greater historical society interest. The New-York Historical Society's collections of the papers of Revolutionary generals Horatio Gates and William Alexander, Lord Sterling, filled more than thirty volumes. In contrast, gifts of lower-ranked men's papers often consisted of individual items (order books, journals, correspondence). The comparatively few gifts documenting lieutenants' services included the New Jersey Historical Society's receipt of the journal of Lieutenant William Barton, while accompanying General James Sullivan to the west in 1779, and donations of some lieutenants' commissions to the Connecticut, Maine, and Rhode Island societies. The Connecticut society also received a highly unusual manuscript letter from an enlisted man. Private Hezekiah Hayden's missive to his parents had especial historical value as a Revolution-era artifact, for it was penned at "Camp N[ew] York, July 4th 1776."[11]

Wives and daughters played critical roles in preserving or destroying personal papers, particularly in the absence of living sons. Most Revolution-era leaders assumed interest in their papers and put thought into their disposition, as did their families. Martha Dandridge Custis Washington famously destroyed most of her correspondence with second husband George following his death. After the death of John Dickinson, his daughters destroyed some of his papers, although Maria Dickinson Logan assured her antiquarian mother-in-law, Deborah Norris Logan, "they burn[ed] nothing of any value." Destruction or preservation of Dickinson's legacy hinged on his daughters' estimation of historical value.[12]

Women in Collections: Creators and Donors

Women played pivotal, albeit often overlooked, roles in contributing to historical society collections. They preserved documents, some created in their own right, which later entered society hands and donated either directly or indirectly through male intermediaries. Opportunities to act in these roles connected to any given woman's race, ethnicity, and station. The wives, sisters, and daughters of professional men of Anglo-American descent contributed where others could not, but even they faced obstacles.

Relatively few men or women gave manuscripts documenting women and their lives. Societies often incorporated women into their collections not as creators of donated materials but recipients. Inasmuch as letters from men to women survived, women implicitly engaged in acts of preservation. The Connecticut Historical Society received a letter merchant Thomas Bidwell of Hartford sent to his wife Prudence Scott from Barbados in 1716, shortly before he was lost at sea. The Historical Society of Pennsylvania received seventeen letters of Hannah Callowhill Penn, wife of colonial founder William, but these were valued as much or more for her husband's name as hers. Other gifts of women's writings took the form of legal documents, with historical interest due to connection to legal history and based on dates of creation; these included a woman's 1731 will and a quitclaim deed.[13]

Given the general dearth of women's documents, exceptions warrant attention. The Connecticut Historical Society received an unusual set of "[s]everal original Letters from the Wife of Colonel Nathaniel Haynes Whiting, late of West Hartford, written to him while serving as an Officer in the Revolutionary Army." These differed from most gifts of Revolutionary correspondence, which contained men's letters from the field treasured at home by wives and mothers. The author, Boston-educated Ruth Hooker of Farmington, was reputedly a "famous belle" due to her "superior education," and her husband evidently treasured her letters. Unfortunately, the Connecticut society held them just over a year before returning them to the family "by request."[14]

A gift to the Rhode Island Historical Society reflected contemporaneous recognition of antislavery petitions and women's involvement. The Rhode Island society received a donation of three original female antislavery petitions for Providence (718 signatures), Lonsdale (115), and Olneyville (166). These were created during a critical moment in the development of women's political activism, when women's engagement in abolition eventually led to organized efforts to obtain the vote. Most petitions were sent to Congress, which set them aside but preserved them among the mass of documents produced in the course of governance. The Rhode Island society accession was a rare act of preservation outside the government records. The petitions came from the estate of former Rhode Island Representative Joseph L. Tillinghast, a Whig, along with letters to the Congressional Library Committee and a petition to end naval spirit rations. Their preservation among Tillinghast's papers may have been accident. His Congressional term ended in March 1843, and he died eighteen months later. Nevertheless, the gift to the Society, by Tillinghast's relative, lawyer Charles F., indicated his appreciation for the petitions' historical value.[15]

Early societies did accept art featuring women. The Massachusetts society received portraits of colonial residents Anne Dison Pollard and Mary Atkinson Shurtleff. The Pollard painting portrayed Anne at the age of a hundred. Maryland Historical Society officer Brantz Mayer gave his organization a painting of Pocahontas with John Smith as part of a gift of portraits. The Connecticut Historical Society received not one but two busts of state luminary and author Lydia Huntley Sigourney.[16]

Historical society donations from women often hinged on connection to the organization—and a man, member or non-member, to serve as a venue of communication. This effectively ruled out most women from the laboring classes or not of Anglo-American descent. Even among the narrower ranks of elite white women, many valued and preserved materials but due to a lack of connection or awareness of a historical society's interest did not donate, although by the end of the nineteenth century, tens of thousands of women would come to participate in local preservationist groups. Women who did donate generally knew members personally or held materials connected to well-known men, in short their wives and daughters.[17]

Most early societies recorded few gifts from women, but this undercounts their actual contributions. Some may have preferred to keep their gifts anonymous. Others did not receive credit due to the ways gifts moved from donors to societies, for women's gifts often passed into the hands of male family members or historical society members before reaching historical society officers. An officer of the Rhode Island Historical Society reported receiving a sizable gift of pamphlets from Baptist minister David Benedict. Benedict had "found" the pamphlets in the possession of his wife's sister, Sally Gano Ludlow, widow of Rev. Peter Ludlow. He also "solicited" additional items from her, which she elected to retain although he expected she would "finally give them up for the Society." The gift of pamphlets thus was as much from Sally Ludlow as from Benedict, although credited to his name.[18]

The Connecticut Historical Society collections suggest a strong connection between women as donors and material artifact donations. The Society had the highest number of known women donors for the 1840s: ninety-two where comparable societies documented ten at best. A third of the Society's female donors gave at least one material artifact, compared to a quarter of male donors. Other societies received artifacts from less than 1 percent (Massachusetts) to 16 (Maryland). The Connecticut society received several material artifacts related to women and their spheres. Mrs. Joseph Rogers contributed three pieces of "ancient Brocade," one formerly the property of Yale president Ezra Stiles's wife. Mrs. William Talcott gave a seventy-year-old window curtain made by Mrs. Priscilla Kingsbury Penroy. "An ancient box Flat iron" came from Miss Electa Kimberly, along with a pair of tongs for smoking. Men also contributed artifacts documenting women's lives and labor. Dr. Henry Holmes gave a portion of the tomb of Lady Alice Apsley Boteler Fenwick, wife of the second governor of the Saybrook colony, and Dr. Timothy P. Beers gave a seventeenth-century embroidered picture.[19]

Donating to historical societies was not a simple matter, particularly for women. Potential donors needed to be aware that such societies existed, through access to notices in newspapers or periodicals or connections to members, and that the organizations were interested in collecting the types of materials the donors possessed. Once these conditions were met, donation further required some degree of confidence in the value of proffered items, assurance the society would accept and take sufficient care of them, and means to deliver the gifts to the society.

Women antiquarians in possession of valued historical materials had reasons to carefully consider whether or not to become donors. The societies relied on volunteer labor and thus access to their collections depended on officer availability. Professional men with suitable connections, particularly past or potential donors, might reasonably expect a degree of accommodation, but women had far less access. Even white women with connections to professional men of wealth and station had limited resources and opportunities. Massachusetts antiquarian Hannah Mather Crocker, descendant of notable colonial ministers, used control of her father's library after his death to ensure continued access to scholarly and historical circles. Her husband was a businessman and not active in antiquarian circles. Noted collector Rev. William Bentley spent time in the library and left with a few manuscripts but first paid "proper visits" to Crocker.[20]

Similar considerations may have contributed to Philadelphia antiquarian Deborah Norris Logan's retention of historical materials during her lifetime.

Shortly after its establishment in 1824, the Historical Society of Pennsylvania considered allowing women a tertiary degree of membership at lawyer William Rawle's instigation, which could have been in the hope of encouraging Logan's support. She controlled a valued collection of documents relating to her husband's ancestor James Logan, secretary to colonial founder William Penn. She negotiated with the American Philosophical Society's historical committee concerning publication of a compilation of correspondence between the men which she had selected and edited, with her husband's consent and support. The work did not appear in print, but the Historical Society of Pennsylvania expressed interest in publishing the volume and representatives visited Logan three times in a single year. She demurred and eventually declined "to save myself the anxiety, and perhaps mortification, which the publication might produce." Her husband had since died, leaving her "unprotected" and deprived of a source of support and authorization inasmuch as she knew the fact of her being a woman would raise questions about the work. Her early negotiations had included a request for a member of the Philosophical society to provide an introduction to the work and thus an implicit endorsement. At the same time, her control of the documents contributed to visits from other antiquarians. Withholding permission to publish during her lifetime allowed her to continue enjoying such visits on her terms.[21]

"As Great in Their Sphere as Their Brother": Hannah Mather Crocker and Hannah Whittelsey's Historical Donations

Close examination of two women donors offers further insights into the complex nature of donation. Early antiquarian Hannah Mather Crocker made multiple donations to the American Antiquarian Society, which helped shape the Society and make it notable for colonial New England manuscripts—including her own. Hannah Whittelsey of Connecticut made a much smaller gift that highlights rhetorical justifications used to advocate adding artifacts of women's creation to historical society collections.

Born in Boston, Hannah Mather Crocker descended on her father's side from famed Mather ministers Richard, Increase, Cotton, and Samuel. Her mother, Hannah Hutchinson Mather, was a sister of Thomas Hutchinson, making Crocker a niece of the loyalist governor and a descendant of Puritan spiritual leader and apostate Anne Hutchinson, expelled from Massachusetts.[22]

As a young unmarried woman, Crocker smuggled Patriot dispatches out of British-occupied Boston by hiding them in her dress in 1775. She recalled in later years that, when faced with a British officer searching the trunks of passengers leaving the city, she dared him to "storm my breast works." Possibly an elaboration, the story is consistent with Crocker's life. In 1778 she founded St. Ann's Lodge, a woman-only organization drawing on a sufficiently deep knowledge of freemasonry to convince modern practitioners she was inducted as a mason. She drafted the North Square Creed, an oath meant for men that declared those with "prudent wives" ought to listen to them. A surviving copy, dated 1787, bears initials including "JC," perhaps indicating the assent of her husband, Joseph Crocker. She published poems on political and masonic topics while raising ten children. With her children grown and husband dead, her involvement in literary and historical pursuits increased. Her later works included longer published works on freemasonry (1815) and temperance (1816) and an 1818 treatise on women's rights.[23]

The process of negotiating gifts, particularly desired materials, was analogous to courtship. Although never elected a member of the Massachusetts Historical Society or American Antiquarian Society, Crocker supported both. Joseph McKean, a member of the historical society, encountered her while she was in negotiation with the antiquarian society to donate materials. He "admonished [her]: not to forsake [her] first lover, alluding to [the Massachusetts Historical Society]." Perhaps meant as a joke, the gendered language compared Crocker to an unfaithful maiden succumbing to the solicitations of a new lover rather than remaining true to her "first lover." The language stung sufficiently that Crocker recalled it nearly a decade later.[24]

Crocker favored the American Antiquarian Society over the Massachusetts Historical Society because the antiquarian society and Isaiah Thomas gave her better returns for her gifts. She donated a portrait of her great-grandfather, Increase, to the historical society by 1798. The society members took no especial notice. After she gave the antiquarian society a few books and familial artifacts, officers appointed Thaddeus Mason Harris, a minister then serving the same Dorchester church that Crocker's great-great-grandfather Richard had once administered, to deliver their thanks. In 1814 she courted the Society through selected gifts, including Cotton's letter-book and Increase's journal. At the time, she was interested in raising money through the sale of parts of her family's library. Thomas purchased one part, giving her at least two hundred dollars. In turn, she donated another part of the library, along with a single gift of "Above Nine Hundred Sermons, in manuscript" plus additional manuscripts including diaries of Increase and Cotton. While Society founder Thomas also gave the Society manuscripts, her contributions dwarfed his. From the vantage point of two hundred years, her donations effectively created the Society as a major repository of early New England manuscripts.[25]

Likewise, from the perspective of two centuries and with the rise of women's history, Crocker's silence about men's dominance of historical writing warrants note. Crocker considered herself an antiquarian and historian. She incorporated extensive references to historical women in her treatise on women's rights and authored unpublished works on antiquarian research and Boston history. The Anglo-American literary world offered several examples of women historians at the time, not least Crocker's New England compatriots Mercy Otis Warren and Judith Sargent Murray. These women and their antebellum successors took behavior considered unfeminine in the heroines of the past and reinterpreted it through gendered conventions. They composed pieces presenting ostensibly demure and deferential women while emphasizing their subjects' intellectual brilliance and agency.[26]

In a similar vein, modern political scientists argue Crocker utilized rhetorical strategies which involved initial concealment. Crocker's essay on antiquarian research used Christian scriptural examples to advocate women's role in preserving historical materials, such as how the biblical Hannah, mother of prophet Samuel, preserved the design for an ancient tunic. In correspondence with the American Antiquarian Society, Crocker described the materials in her gift as "the widow's mite," invoking the biblical tale wherein a poor widow gave a small amount that represented a larger proportion of her assets than rich men, an act Jesus praised. The phrase gave Crocker the appearance of feminine modesty while simultaneously claiming high value.[27]

Of equal importance, Crocker stands as one of the few people of the age who contributed their own unsolicited manuscript writings to institutional collections, thus ensuring inclusion in the historical record. Several authors contributed copies of their printed works to historical societies, as did Crocker. With few exceptions, those who offered manuscripts provided materials written by other individuals. The one group of people who, as a whole, regularly contributed their own contemporary manuscripts to historical societies were members and scholars who had read papers and addresses at society meetings—and they generally contributed copies at the request of the society membership. The American Antiquarian Society possesses most of Crocker's extant manuscript writings, including three drafts of her essay on antiquarian researches. How and when the bulk of these entered the Society collections is unknown. She may well have chosen to include them alongside the writings of her father and other male forbears as a subtle act preserving her writings within a male-dominated collection.[28]

Yet American Antiquarian Society records also document a gift from her in 1820 that included two of her own manuscript essays. The donation was chronologically separated from her other gifts and small enough that Thomas described every component. The entry documents a woman considering her manuscript writings of sufficient value to future generations to warrant preservation in a historical society. The donated essays reflected Crocker's interest in religious themes: a short musing on the biblical tale of Jephthah, explaining his vow to sacrifice his daughter meant turning her over to the temple rather than killing her, and a much longer essay seeking to reconcile Trinitarian and Unitarian Congregational views. Two weeks after entering Crocker's gift of manuscript essays in the Society donation book, Thomas recorded a gift of one of his own manuscripts and later donated other personal manuscripts. So the Society has two of the few, perhaps the only, instances where early authors actively included unsolicited manuscripts in the historical record.[29]

Women donors could not assume acceptance of items into historical society collections even when giving century-old artifacts, as shown by Miss Hannah Whittelsey of Connecticut. The daughter of Deacon Chauncey and Lucy Wetmore Whittelsey of Middletown, she claimed descent through her mother from the locally famous Edwards family of Connecticut, whose members included noted early eighteenth-century theologian Jonathan Edwards. A genealogy of Wetmores, published after Hannah Whittelsey's death, described her as "highly intellectual, well read, and versed not only in polite literature, but in the history of her country." Alongside interest in history, Whittelsey held several treasured artifacts of the Edwards family. She learned in 1840 that the Connecticut Historical Society was interested in items "that would show the Costume and throw light on the early history of the Colony." She promptly donated a pair of shoes worked by her grandmother and great-aunt, a piece of her great-aunt's needlework, and a silk painting also by her great-aunt.[30]

Whittelsey provided three reasons for the Connecticut Historical Society to accept her gift: familial connections to important Connecticut men, intellectual and artistic skills, and evidence of progress. Two sufficiently impressed Recording Secretary Charles Hosmer to appear in the official record of the gift. Whittelsey noted with regret that "the handsomest" examples of her foremothers' labor had not survived the passage of time, but she sent items "of inferior quality which labelled historically may illustrate the character of the times." None of the artifacts portrayed subjects affiliated with men, or were made for men's use, and Whittelsey did not assume the Society would automatically accept them as worthy of inclusion.[31]

First and foremost, Whittelsey named the creators of the artifacts and their father and brother—Hannah, Mary, Timothy, and Jonathan Edwards. The shoes (figure 7) formerly belonged to Whittelsey's grandmother Hannah

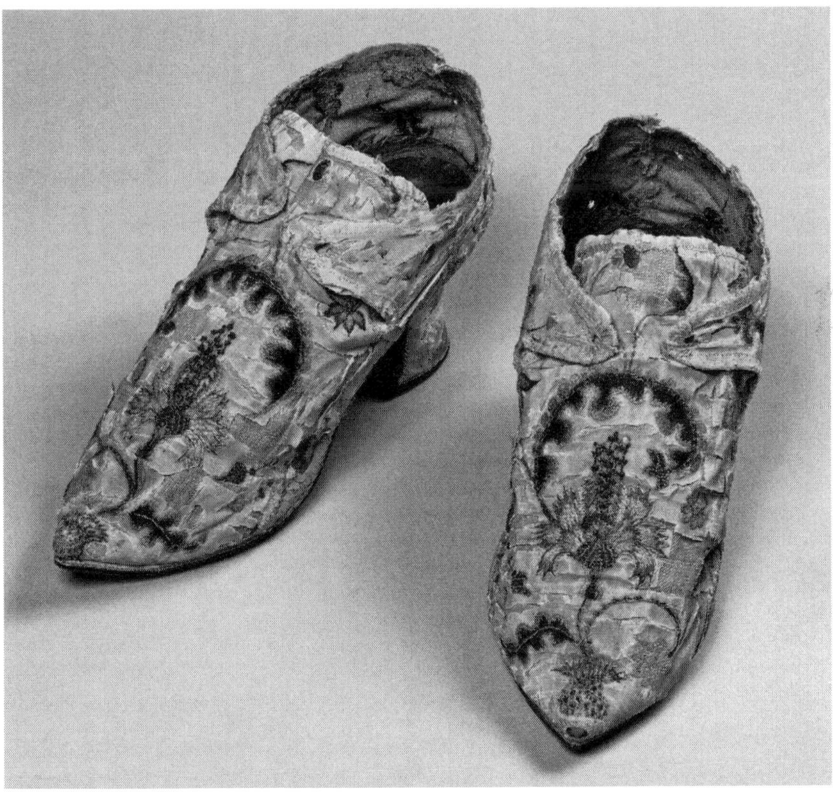

FIGURE 7. Woman's Shoes, originally owned and made by Hannah Edwards, about 1746, handstitched and embroidered silk and metallic threads on silk and linen, leather, and wood; gift of Hannah Whittlesey, 1840.7.1a,b, The Connecticut Historical Society.

Edwards Wetmore and were worked by both Hannah and her older sister Mary for the designs and workmanship show evidence of two different hands. Mary and Hannah were the daughters of Rev. Timothy Edwards, minister in East Windsor, Connecticut, and the sisters of Rev. Jonathan Edwards of Northampton, Massachusetts.[32]

The Society welcomed Whittelsey's invocation of known early Connecticut names, but in recording the donation Hosmer reinforced connections to men over and above women. He named both Timothy and Jonathan alongside Hannah and Mary. This was a logical inclusion as the men were better known. Yet Hosmer added a reference to Hannah's husband, Seth Wetmore of Middletown, Connecticut, emphasizing the artifacts' worth as physical links through women to earlier generations of notable Connecticut men, rather than as artifacts of the women's lives and labors.[33]

Whittelsey also stressed her ancestors' intellects and skills, noting all but one of the Edwards sisters were "as great in their Sphere as their Brother." Utilizing the language of separate spheres characterizing the imagined places of men and women, Whittelsey claimed for her female ancestors a degree of mastership equal to that of her better-known great-uncle. Women historians of the age used similar rhetorical tactics pairing female domesticity and conventional behaviors with claims for intellectual achievement. Indeed, Whittelsey stressed Mary Edwards' intellect further, noting she "went through all the preparatory Studies with her Brother to fit her to enter Colledge and I have heard was equally fit." Mary had artistic skills and exhibited a "fine taste for drawing and painting." The sophisticated and asymmetrical design for the shoes reveals a degree of familiarity with then-current rococo aesthetics. The embroidery fragment, likely originally part of a dress, similarly shows an eye for color, subtle shading, fine stitches, and a sophisticated arrangement of flowers and was sketched first in black ink. For Whittelsey, the donation represented her grandmother and great-aunt's intellectual capabilities and accomplishments. Hosmer largely ignored these in recording the gift.[34]

On the other hand, Hosmer did not ignore evidence of progress as an additional rationale to accept the artifacts. Even as Whittelsey emphasized her great-aunt's intellectual accomplishments, she highlighted the sisters' "self-training and indefatigable Systematic Industry" in what later generations called an Age of Homespun. Whittelsey stressed Mary's involvement in the whole process of creating embroidered works. Mary took wool from sheep, carded it, spun it, dyed it, and "spun and wove the foundation" cloth for her embroidery. Lacking access to prepared dyes or paints, she was forced to make them herself and crafted paintbrushes "from the hairs of the Tail of a Cat." These contrasted with mid-nineteenth-century availability of paints, dyes, brushes, and foundation cloths. The Connecticut Historical Society, vested in ideas of progress and improvement, took note. The accession record reflected that creation of the embroidery required more than stitching, focusing particularly on the need to manufacture brushes, spin cloth, and prepare paints and dyes using "native plants."[35]

Grounded in comparatively industrialized environs, Connecticut society officers appreciated difficulty as an additional rationale for including the works within the historical record. This hinged on Whittelsey's original recitation of the "disadvantages" involved. Without her letter, Hosmer could have accessioned the donation on the basis of the Edwardses' connection alone. With it, the Society embraced the artifacts as emblematic of the state's progress from colonial times, while simultaneously overlooking Mary's and Hannah's intellectual design and creation labor.

The Edwards shoes were relatively unique in appearance and easily identifiable. Other donations—including the needlework and silk painting proffered at the same time—were not so fortunate. Subsequent practices and relocations separated many an early artifact from provenance records. In the 1840s the Connecticut Historical Society received several other items connected with female labor, including an ancient pewter platter and an iron cooking pot, which the Society cannot authoritatively identify. Metal items were particularly susceptible to being separated from their provenance, but the same happened to cloth artifacts. Sufficient doubt exists as to the provenance of Mary Edwards's crewelwork that it is marked as attributed to her. Her silk painting, donated at the same time, may still be in Society hands but cannot be identified. For all the time and space Whittelsey devoted to detailing the rationale for donating her foremothers' work, she never described in detail any of the items accompanying her letter.[36]

The problem of provenance troubled Hosmer, albeit with respect to a different set of shoes. He inscribed "Presented by Mrs. Horatio Fitch" on a pair of shoes donated to the Society in 1843 (figure 8). The shoes were made in 1780 using fabric from a Revolutionary military flag, French given the portion of a fleur-de-lis visible. The story may have served as partial justification for the shoes' inclusion in the Society collections, and he clearly wished to ensure future generations could connect shoes and story. A goodly number of items

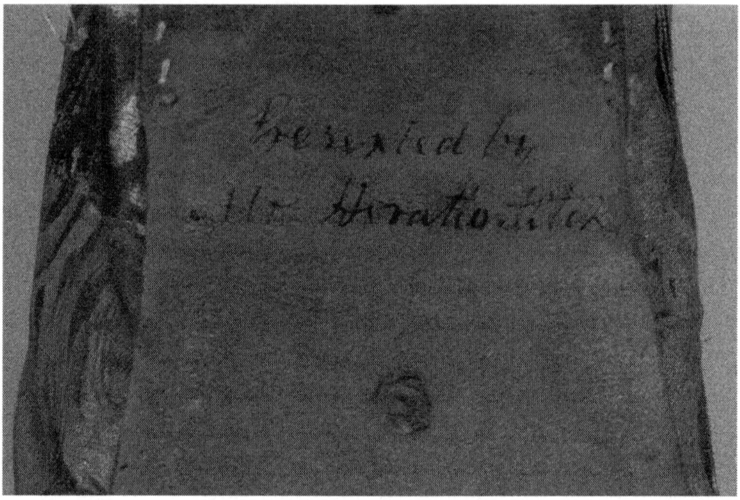

FIGURE 8. Woman's Shoes, about 1780, handstitched painted silk damask, silk tape, wood, and leather; gift of Mrs. Horatio Fitch, 1843.13.0a,b, The Connecticut Historical Society.

affiliated with women's labor came with stories of passage through families and connections to great men and events, although age alone occasionally served as rationale for donation and acceptance of "ancient" shoes.[37]

Together, the Crocker and Whittelsey donations demonstrate the lengths even well-connected women faced to donate women's materials to historical society collections. Crocker valued her own writings sufficiently to ensure the preservation of some in the American Antiquarian Society, although for a long time they served as little more than a sidenote to her better-known male ancestors' writings. Whittelsey's gift documenting her grandmother and great-aunt's intellects and skills became reframed as artifacts of their father, brother, and husband. Nevertheless, the gifts survived along with documentation of their provenance, preserving some measure of the donors' motives.

"An Undistinguished Host": Challenging and Changing Historical Priorities

Crocker and Whittelsey's subversion of the preferences of all male historical societies and their members took place in the archive; others challenged the societies by publishing documents in print. Many externally produced volumes critiqued the historical establishment. Over the second quarter of the nineteenth century, people published numerous documentary collections of papers, alongside memoirs and biographies featuring extensive excerpts from original writings. By the 1820s communities across the nation boasted active printing presses and a maturing distribution network, facilitating the production and spread of independent documentary works and memoirs. Anyone with the ability to fund a publication could preserve documents through print.[38]

Rank or class proved another point of dissension besides gender. "The page of history is resplendent with the names of men who held high rank, or occupied conspicuous stations," Priscilla Maxwell argued in an 1833 memoir of her father, Hugh Maxwell of Massachusetts. A veteran of the French and Indian Wars and the Revolution, Maxwell had risen to the rank of lieutenant colonel. Nevertheless, he was one of "an undistinguished host of subordinate officers and private soldiers" overlooked in favor of generals. Revolution Army veteran Joseph Plumb Martin's autobiography featured recollections of a private as a corrective and counter-story to grand narratives about the Revolution. Similarly, Pennsylvania mill owner Thomas Gilpin used publication to preserve journals documenting the experience of pacifist Quakers removed from patriot-controlled Pennsylvania to Virginia, "with evidences to support them" and ensure they were included in the history of the Revolution.[39]

While less-privileged individuals fought to have their names included in "the page of history," the wealthy and well-connected could reach into their pockets or solicit assistance from subscribers willing to purchase the final product. But poorer individuals still had options. Veterans of the Revolutionary War and their supporters used print to document and affirm wartime service and to encourage petitions for congressional pensions. Veterans' memoirs usually drew on memories and documents in the possession of survivors. By the fiftieth anniversary of the Declaration, a sizable proportion were from the enlisted ranks, those who would have been in their teens or twenties during the war. Thus the passing of time meant celebrations and publications of living individuals from lower classes, contributing to the spread of Jacksonian democracy.[40]

Several external publications also advocated preserving women's Revolutionary memoirs and actions. South Carolina author Caroline Howard Gilman published the letters of Eliza Yonge Wilkinson in 1839 based on grounds of rarity, for "few records exist of American women either before or during the war of the revolution." Her other justifications for publication included the relative lack of materials on the war in the South and those published records that did exist "want the charm of personal narration." Gilman's invocation of charm resembled contemporaneous women historians Lydia Maria Child, Sarah Josepha Hale, and Elizabeth Ellet, who often paired expansion of women's roles with existing gendered conventions of behavior.[41]

Publications of Revolution-era women's manuscripts emphasized ways in which they provided material otherwise wanting. Charles Francis Adams, a member of the Massachusetts Historical Society, echoed Gilman's dismay over the lack of charm. He argued great men were conscious of public performance in the service of public good and wrote under this awareness, blurring distinctions between them to the point that the men "assume a uniform of grave hue." Under his rationale, the growing Victorian doctrine of separate spheres justified preservation of women's history as incorporating sentiment as well as attesting to the "the heroism of the females of the Revolution." Library Company of Philadelphia librarian John Jay Smith privately printed fifty copies of a Revolution-era diary of family member Margaret Hill Morris in 1836, as it was "not designed for the public" and contained details of "daily alarms . . . frequent and often absurd reports" and a "few domestic circumstances." Despite the limited goals, Smith reprinted it as part of a familial documentary history eighteen years later, for the diary "ha[d] exalted considerable interest, even among perfect strangers." The work's popularity suggests the details of alarms, absurd reports, and domestic circumstances spoke to readers.[42]

"No Just Offense to Any One": Tactics of Racial Exclusion

Officers used a variety of tactics to address or overlook the nation's different races. The application of conscious and unconscious exclusionary tactics differed with respect to documenting the histories of Americans descended from enslaved African populations and those related to Native American tribes. Most early historical society collections documented the lives and interests of a small subset of Americans, first and foremost those descended from British colonists and secondarily professional men of wealth and station. Societies located in states with sizable non-Anglo ethnic populations engaged to various degrees in documenting more diverse pasts. Louisiana Historical Society officers sought to incorporate materials relating to French and Spanish pasts, and the New York and New Jersey societies likewise expressed interest in prior Dutch colonies. Nevertheless, on the whole English-language materials and descendants predominated.

A Lack of "Boldness": Avoiding Slavery

Abolitionist and proslavery advocate presences within historical communities complicated efforts to document slavery and abolition. Given the political climate of the time, officers and members could not avoid the issues. Nevertheless, they tried to do so through tactics such as an emphasis on collecting print, focus on slavery at a chronological distance, and a literal separation of present slavery and abolition activities from historical pursuits.

Officers' preference for print and written documents over material culture artifacts meant they did not collect much with respect to slavery. The Massachusetts Historical Society received a silver branding instrument early in the century from an unnamed "Friend," but otherwise societies gathered few slave-related artifacts. The preference for written materials told against enslaved peoples barred from literacy. A number of historical society circulars solicited works on colonization or abolition, but usually within the context of gathering the publications of religious or charitable organizations. The Maryland Historical Society requested "proceedings of Ecclesiastical conventions or councils of all denominations;—narratives of missionaries or of missionary enterprise, histories of colonization, slavery and abolition." In the 1840s the Louisiana Historical Society circular included a rare specific reference to color, inquiring about the "increase and progress of population in your parish, distinguishing blacks and whites; advantages of schools and libraries enjoyed; proportion educated."[43]

Notable references to slavery in historical society publications set the subject at a chronological distance. Historian Jean O'Brien's work on New England demonstrated that nineteenth-century local historians wrote indigenous peoples out by celebrating colonial "firsts" and by mentioning the "last" Native Americans, denying them an ongoing presence. Historical society officers applied similar tactics to slavery, documenting it in terms of the past, preferably the far distant past. The Historical Society of Pennsylvania published Edward Battle's essay on slavery in 1827, celebrating the "various important advances made by [Pennsylvanian] citizens towards meliorating the condition of the oppressed and injured of the human race." Rather than discussing recent occurrences in Pennsylvania or even the experiences of the enslaved, Battle explored white attitudes toward slavery and its progress in the North up to 1770, more than fifty years before he wrote his history. Similarly, William Law of Georgia gave an oration before the Georgia Historical Society, published in 1840 in the first volume of their *Collections*, reviewing

Georgian attitudes toward slavery before the Revolution. In each case, the works avoided recent events and emphasized slavery in terms of white experiences, either as early abolitionists (Battle) or as colonists deprived of the benefits of slavery to their detriment (Law).[44]

Writing histories of slavery required balancing historical information with reception by diverse audiences. New Hampshire Historical Society member, abolitionist, and congressional representative William Plumer Jr. attempted to convince fellow historian and abolitionist John Farmer to write a history of slavery in New England. Plumer considered the prospect manageable but noted if the history were to be published "in a work like our Collections, you would of course confine yourself principally to historical facts, which, fairly stated could give no just offense to any one, however sensitive the subject of the immediate abolition of slavery in the southern states." In short, the work would have to be carefully constructed so as to present controversial information in a neutral way in an attempt not to offend anyone. Farmer declined, pleading the difficulty of obtaining sufficient resources to write such a history. He may also have had the subject's divisive nature in mind.[45]

An unusual set of letters between Farmer and a former New Hampshire resident offer a clear demonstration of one tactic used to avoid conflict over slavery: literal separation. Farmer sent a letter mentioning historical matters and his involvement in abolition to former New Hampshire Historical Society member Richard Bartlett, who had relocated to New York. Bartlett opposed abolition and immediate emancipation and was against racial equality. To Bartlett's mind, Farmer had raised "one topic on which men seldom differ without some display of feeling." Since Farmer asked his opinion, Bartlett sat down and wrote not one but two letters in reply, both with the same date, physically separating discussion of history and slavery. In the letter on slavery and abolition, Bartlett noted he would answer Farmer's questions this once but would not "suffer" further discussion of the subject "to exclude topics more agreeable to my feelings and better suited to familiar correspondence." Farmer took the warning to heart, and the two continued to correspond.[46]

Few societies recorded many slavery-related manuscript donations. Rhode Island Historical Society officers documented perhaps the largest number. Although the Society received six hundred gifts and acquisitions during its first thirty years, based on the written descriptions of these less than 2 percent included manuscript items connected to slavery. The exceptions were largely more than a generation old and chronologically removed from contemporary times, including a seventeenth-century petition for freedom and items from the eighteenth century such as a bill of sale, a letter giving slaves' value, and a letter requesting aid to prevent being unjustly sold as slaves. The Society did receive at least one contemporary item: three recent petitions of Rhode Island women for abolition of slavery in the District of Columbia. Otherwise, the bulk of donated Rhode Island society slavery-related gifts bore old dates. Other societies' records reflected even fewer slavery-related gifts overall.[47]

One member used historical societies' interest in print to forward discussion of slavery and the slave trade. Early societies received a number of print materials on this subject, due to the extent of printing by abolitionist and colonization societies. Judge William Jay sent the New-York Historical Society a lengthy letter in 1843 reminding members of their interest in abolition societies proceedings. Jay favored abolition, had published works on slavery, abolition, and colonization—and gave the Society four-thousand-odd pages of parliamentary materials documenting the slave trade and abolition in the British Empire between 1811 and 1842. The items were geographically removed, speaking to events outside the United States, albeit within the Western Hemisphere, but chronologically contemporaneous. Jay's letter, reprinted in whole in the periodical *The New World* under a section header "Anti-Slavery Selections," discussed the gift at length, with occasional references to the United States, ending with a pointed invitation for others to review the documents particularly with respect to the "result" of the abolition of slavery in the West Indies "in behalf of human happiness and freedom."[48]

At least two historical society presidents mentioned slavery in public addresses. Maryland Historical Society President General John Spear Smith noted the Society's connections with colonization, inasmuch as it was founded in the Colonization Society's meeting rooms, while delivering a presidential address. Although he made no outright reference to slavery, he endorsed colonization. Smith also made a rare reference to free blacks in the context of raising them to a more equal position but did not endorse collecting and preserving historical materials documenting their experiences. When the Society published a memoir of author and naturalist Benjamin Banneker, they considered "a few words . . . to explain why a memoir of a free man of color" should be presented, along with an affirmation of Maryland's dedication to colonization.[49]

Peter Du Ponceau advocated waiting to tackle contentious subjects such as slavery until they were less controversial. He addressed the issues of slavery and abolition, and more broadly the documentation of Americans of African descent, in his inaugural address as president of the Historical Society of Pennsylvania. He framed his discussion within the context of Pennsylvania's abolition of slavery and the absence of legal distinctions between races. Although he suggested collecting and preserving documentation of the history of free and formerly enslaved Pennsylvanians of African descent and referenced the appeals of colonization, he added caveats. There would be "storms and tempests" if what he considered the slow disappearance of slavery was "interfered with," for "too many interests and too acute feelings are involved therein." Therefore, Du Ponceau concluded, "the time has not yet come for touching upon this subject with the boldness of the historian." In short, he considered boldness less important a qualification for historians than caution.[50]

Officers and members of historical societies across the nation evidently agreed with Du Ponceau. General historical society collecting practices and preference for written materials partly explain this lack of action with respect documenting slavery, enslaved peoples, and free peoples of African descent. Nevertheless, the widespread absence of references points to conscious decisions to avoid the controversy as officers preferred to maintain present amity rather than pursue a more complete record of peoples and actions.

Superseding Native American Peoples in the "Discovery" of America

Historical societies sought to preserve materials documenting the spread and development of European American control over the land, past and present. Officers invested more energy in documenting the pasts of Native American peoples than those of African descent to solidify white control of the land versus Native American rights and historic presence. Officers and members' actions reflected prioritization of ties to Great Britain and northern Europe.

Native American peoples were the exception to the societies' general Anglo-American focus. Societies actively solicited information and artifacts. At the same time, officers considered indigenous peoples separate from the builders of mounds in Ohio and Mississippi, thus denying them centuries of habitation. Societies paid unequal attention to indigenous peoples, favoring documentation of their pasts versus contemporaneous presences. Five of the fifty-two topics the Rhode Island Historical Society proposed as subjects for inquiry focused on Native American peoples, but only one acknowledged contemporary presence through a request for information about present

Narragansett peoples' condition. Immediately following this request, the committee asked for "the legislative proceedings relative to the tribe," implicitly connecting contemporaneous presence to government proceedings. Two other queries centered on the earliest colonial times through references to sixteenth- and seventeenth-century leaders Massasoit and Metacomet. Other Native American-related queries focused on burial grounds and the pronunciation of names.[51]

Officers paired interest in Native American peoples in general with marked indifference as to the circumstances of collecting antiquities. Members of the Rhode Island Historical Society actively participated in unearthing remains for use in racial anthropological comparisons. Following a request from a Parisian correspondent, Society officers appointed a committee whose members took time to obtain skulls they considered authentically indigenous. They eventually disinterred three skulls with bits of blanket, bark, and hair, which they sent to Paris.[52]

Even comparatively favorable encounters involved elements of racism. New-York Historical Society member Lewis H. Morgan of Rochester and Dr. Peter Wilson (Wa-o-wa-wâ-na-onk), an Iroquois from the Cayuga Nation, each addressed the New-York Historical Society on the subject of the Iroquois on May 4, 1847. Wilson invoked Iroquois history, appealing for aid on behalf of those relocated westward due to deceptive promises on the part of American agents, as all of the Iroquois wished to return. In the absence of government assistance, members of the Society took up the matter of soliciting donations among themselves and petitioning the state government. Yet these same members did not request a copy of Wilson's talk for the archives, despite doing so for Morgan and others who presented papers throughout the year. Instead, Wilson's words were included in the minutes of the meeting, published in the proceedings for the year, half quotes and half summary. Other papers given that year by European American contributors were either printed in full in the proceedings or summarized in toto, or their copies were requested for the archives.[53]

Moreover, societies minimized Native American land claims and history, and downplayed the continent's non-English immigrant history. The Historical and Philosophical Society of Ohio divided Ohio Valley history into three periods: "discovery and settlement by the French," "discovery and settlement by the English," and "the American dominion, commencing with the Revolution." The Missouri Historical and Philosophical Society asked contributors for information about French and Spanish settlement, but officers connected government of the land to Missouri's status as a United States territory and subsequent statehood. Similarly, the Alabama Historical Society placed Spanish and French presences as part of the transition from Native American control to the United States, asking sequentially about "the earliest notices of Indian tribes," "Spanish adventurers," "French settlements," "Territorial government," and "Formation of the State."[54]

The discovery of America offers a clear demonstration of racial and ethnic negotiations with respect to the history of people on the continent. Officers overlooked the possibility of Native American peoples, or their common ancestors, as discoverers. This drew on a long history of European Americans speculating on who discovered and peopled the Americas. At the American Antiquarian Society's first annual meeting, New England minister and historian William Jenks connected such questions with claims to land ownership, "it being then imagined, that some right in the soil would accrue" to whichever nation had found and peopled the continent. Jenks's use of "then" placed these ideas in the past as far as he was concerned, yet they persisted well into the nineteenth century.[55]

Spain's claim to discovery came under question in the 1830s. The American Historical Society requested "facts relating to the discovery or settlement of America" in the Society's circular. The absence of specific reference to Spain could be taken as an implicit reference to Columbus or an endorsement of recent Central and South American struggles for independence from European powers. The United States was not interested in rival influences within the hemisphere. Historical circles offer a third explanation. The circular appeared at a time when the Royal Society of Antiquaries in Copenhagen corresponded with American societies looking for evidence to document the discovery of America by Vikings before Columbus's arrival. In this context, the American Historical Society might have been deemphasizing Spain's role in establishing a European presence in the Americas.[56]

Rhode Island Historical Society officers' efforts to provide the Royal Society of Antiquaries with materials reflected their interest in supporting claims to European discovery and settlement before Columbus. More than thirty letters and reports document officers' labors. They sought accurate drawings of rocks bearing ancient inscriptions which might be runes; made three visits to the Deighton rock, a boulder bearing petroglyphs located nearby in Massachusetts, and pursued copies of drawings of the petroglyphs made at earlier dates. In addition, they gathered geographic maps, naval charts, and information about tides. Members of the "Committee on Antiquities & Aboriginal History" submitted a report apologizing for not having found "more to offer" and expressing frustration at "spending days and weeks in the pursuit deeming themselves fortunate if at the end of the period they have succeeded in . . . ferreting out from the heap of rubbish they are doomed to examine, one single fact touching the case in point." Nevertheless, the maps, charts, and drawings of petroglyphs the Rhode Island society provided prompted noted antiquarian Charles C. Rafn, writing for the Royal Society of Antiquaries, to send thanks for information "of great importance" and ask for more.[57]

Affirming Viking settlement of America, particularly their presence in or near Rhode Island, offered the Rhode Island society a variety of rewards. It would deemphasize Spain's claims in favor of northern European connections and facilitate reorientation of the history of Europeans in America northward while giving Rhode Island an opportunity to counter neighboring Massachusetts historians in their efforts to make the landing of the Pilgrims the foundational moment in the history of the United States. The earliest reference to Native American peoples on the Rhode Island society's list of historical subjects dated to the sixteenth century, but the last item focused on "probabilities" the "Northmen" wintered in Rhode Island in the eleventh century. Authenticating European presence in the area at a date prior to those associated with the presence of the Wampanoag, Narragansett, and other local tribes potentially offered additional justification for more recent claims to the land by Americans of European descent.[58]

"All the Aged and Wise Antiquarians": Race and Literacy in Preserving and Writing History

Emphasis on writing as a core means of preserving history privileged literate Americans, increasing the number of potential layers between historical actors and historical society collections. Most societies documented Native American lives through the writings of Americans of European descent. For example, the American Antiquarian Society's first two volumes featured extensive discussion of contemporaneous tribes and their mound-builder ancestors. European Americans authored all articles. Until more than a century later Europeans and European Americans dominated historiography about indigenous history and ways of preserving history.[59]

Historical society references to Native American peoples presumed transmission of information and documents through literate people of European descent, rather than through oral histories and indigenous oral traditions. Shortly before addressing the issue of slavery, Du Ponceau celebrated the Historical Society of Pennsylvania's accession of "a Narrative of an embassy to the Western Indians, from the original manuscript of a Native" person. He described it as "a precious document" and expressed a wish the Society might obtain more "of a similar character," but the overall context suggested expectations of communications written by Americans of European descent. The historical societies of Cincinnati and Minnesota, established in midcentury, proclaimed interests in "do[ing] justice to the Indians." Yet on closer examination, justice involved contributors, presumably of European descent, providing "what you may personally know or can gather." The Georgia Historical Society recorded a few gifts related to the development of the Cherokee alphabet, but this was an exception.[60]

Some Native American peoples permitted preservation of their stories through the writings of white writers, although they lacked control over what appeared in print. The autobiography of Sauk leader Ma-ka-tai-me-she-kia-kiak, also known as Black Hawk, involved multiple opportunities for subsequent, unauthorized alterations. He recounted his story in the Sauk language. Government interpreter Antoine LeClair translated it into English, and Illinois newspaper publisher John B. Patterson edited and produced the final version in print in 1833. The interpreter and editor affirmed efforts to maintain accuracy, but some questioned the work, in particular an early Illinois governor, who labeled it a hoax. Nowadays, the Sauk people and scholars accept the work as a genuine production reflecting Ma-ka-tai-me-she-kia-kiak's ideas and memories, albeit mediated through European American minds and hands. Nevertheless, the first version contained extensive, presumably editorial, use of exclamation points and italicization, even for an age during which these were common contrivances. Likewise, the text featured words and phrases for Sauk ideas that a recent scholar considered "poor choices" motivated by a desire "to meet the expectations of Jacksonian-era readers."[61]

Problems of presentation, particularly when reliant on white interpreters, editors, or historians, troubled some potential participants. Missionary Daniel S. Butrick obtained a letter from Cherokee leader Kooweskoowe, also known as John Ross, in 1835, addressed "To Cherokee Antiquarians." Ross

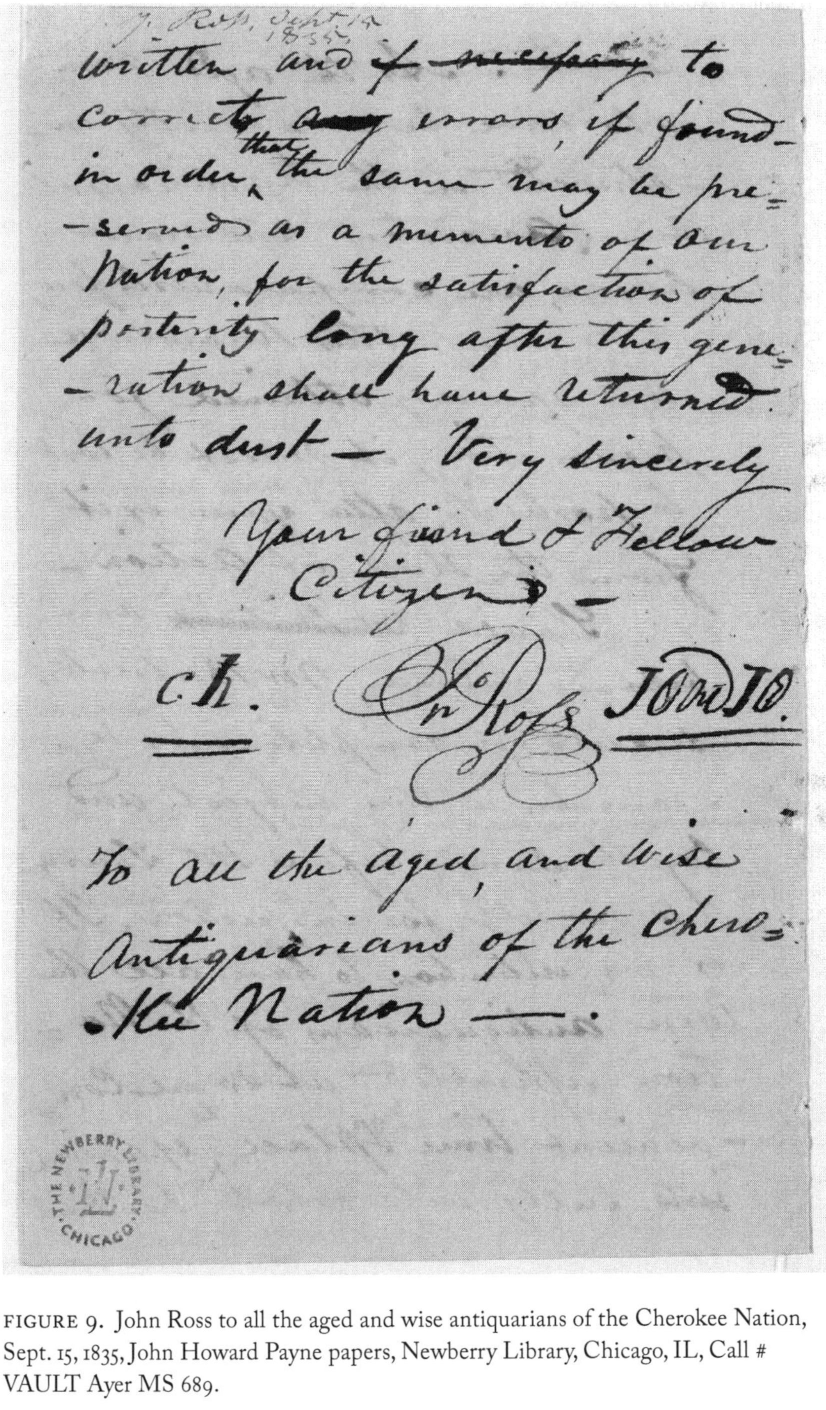

J. Ross, Sept 15, 1835

written and ~~if necessary~~ to correct ~~any~~ errors, if found — in order that the same may be pre-served as a memento of our Nation, for the satisfaction of posterity long after this gene-ration shall have returned unto dust — Very sincerely

Your friend & Fellow Citizen —

Ch. Jno Ross ᎫᏫᏍᎫᏫ.

To all the aged, and wise Antiquarians of the Chero-kee Nation —.

FIGURE 9. John Ross to all the aged and wise antiquarians of the Cherokee Nation, Sept. 15, 1835, John Howard Payne papers, Newberry Library, Chicago, IL, Call # VAULT Ayer MS 689.

endorsed Butrick's efforts to gather and write Cherokee history as an enterprise which would not touch his people's rights and "may be of advantage to us." He approved the plan out of concern for a dwindling pool of men "who have been correctly instructed in the traditions of our ancestors." At the same time, he specified "our beloved Friend has no intention to publish." Furthermore, if Butrick managed to complete gathering information, Ross planned to assemble "all the wise antiquarians of the nation . . . to examine fully into what he has written and to correct errors" before preserving it for the Cherokee Nation (figure 9).[62]

Others participated in Western historical practices more directly—so as to present their views and understandings of treaties and assert authority over their own histories. William Apess, a Pequot, produced several works between 1831 and 1836. Born in poverty, he became an itinerant Methodist preacher ministering to impoverished communities, in particular fellow Pequots and other New England Native Americans. In contrast to the increasingly nationalistic bent of most Americans of European descent, Apess advocated cross-cultural history incorporating recognition of European mistreatment of Native American peoples and how their histories justified these. To do this, he read European-American accounts and reworked them to reflect indigenous experiences. Similarly, William W. Warren, an Ojibwe and a fluent speaker of the language, drew on existing documents to preserve traditional histories. Warren reported receiving encouragement from his grandfather's cousin Buffalo. At a public council of chiefs in 1847, Buffalo told Warren "you are now a man, you know how to write like the whites, you understand what we tell you," suggesting recognition of Warren as an adult familiar with white practices and an understanding of Ojibwe culture. Warren referred to the Ojibwe in the third person plural, showing he maintained a degree of distance between history and sources.[63]

At the same time, many free Americans of African descent used a variety of approaches to critique and counter marginalization within historical cultures. First and foremost, literate individuals articulated responses to European American histories advocating alternative interpretations and explanations. Early African American periodicals featured articles discussing histories of peoples of color and slavery, often focusing on ancient times and practices in Rome, Greece, and Egypt, while others discussed closer events and people such as Toussaint Louverture and the Haitian Revolution in the late eighteenth century. Periodicals supported related book markets. The antebellum periodical *Colored American* began publishing a series on "Sacred Geography and Antiquities" shortly before contributor James W. C. Pennington's *Text-book of the Origin and History of the Colored People* appeared in print. Such publications implicitly advocated readers' familiarity with history as part of "creating an informed African American citizenry." Some free Americans of African descent began to collect materials relating to their history over the second quarter of the nineteenth century, particularly books. The establishment of the Philadelphia Library Company of Colored People in 1833 contributed to the city hosting an active community of scrapbook makers and black bibliophiles.[64]

Ironically, one of the groups largely absent from early historical society collections were officers and members themselves. Many active officers did not consider their own papers as constituting historical materials worth preserving within society collections during their lifetimes or worth bequeathing on their deaths. The papers of Jeremy Belknap, nowadays considered one of the primary forces behind the establishment and early successes of the Massachusetts Historical Society, did not become Society property until sixty years after his death. At that time, the Society valued them first and foremost for his personal collection of historical materials and only later for documentation of the era in which he lived. On the other hand, officers included their fellows in a manner befitting their focus on collecting historical facts and information: they memorialized them through biographical sketches and memoirs.[65]

By the 1830s and 1840s, several societies considered their place in history as organizations. The Massachusetts Historical Society published a volume of proceedings in the 1830s, documenting its activities over the first decades. The New York, New Jersey, and Pennsylvania societies also published proceedings during the 1840s. These drew upon earlier practices of providing minutes and donation lists to local newspapers for dissemination. Yet published proceedings also reflected recognition that historical societies had histories and their records value for historical researchers.

Conclusion

MASSACHUSETTS HISTORICAL SOCIETY FOUNDER John Eliot described the society as embarked on "this business of collecting things which will illustrate the history of our country." Contemporary historical societies still engage in core practices which the early societies established, including officer elections, annual meetings, publications, libraries, collections, and record-keeping. Many remain nonprofit, voluntary associations and struggle with financing competing interests. The early emphasis on collecting facts has given way to the embrace of primary sources, but officers, employees, and members continue to grapple with questions of inclusion and exclusion and whose histories to document. Individuals outside historical establishments continue to comment on and critique activities and collecting within.[1]

The expansion of print over the first half of the nineteenth century facilitated ever more individuals claiming historical space for themselves and others like them. Women, particularly middling and upper-class women of Anglo-Protestant descent, used the press to argue for their place in history. Despite comparatively fewer resources, Native American and African American historians also increasingly published works critiquing the historical publications and activities of historical societies, their members, and researchers. Non-textual activities outside historical society bounds challenged the histories collected within, as laboring classes engaged in commemorative events, celebrations, story-telling, and memorialization.[2]

Likewise, the inaction of existing historical societies with respect to areas of historical inquiry and collecting contributed to the establishment of more historical societies. Societies organized around places (cities, counties, states) predominated, but other societies sought to ensure remembrance of particular faiths, peoples, and ideas. Presbyterians and Baptists established historical societies shortly after midcentury, in 1852 and 1853, followed by other Christian faiths, including the Society of Friends and Roman Catholics in 1873 and 1880, respectively. Jews founded the first ethnic historical society in 1892 and Americans of African descent created the Afro-American Historical Society in 1897. Other people affirmed particular European American heritages, asserting the importance of their ancestors in claiming the country as first settlers, colonists, and farmers. In the early twentieth century, the Southwestern Indiana Historical Society, despite its geographic-oriented name, quickly focused members' attention on elucidating Abraham Lincoln's time in the area as a means to assert importance. After the Civil War, former Confederates established the Southern Historical Society to support their view of the conflict, which contributed to segregation and the subsequent American history of Jim Crow.[3]

The earliest historical society founders sought to document and preserve materials for the history of the nation—but succeeded in fostering interest in documenting and preserving multiple histories. The story of historical societies in the United States mirrored society at large. Early historical societies developed foundational practices including incorporation through states, regular meetings, and active collecting methods. Society officers struggled to define history and set collecting priorities. They chose to separate their work from popular circles, contributing to ongoing differences between scholarly and public history circles.

Of equal importance, the early societies decided what to include and exclude and met with resistance from members and non-members. Citizens of cities, counties, and states responded to the establishment of initial historical societies by founding additional ones within a matter of years or decades. The spread of secular historical societies contributed to the establishment of societies focused on religious denominations. Women, African Americans, and Native Americans worked to preserve materials documenting their histories and affirm their importance.

Nowadays practitioners routinely grapple with core questions. Who should be involved in making decisions? What histories should be preserved? And how will this be accomplished? Many people involved in historical circles work to document and preserve recent and contemporary historical materials. Historical researchers also continue to seek out older materials that remain in private hands or were mislabeled when added to existing collections. Historical societies share interests and spheres of action with a host of other organizations, including governments, archives, libraries, museums, editors, and preservation activists advocating for historic buildings and sites. Collectively, these entities seek to document histories of the Americas and their peoples.

The history of early historical societies contains paradoxes and frustrations, both at the time and from a modern vantage point looking backward. Yet for all the gaps, absences, silences, and other practices that leave modern scholars puzzled or frustrated, the early societies cast a long shadow. At the end of the eighteenth century, a small group of Boston men started a learned society to collect and preserve materials for the writing of history. Dozens of societies across the nation pursued similar objectives by the mid-nineteenth century, conducting business following early precedents. Collectively, these societies amassed extensive materials modern historians use to write histories our predecessors never imagined. While these societies rescued many pasts, they also left questions whose answers are lost to oblivion.

Appendix One

Historical and Related Societies Established in the United States, 1791–1850

These lists are compiled based on Appleton P. C. Griffin, *Bibliography of American Historical Societies* (1896; 2nd ed., revised and enlarged, 1907), supplemented by Leslie W. Dunlap *American Historical Societies, 1790–1860* (1944); and David Van Tassel, *Recording America's Past: An Interpretation of Historical Studies in America, 1607–1884* (1960).

Italics denote societies that differed from societies organized around the collection and preservation of materials for the writing of history—but circulated questionnaires collecting historical information, published proceedings or addresses containing historical information, worked to erect historical monuments, or celebrated historical occasions.

Dates of organization, reorganization, and failure are noted insofar as known. An *x* indicates the specific year is unknown.

BY REGION AND STATE

New England

Connecticut

Connecticut Academy of Arts and Sciences, New Haven, 1799
Connecticut Historical Society, Hartford, 1825–1826, 1839–present

Maine

Maine Historical Society, Brunswick (later Portland), 1822–present

Massachusetts

Massachusetts Historical Society, Boston, 1791–present
American Antiquarian Society, Worcester, 1812–present
Pilgrim Society, Plymouth 1820–present
Essex Historical Society, Salem, 1821, merged with Essex County Natural History Society in 1848 to form Essex Institute (now part of the Peabody-Essex Museum)
Worcester County Historical Society, Worcester, 1825–183x
Plainville Historical Society, 1827–186x
Universalist Historical Society, Cambridge, 1834–x
Bunker Hill Monument Association, Boston, 183x
American Statistical Association, Boston, 1840–present
Dorchester Antiquarian and Historical Society, Dorchester, 1843–1891
New England Historic Genealogical Society, Boston, 1845–present

New Hampshire

New Hampshire Historical Society, Concord, 1823–present

Rhode Island

Rhode Island Historical Society, Providence, 1822–present

Vermont

Vermont Historical and Antiquarian Society, Montpelier, 1838–1846, reorganized as Vermont Historical Society, 1858–present
Middlebury Historical Society, Middlebury, 1843–x

Mid-Atlantic

District of Columbia

Columbian Historical Society, 1833–183x
American Historical Society, 1835–1840

Maryland

Maryland Historical Society, Baltimore, 1844–present

New Jersey

New Jersey Historical Society, Trenton (later New Brunswick), 1845–present

New York

New-York Historical Society, New York City, 1804–present
Deutsche Gesellschaft der Stadt New York, circa 1808
New York Literary and Philosophical Society, New York City, 1815
Historical and Philosophical Society of New York, Schoharie, 1823–182x
Albany Historical Society, later part of the Albany Institute, Albany, 1830

New England Society of the City of New York, New York City, 183x
New Confederacy of the Iroquois, Rochester, 1843
Red Jacket Historical Society, Buffalo, 1844–184x
American Ethnological Society, New York City, 1845
Newburgh Historical Society, Newburgh, 1845–185x
Saint Nicholas Society of New York, New York City, 1847
Protestant Episcopal Historical Society, New York City, 1850–185x

Pennsylvania
Historical and Literary Committee of the American Philosophical Society, 1815–182x
Religious Historical Society, Philadelphia, 1816–182x
Historical Society of Pennsylvania, Philadelphia, 1824–present
Society for the Commemoration of the Landing of William Penn, Philadelphia, 1824–183x
Historical Society of Western Pennsylvania, Pittsburgh, 1834–183x, reorganized 1843–1847, reestablished 1858
Historical Society of the American Lutheran Church, Gettysburg, 1843–x

South

Alabama
Alabama Historical Society, Tuscaloosa, 1850–185x, reorganized 1874–x

Arkansas
Antiquarian and Natural History Society of the State of Arkansas, Little Rock, 1837–1842

Georgia
Georgia Historical Society, Savannah, 1839–present

Kentucky
Kentucky Historical Society, Louisville, 1836–present

Louisiana
Louisiana Historical Society, New Orleans, 1835–183x, reorganized 1846–present

Missouri
Franklin Society of Saint Louis, Saint Louis, 1835
Missouri Historical and Philosophical Society, Jefferson, 1844–bef. 1872

North Carolina
North Carolina Historical Society, 1833–1834
Historical and Literary Society of North Carolina, Raleigh, 1841–1841
Mecklenburg Centennial and Monumental Association, Mecklenburg, 1842
Historical Society of the University of North Carolina, Chapel Hill, 1844–1858

South Carolina

New England Society of Charleston, Charleston, 1819

Charleston Library Society Historical Committee, Charleston, 1833–183x

Tennessee

Tennessee Antiquarian Society, Nashville, 1820–1822

East Tennessee Historical and Antiquarian Society, Knoxville, 1833–186x

Historical Society of Tennessee, 1849–1850, Nashville, reorganized as Tennessee Historical Society, 1857–present

Virginia

Virginia Historical and Philosophical Society, Richmond, 1831–1838, reorganized as Virginia Historical Society, 1846–present

Historical Department of the Society of the Alumni of the University of Virginia, Charlottesville, 1847

Midwest and Western Territories and States

California

Society of California Pioneers, San Francisco, 1850

Illinois

Antiquarian and Historical Society of Illinois, Vandalia, 1827–183x

Illinois Literary and Historical Society, Upper Alton, 1843–1858

Indiana

Indiana Historical Society, Indianapolis, 1830–present

Vincennes Historical and Antiquarian Society, Vincennes, 1839–1841

Historical Society of the County of Vigo, Indiana, 1844–184x

Iowa

Iowa Historical and Geological Institute, Burlington, 1843–x

Michigan

Historical Society of Michigan, Detroit, 1828, reorganized 1857–present

Minnesota

Minnesota Historical Society, Saint Paul, 1849–present

Ohio

Historical and Philosophical Society of Ohio, Columbus, 1822, reorganized 1831, relocated to Cincinnati and merged with Cincinnati Historical Society in 1849

Historical and Philosophical Society of Ashtabula County, Jefferson, 1838–1854

Western Methodist Historical Society, Cincinnati, 1839–x

Logan Historical Society, Chillicothe, 1841–184x

Marietta Historical Association, Marietta, 1841–185x
Historical and Geological Society of Norwalk Seminary, Norwalk, 1841–184x
Cincinnati Historical Society, Cincinnati, 1844–present
New England Society of Cincinnati, 184x

Wisconsin

State Historical Society of Wisconsin, Madison, 1845, reorganized and incorporated 1853–present

BY DATE

1791	Massachusetts Historical Society, Boston
1799	*Connecticut Academy of Arts and Sciences, New Haven*
1804	New-York Historical Society, New York City
1808	*Deutsche Gesellschaft der Stadt New York, New York City*
1812	American Antiquarian Society, Worcester, Massachusetts
1814	*New York Literary and Philosophical Society, New York City*
1815	Historical and Literary Committee of the American Philosophical Society, Philadelphia
1816	Religious Historical Society, Philadelphia, 1816–182x
1819	*New England Society of Charleston, Charleston North Carolina*
1820	Tennessee Antiquarian Society, Nashville, 1820–1822
1820	Pilgrim Society, Plymouth, Massachusetts
1821	Essex Historical Society, Salem, Massachusetts, 1821, merged with Essex County Natural History Society in 1848 to form Essex Institute
1822	Historical and Philosophical Society of Ohio, Columbus, 1822–182x, reorganized 1831, relocated to Cincinnati and merged with Cincinnati Historical Society in 1849
1822	Rhode Island Historical Society, Providence
1822	Maine Historical Society, Brunswick then Portland
1823	Historical and Philosophical Society of New York, Schoharie, 1823–182x
1823	New Hampshire Historical Society, Concord
1824	Historical Society of Pennsylvania, Philadelphia
1824	*Society for the Commemoration of the Landing of William Penn, Philadelphia, 1824–183x*
1825	Worcester County Historical Society, Worcester, Massachusetts, 1825–183x
1825	Connecticut Historical Society, Hartford, 1825–1826, reestablished 1839
1827	*Plainville Historical Society, 1827–186x*

1827	Antiquarian and Historical Society of Illinois, Vandalia, 1827–183x
1828	Historical Society of Michigan, Detroit, 1828, reorganized 1857
1830	Indiana Historical Society, Indianapolis
1830	Albany Historical Society, later part of the Albany Institute, Albany, New York
1831	Virginia Historical and Philosophical Society, Richmond, 1831–1838, reorganized as Virginia Historical Society, 1846
1833	East Tennessee Historical and Antiquarian Society, Knoxville, 1833–186x
1833	Charleston Library Society Historical Committee, Charleston, 1833–183x
1833	North Carolina Historical Society, 1833–1834
1833	Columbian Historical Society, Washington, D.C., 1833–183x
1834	Historical Society of Western Pennsylvania, Pittsburgh, 1834–183x, reorganized 1843–1847, reestablished 1858
1834	Universalist Historical Society, [Cambridge, Massachusetts?], 1834–x
1835	*Franklin Society of Saint Louis, Saint Louis*
1835	Louisiana Historical Society, New Orleans, 1835–x, reorganized 1846
1835	American Historical Society, Washington, D.C., 1835–1840
1836	Kentucky Historical Society, Louisville
1837	Antiquarian and Natural History Society of the State of Arkansas, Little Rock, 1837–1842
1838	Historical and Philosophical Society of Ashtabula County, Jefferson, Ohio, 1838–1854
1838	Vermont Historical and Antiquarian Society, Montpelier, 1838–1846, reorganized as Vermont Historical Society, 1858
1839	Western Methodist Historical Society, Cincinnati, 1839–18xx
1839	Vincennes Historical and Antiquarian Society, Vincennes, Indiana, 1839–1841
1839	Georgia Historical Society, Savannah
183x	*New England Society of the City of New York, New York City*
183x	*Bunker Hill Monument Association, Boston*
1840	*American Statistical Association, Boston*
1841	Historical and Geological Society of Norwalk Seminary, Norwalk, Ohio, 1841–184x
1841	Marietta Historical Association, Marietta, Ohio, 1841–185x
1841	Logan Historical Society, Chillicothe, Ohio, 1841–184x
1841	Historical and Literary Society of North Carolina, Raleigh, 1841–1841

1842 *Mecklenburg Centennial and Monumental Association, Mecklenburg, North Carolina*

1843 Historical Society of the American Lutheran Church, Gettysburg, 1843–x

1843 Iowa Historical and Geological Institute, Burlington

1843 Illinois Literary and Historical Society, Upper Alton, 1843–1858

1843 *New Confederacy of the Iroquois, Rochester, New York*

1843 Middlebury Historical Society, Middlebury, Vermont, 1843–x

1843 Dorchester Antiquarian and Historical Society, Dorchester, Massachusetts, 1843–1891

1844 Missouri Historical and Philosophical Society, Jefferson, 1844–bef. 1872

1844 Cincinnati Historical Society, Cincinnati

1844 Historical Society of the County of Vigo, Indiana, 1844–184x

1844 Historical Society of the University of North Carolina, Chapel Hill, 1844–1858

1844 Red Jacket Historical Society, Buffalo, New York, 1844–184x

1844 Maryland Historical Society, Baltimore

1845 State Historical Society of Wisconsin, Madison

1845 Newburgh Historical Society, Newburgh, New York, 1845–185x

1845 *American Ethnological Society, New York City*

1845 New England Historic Genealogical Society, Boston

1845 New Jersey Historical Society, Trenton (later New Brunswick)

1847 *Historical Department of the Society of the Alumni of the University of Virginia, Charlottesville*

1847 *Saint Nicholas Society of New York, New York City*

1848 Historical Society of the American Lutheran Church, Gettysburg, by 1848

1849 Minnesota Historical Society, Saint Paul

1849 Historical Society of Tennessee, 1849–1850, Nashville, reorganized as Tennessee Historical Society, 1857

184x *New England Society of Cincinnati*

1850 Alabama Historical Society, Tuscaloosa, 1850–185x, reorganized 1874

1850 *Society of California Pioneers, San Francisco*

1850 Protestant Episcopal Historical Society, New York City, 1850–185x

Appendix Two

Mediating the Connecticut Historical Society Visitor Logs

Transcribing the Connecticut Historical Society visitor logs and matching visitors against the 1850 U.S. Census required a degree of interpretation and alteration.

VISITOR RECORDS

The original records were the product of many hands, some more legible than others. The transcription process therefore included intervention in several key areas:

Gender

Signers were presumed male unless the signature included "Mrs." or "Miss" in front of the name or the name was traditionally female (such as Mary, Sarah, Helen).

Missing States

Signers often only listed the town or city of residence. Assignments of place were made under the assumption that if there was a village, town, or city in Connecticut by that name, that was the place intended, absent data to suggest otherwise. Entries of "Portland" alone were interpreted as "Portland, CT." The logs contain enough instances of "Brooklyn L.I." to suggest visitors from Brooklyn, New York, were either aware of the existence of Brooklyn, Connecticut, or elected to specify they came from Long Island.

Signature Type

The logs included references to a number of individuals who did not sign the book themselves. In these cases, the signer included text referring to additional members of his or her party. The most common form was "and lady." Variants included and "wife," "son(s)," "dau.(s)," "children," and "family" or "Mr. and Mrs."

In most cases, the entry did not indicate whether the additional party members shared the same birthplace or residence. Additional party members were

1. added in any overall counts of number of visitors,
2. assumed to share the signer's place of residence and included in counts involving residence,
3. not assumed to share the signer's birthplace and thus excluded from such counts.

With respect to numbers, any signature type indicating a single additional visitor (i.e., "lady") was an added count of one. Any signature type that left in doubt the number of additional visitors (such as "children") was an added count of two, so as to under-count rather than over-count.

MATCHING THE 1850 CENSUS

Visitors were divided into the following categories:

Full Match = Exact or extremely close with no alternate possibilities in census.
Qualified = Match was fairly close, but with a potentially important discrepancy (e.g., missing middle initial in census, different birth state, differing residence) or alternate possibility.
Possible = Too many discrepancies or too many alternate possibilities to identify confidently without extensive research.
Not Found/Identified = Searches returned no hits or far too many potential matches.

The census-related data provided in chapter 5 was based on full and qualified matches only.

TABLE 4. Examples of Visitor Log–Census Comparison

Category	Visitor Log	1850 Census
Full Match	Lavinia Morgan, b. Hartford, res. Hartford	Name, birth state, and residence all match. No other close possibilities.
Qualified	Miss Sarah Burr and Miss Frances Burr, both res. Hartford, sequential signatures	Search resulted in several possible matches. Identification was made as household members Sarah I. and Frances A. Burr, ages eighteen and sixteen, due to proximity of signatures in register.
Possible	Harriett J. Hotchkiss, b. New Haven, res. New Haven	Two possible matches: mother or daughter, neither listed in census with a middle initial.

Notes

ABBREVIATIONS

AAS Donations	"Donations to the American Antiquarian Society with the Names of its Benefactors," March 1813–October 15, 1829, Folio vol. 17.1. American Antiquarian Society Archives, American Antiquarian Society, Worcester, MA.
AAS Proceedings	*Proceedings of the American Antiquarian Society, 1812–1849.* Worcester: Published by the Society, 1912.
APS Transactions	*Transactions of the American Philosophical Society* II–new series III (1786–1830).
CHS Accessions	"Accessions, 1839–1853." Connecticut Historical Society Archives, Connecticut Historical Society, Hartford.
CHS Archives	Connecticut Historical Society Archives, Connecticut Historical Society, Hartford.
CHS eMuseum	Connecticut Historical Society. Online Museum Database. http://emuseum.chs.org/emuseum/.
CHS Logs	Library Visitor Logs. Connecticut Historical Society Archives, Connecticut Historical Society, Hartford.
Farmer Papers	John Farmer Papers. New Hampshire Historical Society, Concord.

History of the Book in America II	*An Extensive Republic: Print, Culture, and Society in the New Nation, 1790–1840: A History of the Book in America,* vol. II, edited by Robert A. Gross and Mary Kelley. Chapel Hill: Published in Association with the American Antiquarian Society by the University of North Carolina Press, 2010.
HSP Archives	Historical Society of Pennsylvania Archives, Historical Society of Pennsylvania, Philadelphia.
HSP Memoirs	*Memoirs of the Historical Society of Pennsylvania* I–IV, part II. 1826–1850.
La. Historical Collections	*Historical Collections of Louisiana.* 5 vols. New York: Wiley and Putnam, 1846–1853.
MHS Archives	Massachusetts Historical Society Archives. Massachusetts Historical Society, Boston.
MHS Collections	*Collections of the Massachusetts Historical Society* I–5th series III. 1792–1877.
MHS Proceedings	*Proceedings of the Massachusetts Historical Society* I–3rd series 54. 1879–1920/1921.
Moore Papers	Jacob Bailey Moore Papers. Houghton Library, Harvard University, Cambridge, MA.
NHHS Collections	*Collections of the New Hampshire Historical Society* I–VI. 1824–1850.
NJHS Proceedings	*Proceedings of the New Jersey Historical Society* I–IV. 1846 (reprint, 1968)–1849.
N-YHS Collections	*Collections of the New-York Historical Society* 1st series I–2nd series II. 1811–1848.
Plumer Papers	*The Papers of William Plumer (1759–1850) and William Plumer, Jr (1789–1854).* Concord, NH: New Hampshire Historical Society; Washington, D.C.: National Historical Publications and Records Commission; Sanford, NC: Microfilming Corporation of America, distributor, 1981.
RIHS Archives	Rhode Island Historical Society Archives. Rhode Island Historical Society, Providence.
RIHS Collections	*Collections of the Rhode Island Historical Society* I–V. 1827–1843.
Sparks Collection	Jared Sparks Collection of American Manuscripts. Houghton Library, Harvard University, Cambridge, MA.

INTRODUCTION

1. John Eliot to [Benjamin Trumbull?], Dec. 11, 1790, *MHS Proceedings* II (1880): viii; "Literary Notice," *APS Transactions*, new series I (1818): xii.
2. John Farmer to Isaac Hill, Mar. 10, 1837, Farmer Papers; Elizabeth H. Dow, "Seeds of Conflict: Public Record Keeping in the Past," *Manuscripts* 63, no. 2 (2011): 105–16.

CHAPTER ONE: "THE LUMBER YARD OF HISTORY"

1. "First Settlement of Cincinnati," *American Pioneer: A Monthly Periodical, Devoted to the Objects of the Logan Historical Society; Or, to Collecting and Publishing Sketches Relative to the Early Settlement and Successive Improvement of the Country*, 2 vols. (Cincinnati: Edited and Published by John S. Williams, 1842–43), vol. 2, 400; Government Publication Office, "Snapshots of the FDLP (August 2000)," https://www.fdlp.gov/about-the-fdlp/mission-and-history/2500-snapshots-of-the-fdlp-august-2000.
2. Hannah Mather Crocker, "Antiquarian Researches," in *Observations on the Real Rights of Women*, ed. Constance J. Post (Lincoln: University of Nebraska Press, 2011), 27–36, esp. 32; Hannah Mather Crocker, "Antiquarian Researches," (3 drafts), Folder 4, Box 10, Mather Family Papers, American Antiquarian Society, Worcester, MA.
3. Scholarship on historical societies includes Tom Glynn, *Reading Publics: New York City's Libraries, 1754–1911* (New York: Fordham University Press, 2015), 66–100; Philip F. Gura, *The American Antiquarian Society, 1812–2012: A Bicentennial History* (Worcester: American Antiquarian Society, 2012); Melvin I. Urofsky, "The Virginia Historical Society: The First 175 Years, 1831–2006," *Virginia Magazine of History and Biography* 114, no. 1 (2006); Terry A. Barnhart, "'Elegant and Useful Learning': The Antiquarian and Historical Society of Illinois, 1827–1829," *Journal of the Illinois State Historical Society* 95, no. 1 (2002): 7–32; Louis Leonard Tucker, *The Massachusetts Historical Society: A Bicentennial History, 1791–1991* (Boston: The Society; Distributed by Northeastern University Press, 1996); John A. Schutz, *A Noble Pursuit: The Sesquicentennial History of the New England Historic Genealogical Society, 1845–1995* (Boston: New England Historic Genealogical Society, 1995); *Historical Consciousness in the Early Republic: The Origins of State Historical Societies, Museums, and Collections, 1791–1861*, ed. H. G. Jones (Chapel Hill: North Caroliniana Society and North Carolina Collection, 1995); Walter M. Whitehill, *Independent Historical Societies* (Boston: Boston Athenaeum, 1962); David Van Tassel, *Recording America's Past: An Interpretation of Historical Studies in America, 1607–1884* (Chicago: University of Chicago Press, 1960); Leslie W. Dunlap, *American Historical Societies, 1790–1860* (Madison, WI: Cantwell Printing Co., 1944); Julian P. Boyd, "State and Local Historical Societies in the United States," *American Historical Review* 40, no. 1 (1934): 10–37. For work on historical sites and cities, see John D. Seelye, *Memory's Nation:*

The Place of Plymouth Rock (Chapel Hill: University of North Carolina Press, 1998); Charlotte Mires, *Independence Hall in American Memory* (Philadelphia: University of Pennsylvania Press, 2002); Gary B. Nash, *First City: Philadelphia and the Forging of Historical Memory* (Philadelphia: University of Pennsylvania Press, 2002); Jennifer Erga Steenshorne, "Past, Present, and Future: History and Memory in New York City, 1800–1860" (Ph.D. diss., University of California, Irvine, 2002); Michael C. Batinski, *Pastkeepers in a Small Place: Five Centuries in Deerfield, Massachusetts* (Amherst: University of Massachusetts Press, 2004).

4. Cadwallader Colden, *The History of the Five Indian Nations Depending on the Province of New-York in America* (New York: Printed and Sold by William Bradford, 1727), vii; Jeremy Belknap, *The History of New Hampshire, Volume I* (Philadelphia: Printed for the Author by Robert Aitken, in Market Street, Near the Coffee-House, 1784), iii.
5. Thomas Hutchinson, *The History of the Colony of Massachusetts-Bay . . . .* (Boston: Printed by Thomas and John Fleet, at the Heart and Crown in Cornhill, 1764), i; Dow, "Seeds of Conflict," 105–16.
6. *The Public Records of the Colony of Connecticut*, ed. James H. Trumbull and Charles H. Hoadly, 15 vols. (Hartford: Press of the Case, Lockwood, and Brainard Company, 1850–90), vol. 13, 247, 304, 355–67, 424; Christopher P. Bickford, "Public Records and the Private Historical Society: A Connecticut Example," *Government Publications Review* 6A, no. 4 (1981): 313–14; Tucker, *Massachusetts*, 64–65, 104–6, 316–18.
7. David Trumbull to Jeremy Belknap, Apr. 15, 1794, Volume I: 1791–1798, Box 24, Correspondence Second Series, Corresponding Secretary Records, MHS Archives; Thomas D. Walker, "The State of Libraries in Eighteenth-Century Europe: Adalbert Blumenschein's 'Beschreibung Verschiedener Bibliotheken in Europa,'" *Library Quarterly* 65, no. 3 (1995): 269–94; Ross W. Beales and James N. Green, "Libraries and Their Users," in *A History of the Book in America, Volume I: The Colonial Book in the Atlantic World*, ed. Hugh Amory and David D. Hall (Chapel Hill: University of North Carolina Press in association with the American Antiquarian Society, 2007), 400; David S. Zubatsky, *The History of American Colleges and Their Libraries in the Seventeenth and Eighteenth Centuries: A Bibliographical Essay* (Champaign: University of Illinois Graduate School of Library Science, 1979), 25, 30, 34; Dunlap, *American*; Van Tassel, *Recording*, 4–5; Ian Philip, *The Bodleian Library in the Seventeenth and Eighteenth Centuries* (Oxford: Clarendon Press, 1983), 97.
8. Fred Shelley, "Ebenezer Hazard: America's First Historical Editor," *William and Mary Quarterly*, 12, no. 1 (1955): 44–73; Rosemary Sweet, *Antiquaries: The Discovery of the Past in Eighteenth-Century Britain* (New York: Hambledon and London, 2004), 91–93, 280–84. See also George Pilcher, "Ebenezer Hazard and the Promotion of Historical Scholarship in the Early Republic," *Pennsylvania History* 56, no. 1 (1989):

3–14; Russell M. Lawson, *Ebenezer Hazard, Jeremy Belknap and the American Revolution* (London: Pickering and Chatto, 2011), 1–5, 27–28, 32–33, 43.

9. Hutchinson, *History*, i; Van Tassel, *Recording*, 19–20; William Stith, *The History of the First Discovery and Settlement of Virginia, Being an Essay towards a General History of This Colony* (Williamsburg: Printed by William Parks, 1747), [iii].

10. Julius Herbert Tuttle, "The Libraries of the Mathers," *American Antiquarian Society Proceedings* 20 (Apr. 1910): 268–356; Alea Henle, "The Widow's Mite: Hannah Mather Crocker and the Mather Libraries," *Information and Culture: A Journal of History* 48, no. 3 (2013): 323–43; *Catalogue of the Collection of Books and Manuscripts Which Formerly Belonged to the Reverend Thomas Prince* (Boston: Alfred Mudge and Son, City Printers, 1870), ix–xiii; Peter Knapp, "The Rev. Thomas Prince and the Prince Library," *American Book Collector* 22, no. 2 (1971): 20; William H. Whitmore, *Catalogue of the American Portion of the Library of the Rev. Thomas Prince : with a Memoir, and List of his Publications* (Boston: J. K. Wiggin and W. P. Lunt, 1868), v–x; "Quarterly Meeting," Jul. 1793, *MHS Proceedings* I (1879): 52n; Karin Wulf, "Ancestry as Social Practice in Eighteenth-Century New England: The Origins of Early Republic Genealogical Vogue," unpublished paper, 22–28.

11. Jeremy Belknap to Andrew Eliot, Jun. 18, 1774, draft letter, quoted in Louis Leonard Tucker, *Clio's Consort: Jeremy Belknap and the Founding of the Massachusetts Historical Society* (Boston: The Society; Distributed by Northeastern University Press, 1990), 62–63, see also 3–20, 22–36, 60–63, 66–67; Belknap, *History of New Hampshire*, I:iii.

12. Jeremy Belknap to Ebenezer Hazard, May 18, 1877, *MHS Collections*, 5th series, vol. II (1877): 481; Tucker, *Clio's*, 70–73.

13. Belknap to Hazard, May 18, 1877; Tucker, *Clio's*, 70–73.

14. David Shields, "The Learned World," in *History of the Book in America* II:247–68; Tucker, *Clio's*, 80–93; "Constitution of the Historical Society," Jan. 24, 1791, *MHS Proceedings* I (1879): 2.

15. "Introduction," *MHS Proceedings* I (1879): xii–xiii; Jeremy Belknap to Ebenezer Hazard, Aug. 10, 1789, and Feb. 19, 1791, *MHS Collections*, 5th series, III (1877): 157, 245; Tucker, *Clio's*, 80–93; Joan Evans, *A History of the Society of Antiquaries* (Oxford, Printed at the University Press by Charles Batey for the Society of Antiquaries, Burlington House, London, 1956), 179; David Allan, "The Scottish Enlightenment and the Politics of Provincial Culture: The Perth Literary and Antiquarian Society, ca. 1784–1790," *Eighteenth-Century Life* 27, no. 3 (2001): 1–30.

16. "Constitution of the Historical Society," 2–4; Tucker, *Clio's*, 92–93; Richard D. Brown, *The Strength of a People: The Idea of an Informed Citizenry in America, 1650–1870* (Chapel Hill: University of North Carolina Press, 1996), 95.

17. Massachusetts Historical Society, *The Act of Incorporation, the Laws, and the Circular Letter of the Massachusetts Historical Society, with an Appendix* (Boston: Printed at

the Apollo Press by Joseph Belknap, 1794), 1–2; Johann N. Neem, *Creating a Nation of Joiners: Democracy and Civil Society in Early National Massachusetts* (Cambridge, MA: Harvard University Press, 2008), 18–29; Oscar Handlin and Mary Flug Handlin, *Commonwealth: A Study of the Role of Government in the American Economy, 1774–1861, Revised Edition* (Cambridge, MA: Belknap Press of Harvard University, 1969), 96–97; Richard D. Brown, "The Emergence of Urban Society," *Journal of American History* 61, no. 1 (1974): 29–51; Peter Clark, *British Clubs and Societies, 1580–1800: The Origins of an Associational World* (Oxford: Oxford University Press, 2000), 388–420; Stefan-Ludewig Hoffmann, "Democracy and Associations in the Long Nineteenth-Century: Toward a Transnational Perspective," *Journal of Modern History* 75, no. 2 (2003): 269–99; Tucker, *Massachusetts*, 23.

18. Massachusetts Historical Society, *Act*, 1–2, emphasis added.
19. Massachusetts Historical Society, *Act*, 5; Tucker, *Massachusetts*, 27; *MHS Collections*, first to third series (1792–1849).
20. New-York Historical Society, *The Constitution and Bye-Laws of the New-York Historical Society: Instituted in the City of New-York the 10th Day of December, 1804* (New-York: Printed by T. and J. Swords, 1805), 3–7; R. W. G. Vail, *Knickerbocker Birthday: A Sesqui-Centennial History of the New-York Historical Society, 1804–1954* (New York: New-York Historical Society, 1954), 457–58, 475–81.
21. New-York Historical Society, *Constitution*, 3, 9; *N-YHS Collections*, first series, I–V, and second series, I–II, part I (1811–48); Glynn, *Reading*, 66–100; Steenshorne, "Past," 30–31.
22. Timothy Alden to Samuel Burnside, Oct. 21, 1813, Documents and Correspondence, American Antiquarian Society Archives, American Antiquarian Society, Worcester, MA; John Lowell quoted in "Petition to the Legislature of Massachusetts," and "Act of Incorporation," *AAS Proceedings*, 4n; Tucker, *Massachusetts*, 541, 457; Vail, *Knickerbocker*, 41.
23. Isaiah Thomas, "An Account of the American Antiquarian Society," *AAS Proceedings*, 15–16; Peter Onuf, "American Antiquarian: Isaiah Thomas and the New Nation's Future," unpublished paper.
24. Ebenezer Hazard to Jeremy Belknap, Jan. 14, 1791, *MHS Collections*, 3rd series, vol. III (1877): 242; William Tilghman, "Report of the Historical and Literary Committee to the American Philosophical Society, Read 9th Jan. 1818," *APS Transactions*, new series, I (1818): xi–v; E. Digby Baltzell, *Puritan Boston and Quaker Philadelphia: Two Protestant Ethics and the Spirit of Class Authority and Leadership* (New York: The Free Press, 1979), 48; Van Tassel, *Recording*, 64.
25. Tilghman, "Report," xii; Whitfield J. Bell Jr., "As Others Saw Us: Notes on the Reputation of the American Philosophical Society," *Proceedings of the American Philosophical Society* 116, no. 3 (1972): 273–74; Edward C. Carter II, *"One Grand Pursuit": A*

Brief History of the American Philosophical Society's First 250 Years, 1743–1993 (Philadelphia: American Philosophical Society, 1993), 19–27.

26. Tilghman, "Report," xi–xiii; Peter S. Du Ponceau to William Barton, Jan. 20, 1816, letter draft, Peter Stephen Du Ponceau Collection, American Philosophical Society Archives, American Philosophical Society, Philadelphia.
27. "Literary Notice," ix; Tilghman, "Report," xii–xiii; Peter S. Du Ponceau to John Vaughan, Mar. 11, 1816, American Philosophical Society Archives.
28. Historical Society of Pennsylvania, "Society Minutes, 1824–1843," Box I-1–2, HSP Archives.
29. Trish Loughran, *The Republic in Print: Print Culture in the Age of U.S. Nation Building, 1770–1870* (New York: Columbia University Press, 2007); Robert A. Gross, "Introduction: An Extensive Republic," in *History of the Book in America* II:1–6; Robb Haberman, "Provincial Nationalism: Civic Rivalry in Postrevolutionary American Magazines," *Early American Studies* 10, no. 1 (2012), 162–193; David Waldstreicher, *In the Midst of Perpetual Fetes: The Making of American Nationalism, 1776–1820* (Chapel Hill: University of North Carolina Press, 1997); Stephanie Kermes, *Creating an American Identity: New England, 1789–1825* (New York: Palgrave Macmillan, 2008); Randall C. Jimerson, "Documents and Archives in Early America," *Archivaria* 60 (2005): 235–58.
30. See appendix 1.
31. Brent Taylor, "Making History in Virginia," *Virginia Magazine of History and Biography* 115, no. 1 (2007): 2–55; Michael Kraus, *The Writing of American History* (Norman: University of Oklahoma, 1953), 90; William M. E. Rachal, ed., "Early Records of the Virginia Historical Society, 1831–1833," *Virginia Magazine of History & Biography* 67, no. 1 (1959): 8–9, 13.
32. David James Kiracofe, "The Jamestown Jubilees: 'State Patriotism' and Virginia Identity in the Early Nineteenth Century," *Virginia Magazine of History and Biography* 110, no. 1 (2002): 35–68.
33. Urofsky, "Virginia," 20–21; William M. E. Rachal, "The Formation of the Virginia Historical Society," in *The Old Dominion: Essays for Thomas Perkins Abernethy*, ed. Darrett Bruce Rutman (Charlottesville: University Press of Virginia, 1964), 171–86.
34. Jonathan Cushing, "For the Lit. and Evan. Magazine," *Literary and Evangelical Magazine*, Jan. 1, 1824, emphasis in original.
35. Rachal, "Early," 8–9, 13; Urofsky, "Virginia," 12, 20–24; Rachal, "Formation," 171, 173; Gerald F. Morris and Maris A. Vinovskis, "Schools," in *History of the Book in America* II:292.
36. Taylor, "Making"; Urofsky, "Virginia," 29–36; Rachal, "Foundation," 185–86.
37. See chapter 2, pages 56–61, for discussion of the American Antiquarian Society as a national organization.

38. Clark, *British*, 388–420.
39. "Constitution," *MHS Proceedings* I (1879): 2–4; Massachusetts Historical Society, *Act*, 2; Tucker, *Clio's*, 87–97; Scott Derks and Tony Smith, *The Value of a Dollar: Colonial Era to the Civil War, 1600–1865* (Millerton, NY: Grey House, 2005), 155.
40. "Constitution," *MHS Proceedings* I (1879): 2–4; Massachusetts Historical Society, *Act*, 2; Tucker, *Clio's*, 87–97; for Isaiah Thomas's gifts, see *MHS Proceedings* I (1879): 48, 60, 79, 111, 112, 130, 138, 147, 154, 168, 202, 218, and for nomination and membership election see 220, 221; Isaiah Thomas, *The History of Printing in America, with a Biography of Printers, and an Account of Newspapers*, 2 vols. (Worcester, MA: From the Press of Isaiah Thomas, Jun., Isaac Sturtevant, Printer, 1810); Gura, *American*, 13–14; Onuf, "American," 9.
41. Analysis of officers based on American National Biography Online, Feb. 2000, https://www.anb.org/; Allen Johnson, ed., *Dictionary of American Biography, under the Auspices of the American Council of Learned Societies*, 20 vols. (New York: Charles Scribner's Sons, 1928); James Grant Wilson and John Fiske, eds. *Appleton's Cyclopædia of American Biography*, 7 vols. (New York: D. Appleton and Company, 1888); Clifford K. Shipton, *Sibley's Harvard Graduates*, 18 vols. (Boston: Massachusetts Historical Society, 1951–99); Franklin Bowditch Dexter, *Biographical Sketches of the Graduates of Yale College: With Annals of the College History*, 6 vols. (New York: Hold, 1885–1912); Tucker, *Massachusetts*, 540–47; Conrad Edick Wright and Edward W. Hanson, *Sibley's Harvard Graduates* XVIII (1999), 63; Joseph McKean, *Memoir towards a Character of Rev. John Eliot, S.T.D.* (Boston: [s.n.], 1813).
42. John Kelly to John Farmer, Sept. 19, 1823, Farmer Papers; Donald M. Scott, *From Office to Profession: The New England Ministry, 1750–1850* (Philadelphia: University of Pennsylvania, 1978), 18–35.
43. Gura, *American*, 21.
44. The five European-born New-York Historical Society founders were Peter Wilson and John Kemp from Scotland, John Bowden of Ireland, Charles Wilkes of England, and John C. Kunze of Germany.
45. Crocker, "Antiquarian Researches," 27–36, esp. 31 in Post, *Observations*.
46. "Society Minutes, 1824–1843," May 2 and Nov. 7, 1825, Box I-1–3, HSP Archives; Deborah Norris Logan to Sarah F. Watson, Jan. 6, 1826, Folder 5, Maria Dickinson Logan Family Papers, Historical Society of Pennsylvania, Philadelphia.
47. Tucker, *Massachusetts*, 55–58.
48. Leon Jackson, *The Business of Letters: Authorial Economies in Antebellum America* (Stanford: Stanford University Press, 2008), 95–96.
49. New-York Historical Society, *Act*, 8; James M. Olney to W. R. Staples, Jun. 5, 1823, "Correspondence and Reports, 1822–1838," vol. 59 (aka I), 35, RIHS Archives.
50. "Special Meeting," Jan. 1794, and "Special Meeting," Apr. 4, 1794, *MHS Proceedings* I (1879): 57–59, 65; Tucker, *Massachusetts*, 20–22, 47–51; Isaiah Thomas, *Public Bequests:*

The Following Extracts from the Will and Codicils of the Late Isaiah Thomas, L.L. D., of Worcester (Mass.) Shew the Amount Bequeathed by Him for Public Purposes (Worcester, MA: s.n., 1831).

51. "Adjourned Meeting," Nov. 26, 1793, and "Quarterly Meeting," Jan. 28, 1794, *MHS Proceedings* I (1879): 59, 61; "Meeting of October 24, 1814," and "Meeting of December 29, 1821," *AAS Proceedings*, 49, 175; Tucker, *Massachusetts*, 20–21, 36.
52. Tucker, *Massachusetts*, 43–51, 72–73; Trustees Report, Jul. 19, 1839, Jul. 19, 1844, and Jul. 19, 1845, "Correspondence and Reports, 1838–1845," vol. 61 (aka III), 52, 136, 148, RIHS Archives; Gura, *American*, 94.
53. "Introduction" and "Fourth Annual Meeting," *Annals of the Missouri Historical and Philosophical Society, No. 1* (Jefferson City: Metropolitan Print, 1848), 3, 24; Christopher P. Bickford, *The Connecticut Historical Society, 1825–1975: An Illustrated History* (Hartford: Connecticut Historical Society, 1975), 6–23.
54. AAS Donations, 90, 128, 153.
55. "Annual Meeting," Apr. 1825, *MHS Proceedings* I (1879): 380; Clark, *British*, 257–59; Tucker, *Massachusetts*, 36; "Meeting of October 23, 1821," "Meeting of October 23, 1823," "Meeting of October 23, 1826," "Meeting of November 23, 1826," and "Meeting of October 23, 1827," *AAS Proceedings*, 171, 202, 212, 215, 218; Dunlap, *American*, 35, 51–53, 62–64.
56. Tucker, *Clio's*, 90n107; "Special Meeting," Apr. 4, 1794, "Quarterly Meeting," Jan. 30, 1798, and "Special Meeting," Aug. 20, 1801, *MHS Proceedings* I (1879): 65, 111, 142; *MHS Collections*.
57. "Special Meeting," Aug. 20, 1801, *MHS Proceedings* I (1879): 142; Ronald Story, *The Forging of an Aristocracy: Harvard and the Boston Upper Class, 1800–1870* (Middletown, CT: Wesleyan University Press, 1980), 28, 160–61; Tucker, *Massachusetts*, 49.
58. Isaiah Thomas, *The Diary of Isaiah Thomas, 1805–1828*, ed. Benjamin Hill, 2 vols. (Worcester: American Antiquarian Society, 1909), 2:15–16; Gura, *American*, 41; Isaiah Thomas to John Farmer, Nov. 3, 1821, Feb. 27, 1822, and Jul. 4, 1822, Farmer Papers.
59. Thomas, *Public*; Vail, *Knickerbocker*, 74.
60. New-York Historical Society, *Constitution*, 4; Massachusetts Historical Society, *Act*, 2; Derks and Smith, *Value*, 232; Vail, *Knickerbocker*, 451; New-York Historical Society, *New-York Historical Society [Memorial]* (s.n., 1827), 8; Tucker, *Massachusetts*, 62; "Monthly Meeting," Nov. 26, 1839, *MHS Proceedings* II (1880): 143; "Quarterly Meeting," Oct. 31, 1811, and "Annual Meeting," Apr. 1813, *MHS Proceedings* I (1879): 224, 232.
61. Gura, *American*, 45–128; "Annual Meeting," Apr. 1837, *MHS Proceedings* II (1880): 81–82, 357; Vail, *Knickerbocker*, 90; Dunlap, *American*, 30–32, 41–42; Bickford, *Connecticut*, 28, 35, 37; Bruce A. Kimball, *The "True Professional Ideal" in America: A History* (Cambridge: Blackwell, 1992), 169–70.
62. "Quarterly Meeting," Jan. 31, 1797, and "Annual Meeting," Apr. 1815, *MHS Proceedings* I (1879): 105, 247; "Laws of the American Antiquarian Society," 1815, "Meeting

of October 23, 1819," and "Meeting of January 27, 1820," *AAS Proceedings*, 75, 149, 151; Clark, *British*, 242.

63. Tucker, *Clio's*, 106–7; "Annual Meeting," April 1796, "Quarterly Meeting," Oct. 25, 1796, "Quarterly Meeting," Jan. 30, 1798, "Quarterly Meeting," Jan. 1799, "Quarterly Meeting," Jan. 1800, "Quarterly Meeting," Jan. 1801, "Quarterly Meeting," Jan. 1802, and "Quarterly Meeting," Jan. 1809, *MHS Proceedings* I (1879): 97, 102, 111, 123, 130, 138, 145, 201; William Plumer, *William Plumer's Memorandum of Proceedings in the United States Senate, 1803–1807*, ed. Everett Somerville Brown (New York: Macmillan, 1923), 537–39; Tucker, *Massachusetts*, 26.
64. "Petition to the Legislature of Massachusetts," Isaiah Thomas, "Communication from the President," "Meeting of October 23, 1815," and Oliver Fiske, "Address to the Members of the American Antiquarian Society," *AAS Proceedings*, 2, 55, 79–80, 139; Gura, *American*, 30, 380n.
65. *Statutes at Large*, 13th Congress, 2nd Session, Joint Resolution of Dec. 27, 1813, on Library of Congress's American Memory; Isaiah Thomas, *An Account of the American Antiquarian Society, Incorporated October 24th, 1812* (Boston: Isaiah Thomas, 1813), 8; Clarence E. Carter, "The United States and Documentary Historical Publication," *Mississippi Valley Historical Review* 25, no. 1 (1938), 3–24; Government Publication Office, "Snapshots."
66. Vail, *Knickerbocker*, 30; Larry E. Sullivan, "Books, Power, and the Development of Libraries in the New Republic: The Prison and Other Journals of John Pintard of New York," *Journal of Library History* 21, no. 2 (1986), 406–24, esp. 408–10; David L. Sterling, "William Duer, John Pintard, and the Panic of 1792," in *Business Enterprise in Early New York*, ed. Joseph R. Frese and Jacob Judd (Tarrytown, NY: Sleepy Hollow Press, 1979), 101.
67. Kenneth Robert Nodyne, "The Role of De Witt Clinton and the Municipal Government in the Development of Cultural Organizations in New York City, 1803 to 1817" (Ph.D. diss., New York University, 1969); Tammany Society, *American Museum . . . . June 1, 1791* (New York: Printed by Thomas and James Swords, 1791); Dunlap, *American*, 51; Tucker, *Massachusetts*, 23.
68. Nodyne, "Role," 19–38.
69. De Witt Clinton to John Pintard, Mar. 22, 1810, and Samuel L. Mitchill to John Pintard, Apr. 3, 1810, as quoted in Vail, *Knickerbocker*, 39; Vail, *Knickerbocker*, 458; Massachusetts Historical Society, *Act*, 1–2; "Act of Incorporation," *AAS Proceedings*, 3–5.
70. Nodyne, "Role," 98–126; Vail, *Knickerbocker*, 41.
71. Vail, *Knickerbocker*, 43; Dunlap, *American*, 51–53; "Quarterly Meeting," Jan. 31, 1797, *MHS Proceedings* I (1879): 104–5; New-York Historical Society, *Memorial of the New-York Historical Society to the Honourable the Legislature of the State of New York* (New York: C. S. Van Winkle, 1814); Gura, *American*, 30, 380n.

72. Sullivan, "Books"; Vail, *Knickerbocker*, 33–34; James J. Heslin, "New York," 51–58, esp. 53, in Jones, *Historical Consciousness in the Early Republic.*
73. "Festival of St. Nicholas," *Commercial Advertiser*, Dec. 11, 1810; Vail, *Knickerbocker*, 368–70; Heslin, "New York," 53; "Adjourned Meeting," Dec. 22, 1813, *MHS Proceedings* I (1879): 235; Tucker, *Clio's*, 134.
74. Vail, *Knickerbocker*, 41–44, 52–54; Joel J. Orosz, *Curators and Culture: The Museum Movement in America, 1740–1870* (Tuscaloosa: University of Alabama Press, 1990), 136; Heslin, "New York," 53–54; New-York Historical Society, *New-York Historical Society [Memorial]* (s.n., 1827), 6–10.
75. Vail, *Knickerbocker*, 43–44, 52–54, 58; Heslin, "New York," 53–54; New-York Historical Society, *New-York*, 6–10; Glynn, *Reading*, 88.
76. Heslin, "New York," 54; Vail, *Knickerbocker*, 43, 52, 58, 61, 63–65, 480; New-York Historical Society, *New-York*, 6–10; Glynn, *Reading*, 88.
77. "New-York Historical Society," *Boston Weekly Messenger*, May 12, 1825; "New-York Historical Library," *New-York American*, May 3, 1825; "Historical," *New York Spectator*, May 6, 1825; *National Gazette*, May 7, 1825; "New York Historical Society," *Providence Gazette*, May 11, 1825. See also "Sale of Valuable Books," *New-York Evening Post*, May 4, 1825; "Historical Society's Library," *New York Spectator*, May 10, 1825.
78. John Farmer to John Kelly, May 10, 1825, and John Kelly to John Farmer, May 13, 1825, Farmer Papers.
79. Vail, *Knickerbocker*, 67; Orosz, *Curators*, 134–38; Glynn, *Reading*, 89.
80. "Historical," *New York Spectator*, May 6, 1825; Orosz, *Curators*, 137.
81. New York Historical Society Act of Incorporation, as quoted in Vail, *Knickerbocker*, 457–59.
82. "Report of the Senate. Report from the Committee on Literature on the Memorial of the New-York Historical Society," in New-York Historical Society, *New-York*, 9–10, emphasis added; Vail, *Knickerbocker*, 67–68, 457–59; Sullivan, "Books"; Orosz, *Curators*, 137–38; Glynn, *Reading*, 89–90.
83. John Pintard to Jeremy Belknap, Apr. 6, 1791, *MHS Collections*, 6th series, IV (1891): 491.
84. Tammany Society, *American Museum . . . . June 1, 1791* (New York: Printed by Thomas and James Swords, 1791); Sterling, "William Duer," 101; Whitehill, *Independent*, 5; "Letter from Samuel L. Mitchell, Esq. to John Pintard," *New-York Magazine; or Literary Repository*, Jun. 1, 1791; Orosz, *Curators*, 58–59.
85. Orosz, *Curators*, 60–61; Sterling, "William Duer," 99–132; Sullivan, "Books," 410.
86. American Museum, "The King of Vultures" (New York, 1793); Tammany Museum, *Tammany Museum, Belonging to Gardiner Baker* (New York: Printed by John Harrison, n.d.); Orosz, *Curators*, 59–74; Whitehill, *Independent*, 6.
87. Peter S. Du Ponceau to Mr. Morandini, Nov. 29, 1824, letter-book copy, "Letter Books (VIII.5)," vol. 3, 30–31, Historical and Literary Committee, American

Philosophical Society Archives; *Transactions of the Historical and Literary Committee of the American Philosophical Society* I (1819)–II (1838).

88. Roberts Vaux to John F. Watson, Sept. 28, 1824, "Letters & Communications to John F. Watson, 1823–1828," 46 (Am 30163), Historical Society of Pennsylvania, Philadelphia, emphasis in original.
89. Bickford, *Connecticut*, 13–29; Boyd, "State," 10–37; Dunlap, *American*, 3–20; Van Tassel, *Recording*, 96–102.
90. Isaiah Thomas to John Farmer, Apr. 7, 1829, Farmer Papers.
91. "Dorchester Antiquarian & Historical Society Records, 1641–1904, Guide to the Collection," Massachusetts Historical Society, Boston, http://www.masshist.org/collection-guides/view/fa0202.
92. Samuel Brown Wylie, *The First Annual Address, Read Before the Religious Historical Society* (Philadelphia: John W. Scott, 1818), 3, [17], 19; *Religious Remembrancer* (Philadelphia: J. W. Scott, 1813–23). See also Religious Historical Society of Philadelphia, *Constitution of the Religious Historical Society of Philadelphia* (Philadelphia, s.n., 1816).
93. Wylie, *First*, 3, [17], 19; *Religious Remembrancer.*
94. Wylie, *First*, 6, 8.
95. James B. Finley, "Story of Methodism in the West," *Western Christian Advocate* 5, 38 (Jan. 11, 1839); Walter Stix Glazer, *Cincinnati in 1840: The Social and Functional Organization of an Urban Community during the Pre-Civil War Period* (Columbus: Ohio State University Press, 1999), 44–49.
96. Western Methodist Historical Society, *Proceedings of the Board of Managers of the Western Methodist Historical Society in the Mississippi Valley; Containing an Account of the Origin of the Society, its Organization, Constitution, Address, Circular, &c* (Cincinnati: Printed at the Methodist Book Room, 1839), 8, 10, emphasis in original; David B. Malone, "The 'Western Christian Advocate': A Voice in the Wilderness," *Queen City Heritage* 51, no. 4 (1993): 23–29; "History of the Methodist Episcopal Church in the Valley of the Mississippi," *Western Christian Advocate* 5, no. 38 (Jan. 11, 1839).
97. "History," *Western Christian Advocate*; "Proceedings of the Universalist Historical Society," *Star in the West and Glad Tidings*, Nov. 13, 1841; Western Methodist Historical Society, *Proceedings*, 9.

CHAPTER TWO: "SO DIVIDED AND SUBDIVIDED"

1. J. D. B. De Bow, "An Account of the Louisiana Historical Society," *La. Historical Collections* II (1850): 8–9; Faye Phillips, "Writing Louisiana Colonial History in the Mid-Nineteenth Century: Charles Gayarré, Benjamin Franklin French, and the Louisiana Historical Society," *Louisiana History* 49, no. 2 (2008): 170.
2. "Louisiana Historical Society: Foreign Documents and Records Relating to the History of Louisiana," *Commercial Review of the South and West* VIII, new series II, no. 1 (1850): 98; De Bow, "Account," 2, 9–11; "An Analytical Index of All the Public

Documents in Paris relating to the Discovery and Early Settlement of Louisiana," *La. Historical Collections* II (1850): 43–90; Phillips, "Writing," 170.

3. James E. Snead, *Relic Hunters: Archaeology and the Public in Nineteenth-Century America* (Oxford, UK: Oxford University Press, 2018) 6.
4. See appendix 1.
5. Philippa Levine, *The Amateur and the Professional: Antiquarians, Historians, and Archaeologists in Victorian England, 1838–1886* (New York: Cambridge University Press, 1986), 67; F. M. Powicke, "English Local Historical Societies," *Canadian Historical Review* 13, no. 3 (1932): 258; Louis Blake Duff, "The Problems and Opportunities of Canadian Historical Societies," *Canadian Historical Review* 13, no. 3 (1932): 253–54; Susan A. Crane, *Collecting and Historical Consciousness in Early Nineteenth-Century Germany* (Ithaca, NY: Cornell University Press, 2000), 81–86.
6. Boyd, "State," 10–37; Dunlap, *American*, 3–20; Van Tassel, *Recording*, 96–102; Gregory M. Pfitzer, *Popular History and the Literary Marketplace, 1840–1920* (Amherst: University of Massachusetts Press, 2008), 41; Peter Fritzsche, *Stranded in the Present: Modern Time and the Melancholy of History* (Cambridge, MA: Harvard University Press, 2004), 184.
7. Boyd, "State," 10–37; Dunlap, *American*, 3–20; Urofsky, "Virginia," 12, 20–24; Lana Ruegamer, *History of the Indiana Historical Society, 1830–1980* (Indianapolis: The Society, 1980), 8–9, 24–25.
8. Tilghman, "Report," xi–v; New-York Historical Society, *Constitution*, 3, 8.
9. Jacob B. Moore to William Plumer Jr., Dec. 18, 1821, Plumer Papers; "Historical Society, Circular," *Rhode-Island American and General Advertiser*, Sept. 3, 1822.
10. "Historical," *Rhode-Island American*; James David Butler, *Deficiencies in Our History: An Address Delivered before the Vermont Historical and Antiquarian Society at Montpelier, October 16, 1846* (Montpelier: Eastman and Danforth, 1846), 7, 26–27.
11. Randolph Roth, "Why Are We Still Vermonters? Vermont's Identity Crisis and the Founding of the Vermont Historical Society," *Vermont History* 59, no. 1 (1991): 197–211.
12. Boyd, "State," 14–16; Dunlap, *American*, 26; Ruegamer, *History*, 13–24; Thomas E. Stephens, "'A Glorious Birthright to Guard': A History of the Kentucky Historical Society," *Register of the Kentucky Historical Society* 101, no. 1 (2003), 8–10; *Historical Collections*, III:5–7.
13. John R. Bartlett to Thomas Webb, Apr. 17, 1837, "Correspondence and Reports, 1835–1838," vol. 61 (aka III), 22, RIHS Archives.
14. I. J. Tefft to Rhode Island Historical Society, Jun. 26, 1839, "Correspondence and Reports, 1845–1852," vol. 61 (aka IV), 61, RIHS Archives, emphasis in original; "The Virginia Historical Society," *Southern Literary Messenger* XIV, no. 1 (Jan. 1848): 54; and *Virginia Historical Register* I, no. 1 (1848), 7.
15. Boyd, "State," 10–37; Dunlap, *American*, 10–21; Van Tassel, *Recording*, 95–102; Whitehill, *Independent*; David J. Russo, *Keepers of the Past: Local Historical Writing*

in the United States, 1820s–1930s (Westport, CT: Greenwood, 1988), 4, 11–28; David Hall, and Alan Taylor, "Reassessing the Local History of New England," in *New England: A Bibliography of Its History*, ed. Roger Parks, vol. 7, xix–xlviii, esp. xxiv–xxx (Hanover: University Press of New England, 1989); Jones, *Historical Consciousness in the Early Republic.*

16. Pilgrim Society, *The Constitutional Articles of the Pilgrim Society, Incorporated February 24, 1820* (Plymouth: Printed by Allen Danforth, 1823), 5; Essex Historical Society, *Essex Historical Society, Incorporated June 11, 1821* (Salem, MA: s.n., 1821), 1–2; David Jaffee, *People of the Wachusett: Greater New England in History and Memory, 1630–1860* (Ithaca: Cornell University Press, 1999), 240.
17. Essex Historical Society, *Essex*, 1, 7, emphasis added.
18. "[Front Matter]," *Worcester Magazine and Historical Journal* 2, no. 1 (May 1826): 1; *Private and Special Statutes of the Commonwealth of Massachusetts, from May 1830, to April 1837: Revised and Published by the Authority of the Legislature*, vol. VII (1837), 36; William Lincoln, *History of Worcester, Massachusetts, from Its Earliest Settlement to September, 1836: With Various Notices Relating to the History of Worcester County* (Worcester: Moses D. Phillips, 1837); "Library Records circa 1845–1858," vol. I, Dorchester Antiquarian and Historical Society Archives, Massachusetts Historical Society, Boston.
19. Benjamin Tappan, "Address Delivered before the Society, At Its Annual Meeting, Held in Columbus, December 22, 1832," *Journal of the Historical and Philosophical Society of Ohio* (Columbus: Printed for the Society, 1838; reprint, Cincinnati: R. Clarke, 1872), 14, 28–29; Virginius C. Hall, "Historical and Philosophical Society of Ohio: A Short History," *Bulletin of the Historical and Philosophical Society of Ohio* 14, no. 2 (1956): 87–104; James H. Perkins and G. Williams Kendall, "A Historical Sketch of the Historical Societies of Ohio," in William D. Gallagher, *Facts and Conditions of Progress in the North-West: Being the Annual Discourse for 1850, before the Historical and Philosophical Society of Ohio* (Cincinnati: Published by H. W. Derby, 1850), 77–85.
20. Perkins and Kendall, "Historical," 78–79; "The Marietta Historical Association," *American Pioneer* I:198–199.
21. "Ephraim Cutler," *Ohio History Central: An Online Encyclopedia of Ohio History*, Jul. 1, 2005, http://www.ohiohistorycentral.org/entry.php?rec=61; Julia Perkins Cutler, *Life and Times of Ephraim Cutler, Prepared From His Journals and Correspondence* (Cincinnati: Robert Clarke, 1890), 242–61.
22. "The Logan Historical Society," *American Pioneer* I:5–24; "Marietta," 198–99; Jean M. O'Brien, *Firsting and Lasting: Writing Indians out of Existence in New England* (Minneapolis: University of Minnesota Press, 2010).
23. "Marietta," 198–99.
24. Perkins and Kendall, "Historical," 77.
25. Perkins and Kendall, "Historical," 78–79, 82; "Marietta," 198.

26. "Proceedings at Trenton, January 21st, 1847," "Proceedings at Newark, May 27th, 1847," and "Proceedings at New Brunswick, June 25th, 1847," *NJHS Proceedings* II (1848): 52–53, 55, 70, 72–73, 92.
27. Brantz Mayer to John Jay, Esq., Mar. 21, 1844, letter-book copy, "Corresponding Secretary Letter-Book, 1844–1888," Box 46, Maryland Historical Society Archives, Maryland Historical Society, Baltimore.
28. "Meeting of October 23, 1827," *AAS Proceedings*, 220; "Constitution and By-Laws of the Cincinnati Historical Society," *Annals of the Cincinnati Historical Society* (Cincinnati: Printed by R. P. Donogh, 1845), 9; Isaiah Thomas to John Farmer, Apr. 7, 1829, Farmer Papers.
29. Joseph Willard to John Farmer, Jul. 10, 1831, Farmer Papers.
30. "Petition to the Legislature of Massachusetts," "Act of Incorporation," Isaiah Thomas, "An Account of the American Antiquarian Society," and Isaiah Thomas, "Communication from the President," *AAS Proceedings*, 1–3, 3–5, 19, 56.
31. Richard F. Hixson, "Isaiah Thomas," American National Biography Online, Feb. 2000; Tucker, *Massachusetts*, 530; "Petition," *AAS Proceedings*, 3.
32. Isaiah Thomas to John Farmer, Dec. 1, 1820, Feb. 24, and Nov. 3, 1821, and Jul. 4, 1822, Farmer Papers; AAS Donations; "Petition," "Meeting of February 3, 1813," "Meeting of October 23, 1819," and "Meeting of October 23, 1821," *AAS Proceedings*, 3, 9, 149, and 170.
33. Thomas, "Account," *AAS Proceedings*, 16–17; Onuf, "American"; Carl Ostrowski, *Books, Maps, and Politics: A Cultural History of the Library of Congress, 1783–1861* (Amherst: University of Massachusetts Press, 2004), 28.
34. Thomas, "Account" and "Council Meeting of October 16, 1813," and William Jenks, "Address," *AAS Proceedings*, 19, 25, and 33; American Antiquarian Society, *Archaeologia Americana: Transactions and Collections of the American Antiquarian Society, Volume I* (Worcester: Printed for the American Antiquarian Society by William Manning, 1820).
35. Thomas, "Communication from the President," *AAS Proceedings*, 55; "Laws of the American Antiquarian Society," 1812, and Thomas, "Account," *AAS Proceedings*, 10, 18; Gura, *American*, 28–30.
36. Thomas, "Communication," *AAS Proceedings*, 53–55, emphasis in original; Gura, *American*, 29.
37. "Laws of the American Antiquarian Society," 1812 and 1815, *AAS Proceedings*, 10, 71–77, 80.
38. "Laws," 1812 and 1815, *AAS Proceedings*, 10, 71–77, 80.
39. "Meeting of June 30, 1831," and "Laws of the American Antiquarian Society, 24 Oct., 1831," *AAS Proceedings*, 241, 244–48.
40. Haberman, "Provincial"; Gross, "Introduction," 4–6; Rejoice Newton to William Plumer Sr., Nov. 20, 1821, and William Plumer Sr., to Rejoice Newton, Dec.

14, 1821, Plumer Papers; Christopher Columbus Baldwin to Samuel Starkweather, Aug. 24, 1832, letter-book copy, "Letters from the Librarian, Volume I (1 April 1831–8 November 1833)," Christopher Columbus Baldwin Papers, American Antiquarian Society, Worcester, MA.

41. Christopher Columbus Baldwin to Matthew St. Clair Clarke, Oct. 28, 1833, letter-book copy, "Letters from the Librarian, Volume I (1 April 1831–8 November 1833)," Christopher Columbus Baldwin Papers, American Antiquarian Society; Christopher Columbus Baldwin, *A Place in My Chronicle: A New Edition of the Diary of Christopher Columbus Baldwin, 1829–1835*, ed. Jack Larkin and Caroline Sloat (Worcester, MA: American Antiquarian Society, 2010), xii; Christopher Columbus Baldwin to John Farmer, Jun. 3, 1834, Joseph Worcester to John Farmer, Sept. 16, 1834, and Joseph Willard to John Farmer, Nov. 17, 1834, Farmer Papers, emphasis in original; Gura, *American*, 39, 45–77. See also Christopher Columbus Baldwin to John Farmer, Aug. 14, 1834, Farmer Papers.

42. American Historical Society, *Transactions of the American Historical Society: Instituted at the City of Washington, October 12, 1835, Vol. 1* (Washington: Printed by Jacob Gideon Jr., 1839), 3–7; Dunlap, *American*, 145; Whitehill, *Independent*, 173–74; Gross, "Introduction," 4–6.

43. "Peter Force," in Wilson and Fiske, *Appleton's Cyclopædia*, II:499; Dunlap, *American*, 145; Whitehill, *Independent*, 173–174; Carolyn Hoover Sung, "Peter Force: Washington Printer and Creator of the 'American Archives'" (Ph.D. diss., George Washington University, 1985).

44. Sung, "Peter," xviii, 141–44.

45. American Historical Society, *Transactions*, 3–7; Dunlap, *American*, 145; Whitehill, *Independent*, 173–74.

46. Boyd, "State"; Clarence E. Carter, "The United States and Documentary Historical Publication," *Mississippi Valley Historical Review* 25, no. 1 (1938): 3–24; Dunlap, *American*, 54–60; Lyman H. Butterfield, "Archival and Editorial Enterprise in 1850 and in 1950: Some Comparisons and Contrasts," *Proceedings of the American Philosophical Society* 98, no. 3 (1954): 159–70; Francis L. Berkeley Jr., "History and Problems of the Control of Manuscripts in the United States," *Proceedings of the American Philosophical Society* 98, no. 3 (1954): 171–78; G. Philip Bauer, "Public Archives in the United States," and David Van Tassel and James A. Tinsley. "Historical Organizations as Aids to History," in *In Support of Clio: Essays in Memory of Herbert A. Kellar*, ed. William B. Hesseltine and Donald R. McNeil (Madison: State Historical Society of Wisconsin, 1958), 49–76 and 127–52; Van Tassel, *Recording*, 103–8; Lawrence Burnette Jr., *Beneath the Footnote: A Guide to the Use and Preservation of American Historical Sources* (Madison: State Historical Society of Wisconsin, 1969), 7–8, 45–50, 135–36; H. G. Jones, *The Records of a Nation: Their Management, Preservation, and Use; With an Introduction by Wayne C. Grover* (New York: Atheneum, 1969), 3–5.

47. New-York Historical Society, *Memorial of the New-York Historical Society to the Honourable the Legislature of the State of New York* (New York: C. S. Van Winkle, 1814).
48. Richard J. Cox, "Sparks, Jared," American National Biography Online, Feb. 2000, https://doi.org/10.1093/anb/9780198606697.article.1400580; Jared Sparks, "Journal of Three Southern Tours made for Historical Researches," MS Sparks 123, Sparks Collection.
49. Jared Sparks, "Memoirs of the Historical Society of Pennsylvania," aka "Materials for American History," *North American Review* 23, no. 53 (1826): 275–95, esp. 276–78, 286–87, 291–92.
50. Dutee Jerauld Pearce to W. R. Staples, Jan. 11 and 21, 1827, "Correspondence and Reports, 1822–1838," vol. 59 (aka I), 66, 67, and "Trustee Records, 1822–1848," vol. 25, 16, RIHS Archives; M. St. Clair Clarke and Peter Force, *Report Made to the Hon. John Forsyth, Secretary of State of the United States, On the Subject of the Documentary History of the United States* (Washington, 1834), 11–12.
51. "Seventh Meeting," Dec. 1791, "Quarterly Meeting," Jan. 1793, "Special Meeting," Jan. 1794, "Quarterly Meeting," Jan. 1794, "Quarterly Meeting," Jan. 1795, "Quarterly Meeting," Jan. 1796, "Special Meeting," Jun. 6, 1796, "Quarterly Meeting," Jan. 31, 1797, "Quarterly Meeting," Jul. 20, 1797, "Special Meeting," Jan. 1798, "Quarterly Meeting," Oct. 28, 1800, "Special Meeting," Jul. 13, 1801, "Annual Meeting," 1814, "Quarterly Meeting," Aug. 1814, "Annual Meeting," 1815, "Annual Meeting," 1819, "Quarterly Meeting," Oct. 28, 1819, "Annual Meeting," 1820, "Annual Meeting," 1824, "Quarterly Meeting," Oct. 27, 1825, "Quarterly Meeting," Jan. 1827, and "Appendix," *MHS Proceedings* I:28, 49, 59, 61, 81, 94–96, 99, 104–5, 107, 109, 135, 141, 239–40, 242–43, 247, 280, 284, 326, 374–76, 385, 396, 505–6.
52. Clarke and Force, *Report*, 23–26.
53. Ibid., 23–26.
54. "Circular," Nov. 1, 1830, "Correspondence and Reports, 1822–1838," vol. 59 (aka I), 99, 104, RIHS Archives; Clarke and Force, *Report*, 11–12; U.S. Congress, *Journal of the House of Representatives of the United States*, 19th Cong., 2nd sess., Feb. 24, 1827, 327.
55. Ostrowski, *Books*, 87–89, 103–5.
56. "Trustee Records, 1822–1848," vol. 25, 14, 17, 20, 25, RIHS Archives.
57. J. L. Clark to Rhode Island Historical Society, Dec. 6, 1830, Committee report, Jan. 1, 1831, Col. Henry Cruger to Rhode Island Historical Society, Dec. 7, 1830, Connecticut Academy of Arts and Sciences to Rhode Island Historical Society, Dec. 29, 1831, Circular, Nov. 11, 1830, Nehemiah Knight to Rhode Island Historical Society, Dec. 17, 1830, and John Farmer to Rhode Island Historical Society, Jan. 8, 1831, "Correspondence and Reports, 1822–1838" vol. 59 (aka I), 94–101, and "Trustee Records, 1822–1848," vol. 25, 14, 17, 20, 25, 32, 35, 39, RIHS Archives.
58. Van Tassel, *Recording*, 103–6; E. Merton Coulter, *Joseph Vallance Bevan: Georgia's First Official Historian* (Athens: Wormsloe Foundation Publications, University of Georgia Press, 1964), 78–83; Clarke and Force, *Report*, 11, 15–18.

59. N[ehemiah Rice] Knight to the Rhode Island Historical Society, Feb. 2, 1831, "Correspondence and Reports, 1822–1838," vol. 59 (aka I), 102, RIHS Archives.
60. John R. Brodhead, "An Address, Delivered before the New York Historical Society, at its Fortieth Anniversary, 20th November, 1844," *Proceedings of the New-York Historical Society for the Year of 1844*, 3 [2nd]; Coulton, *Joseph*, 123–26; Vail, *Knickerbocker*, 86–87; Butterfield, "Archival," 160–61.
61. Benjamin Penley Poore to Jared Sparks, Mar. 28, 1844, emphasis in original, MS Sparks 153, Sparks Collection.
62. Henry Stevens to Jared Sparks, Jan. 1, 1846, MS Sparks 153, Sparks Collection. See also Carter, "United States"; Boyd, "State"; Dunlap, *American*, 54–60; "Newark, May 27th, 1847," *NJHS Proceedings* II (1847): 72; "Princeton, September 27th, 1748," *NJHS Proceedings* III (1848): 125; "To Henry Stevens, Esq., London," *NJHS Proceedings* IV (1849): 8–12.
63. "Some Extracts, &c.," *HSP Memoirs* I, part II (1826): 323–33; Southern District Cabinet Keeper Reports for 1833 and 1834, "Correspondence and Reports, 1822–1838," vol. 59 (aka I), 119, 133, Southern District Cabinet Keeper Report for 1838, "Correspondence and Reports, 1835–1838," vol. 60 (aka II), 144, Southern District Cabinet Keeper Report for 1839, "Correspondence and Reports, 1838–1845," vol. 61 (aka III), 49, and "Trustee Records, 1822–1848," vol. 25, 42, 44–45, 140–42, RIHS Archives; "Minutes 1823–1867," 58, New Hampshire Historical Society Archives, New Hampshire Historical Society, Concord; "Penacook Papers, 1659–1668," *NHHS Collections* III (1832): 212–24.
64. Plumer, *Memorandum*, 537–39; Edmund Berkeley and Dorothy Smith Berkeley, "The First Librarian of Congress; John Beckley," *Quarterly Journal of the Library of Congress* 32, no. 2 (1975): 83–117.
65. Plumer, *Memorandum*, 538–39; Charles F. Mullett, "The 'Better Reception, Preservation, and More Convenient Use' of Public Records in Eighteenth-Century England," *American Archivist* 27, no. 2 (1964): 195–217, esp. 212.
66. U.S. House of Representatives, *Report of the Committee Appointed to Inquire into the State of the Ancient Public Records and Archives of the United States* (Washington City: Printed by R. C. Weightman, 1810), [3], [6]–7; *Journal of the House of Representatives of the United States, at the First Session of the Eleventh Congress, Volume VII* (Washington: Printed by Gales and Seaton, 1826), 240.
67. U.S. House of Representatives, *Report*, [3], 7; Burnette, *Beneath*, 7–8; Jones, *Records*, 3–5.
68. "Meeting of October 23, 1816," *AAS Proceedings*, 99n–100n.
69. "Trustee Records, 1822–1848," vol. 25, 61, RIHS Archives.
70. Richard Bartlett to John Farmer, Aug. 26, 1836, in Jacob B. Moore, *Memoir and Letters of the Late Richard Bartlett, Esq. of New York*, mss. volume, Moore Papers; Richard Bartlett, *Remarks and Documents Related to the Preservation and Keeping*

of the Public Archives (Concord, NH: Printed by Asa M'Farland, 1837); Richard G. Wood, "Richard Bartlett, Minor Archival Prophet," *American Archivist* 17, no. 1 (1954): 13–18.

71. Richard Bartlett to John Farmer, Apr. 3, 1837, Moore Papers; Wood, "Richard," 13–18.
72. Wood, "Richard," 13–14; Richard Bartlett to John Farmer, Apr. 17, 1833, Farmer Papers.
73. Richard Bartlett to John Farmer, Feb. 10, and Dec. 6, 1834, Farmer Papers.
74. Bartlett, *Remarks*; Richard Bartlett to John Farmer, Aug. 6, 1836, John Farmer to Caleb Stark Jr., Jun. 29, 1837, and John Farmer to Isaac Spalding, Aug. 20, 1837, Farmer Papers; "Minutes, 1823–1867," New Hampshire Historical Society Archives.
75. Bartlett, *Remarks*; Richard Bartlett to John Farmer, Dec. 22, 1836, Moore Papers.
76. Bartlett to Farmer, Aug. 26, 1836, Moore Papers; Bartlett, *Remarks*, 32; Maryland State Library, *Report of D. Ridgely, State Librarian, to the Executive of Maryland, in Relation to the Collection of Documents, Papers, &c. Ordered to be Deposited in the Council Chamber* (Annapolis: Jeremiah Hughes, 1836); Maryland State Library, *Second Report of D. Ridgely, State Librarian, to the Executive of Maryland, in Relation to the Collection of Documents, Papers, &c. Ordered to be Deposited in the Council Chamber* (Annapolis: Jeremiah Hughes, 1836); Maryland State Library, *Third Report of D. Ridgely, State Librarian, to the Executive of Maryland, in Relation to the Collection of Documents, Papers, &c. Ordered to be Deposited in the Council Chamber* (Annapolis: Jeremiah Hughes, 1836).
77. Charles W. Cady to John Farmer, Sept. 25, 1837, Farmer Papers, emphasis in original; Bartlett, *Remarks*; Richard Bartlett to John Farmer, Jan. 10 and 21, 1837, Moore Papers.
78. Richard Bartlett to John Farmer, Apr. 23, 1837, Moore Papers; John Farmer to Isaac Hill, Mar. 10, 1837, Farmer Papers; "Minutes 1823–1867," 37, New Hampshire Historical Society Archives; Dow, "Seeds of Conflict," 105–16.
79. Tucker, *Massachusetts*, 64–65, 104–6, 316–18; "Monthly Meeting," Nov. 19, 1846, *MHS Proceedings* II (1880): 357; "Return of the Trumbull Papers," *MHS Proceedings*, 3rd series, 54 (1920–1921): 352–57; Bickford, "Public," 311–20.
80. Massachusetts Secretary of the Commonwealth, *Commonwealth of Massachusetts, Secretary's Office, April 17, 1821* (Boston: s.n., 1821), 11–12; Tucker, *Massachusetts*, 479; Massachusetts Historical Society, *MHS Proceedings* I (1879): 285–87.
81. Sweet, *Antiquaries*, 280; Van Tassel, *Recording*, 105; Crane, *Collecting*, 79; Carter, "United States," 3–24.
82. American Philosophical Society and Historical Society of Philadelphia, *Memorial of the American Philosophical Society, and of the Historical Society of Philadelphia, Recommending the Publication of Certain Ancient Records; and the Report of a Committee of the House of Representatives, upon the Same Subject* (Harrisburg: Printed by Samuel

D. Patterson, 1836) (henceforth APS-HSP Memorial); Burnette, *Beneath*, 49–50; Carter, "United States," 3–24.

83. Hampton L. Carson, *A History of the Historical Society of Pennsylvania*, 2 vols. (Philadelphia: Published by the Society under the special centennial publication fund, 1940), I:160–63; APS-HSP Memorial, 5.
84. APS-HSP Memorial, 6–8; Carson, *History*, I:163–65.
85. *Minutes of the Provincial Council of Pennsylvania, from the Organization to the Termination of the Proprietary Government*, 16 vols. (Harrisburg, PA: Published by the State, Printed by Theophilus Fenn, 1838), I:i–vii; Carson, *History*, I:165–66; Butterfield, "Archival," 161.
86. Vail, *Knickerbocker*, 87; "Annual Report," *Proceedings of the New-York Historical Society for the Year of 1845*, 12–14; "Annual Report," *Proceedings of the New-York Historical Society for the Year of 1846*, 15–16.
87. Bauer, "Public," 57–58; *Historical Collections*; Phillips, "Writing."
88. "Trustee Records, 1822–1848," 25:79, 84, report of the committee regarding the Coddington House, Jul. 20, 1835, Thomas Webb's report on the Bishop Berkeley building, Nov. 5, 1835, Jeremiah Day to Thomas Webb, Aug. 9, 1835, "Correspondence and Reports, 1835–1838," vol. 60 (aka II), 6, 89, 90, and Northern District Cabinet Keeper's report, Jul. 19, 1842, "Correspondence and Reports, 1838–1845," vol. 61 (aka III), 114, RIHS Archives; Colonial Dames of America in the State of Rhode Island, "History of the Whitehall Property," http://www.whitehallmuseumhouse.org/history-of-the-whitehall-property/.
89. Whitney Martinko, "Progress and Preservation: Representing History in Boston's Landscape of Urban Reform, 1820–1860," *New England Quarterly* 82, no. 2 (2009): 304–34; "Library Accession Book I, 1825–1862," 17, 32, vol. I-7–45, HSP Archives; "Librarian's Record of Donations to the N.H. Historical Society," 42, New Hampshire Historical Society Archives. See also Batinski, *Pastkeepers*, 86, 103–4; Charles B. Hosmer Jr., *Presence of the Past: A History of the Preservation Movement in the United States before Williamsburg* (New York: Putnam, 1965); Denise D. Meringolo, *Museums, Monuments, and National Parks: Toward a New Genealogy of Public History* (Amherst: University of Massachusetts Press, 2012), 11–12; Matthew Mason, "'The Sacred Ashes of the First of Men': Edward Everett, the Mount Vernon Ladies Association of the Union and Late Antebellum Unionism," in *Remembering the Revolution: Memory, History, and Nation Making from Independence to the Civil War*, ed. Michael A. McDonnell, Clare Corbould, Frances M. Clarke, and W. Fitzhugh Brundage (Amherst: University of Massachusetts Press, 2013), 265–79.
90. Whitehill, *Independent*, 243–48; Clifford L. Lord and Carl Ubbelohde, *Clio's Servant: The State Historical Society of Wisconsin, 1846–1954* (Madison: State Historical Society of Wisconsin, 1967), 3–27; William B. Hesseltine, *Pioneer's Mission: The Story of Lyman Copeland Draper* (Madison: State Historical Society of Wisconsin, 1954).

91. Amanda Laugesen, *The Making of Public Historical Culture in the American West, 1880–1910* (Lewiston, NY: Edwin Mellen Press, 2006).

CHAPTER THREE: "PROVIDING MATERIALS FOR HISTORY"

1. Lemuel Shattuck, "A Plan for Providing Materials for History," *NHHS Collections* III (1832): 233–37.
2. New Hampshire Historical Society, Circular, 1823, see Mar. 30, 1827, Farmer Papers; Board of Trustees Report, 1825, "Correspondence & Reports, 1822–1838," vol. 59 (aka I), 39, RIHS Archives.
3. Board of Trustees Report, Jul. 19, 1839, "Correspondence & Reports," vol. 61 (aka III), 52, RIHS Archives; Andrew H. Ward to Ebenezer Clapp, May 29, 1843, Dorchester Historical and Antiquarian Society Archives, Massachusetts Historical Society, Boston; Steenshorne, "Past," 42.
4. Tucker, *Massachusetts*, 25–26, 40–44.
5. Jutta Reed-Scott, "Collection Management Strategies for Archivists," *American Archivist* 47, no. 1 (1984): 24.
6. Jeremy Belknap to Ebenezer Hazard, Mar. 2, 1793, *MHS Collections*, 5th series, III (1877): 322, emphasis in original.
7. "Constitution of the Historical Society," 2, emphasis added; Tucker, *Clio's*, 95.
8. "Introduction," and "Adjourned Meeting" Jun. 1794, *MHS Proceedings* I (1879): xx–xxi, 67; Tucker, *Massachusetts*, 26–27; "Circular Letter of the Historical Society," *Massachusetts Spy*, Feb. 28, 1793; Massachusetts Historical Society, *Act*; "Circular Letter of the Massachusetts Historical Society, Respectfully Addressed to Every Gentleman," *South-Carolina State Gazette and Timothy's Daily Advertiser*, Oct. 29, 1794; "Miscellany," *Nantucket Inquirer*, Apr. 22, 1823.
9. "Introduction," *MHS Proceedings* I (1879): xx–xxi, 67; Thomas Prince, "Boston, April 10, 1729. Reverend Sir" (Boston: s.n., 1729); Massachusetts Historical Society, *Act*; Sweet, *Antiquaries*, 89–91; Allan, "Scottish Enlightenment," 22.
10. "Introduction," *MHS Proceedings* I (1879): xx–xxi; "Circular," *Massachusetts Spy*, Feb. 28, 1793; Massachusetts Historical Society, *Act*, 7–8; "Miscellany," *Nantucket Inquirer*.
11. "Introduction," *MHS Proceedings* I (1879): xx–xxi; "Circular," *Massachusetts Spy*, Feb. 28, 1793; Massachusetts Historical Society, *Act*, 7–8; "Miscellany," *Nantucket Inquirer*; Russo, *Keepers of the Past*, 45–47.
12. "Introduction," *MHS Proceedings* I (1879): xx–xxi; "Circular," *Massachusetts Spy*, Feb. 28, 1793; Massachusetts Historical Society, *Act*, 7–8; "Miscellany," *Nantucket Inquirer*.
13. John Whiting to James Sullivan, Apr. 19, 1793, Corresponding Secretary Records, second series, vol. I, and Benjamin Trumbull to John Eliot, Feb. 9, 1801, Corresponding Secretary Records, first series, vol. I, MHS Archives.
14. "Introduction," *MHS Proceedings* I (1879): xx–xxi; "Circular," *Massachusetts Spy*, Feb. 28, 1793; Massachusetts Historical Society, *Act*, 7–8; "Miscellany," *Nantucket Inquirer*,

Apr. 22, 1823; George Callcott, *History in the United States, 1800–1860: Its Practice and Purpose* (Baltimore: Johns Hopkins University Press, 1970), 15.

15. For examples of historian circulars, see Timothy Alden to Rev. Samuel M. Burnside, Oct. 21, 1813, Documents and Correspondence, American Antiquarian Society Archives; Thomas Peters, "Circular," Nov. 15, 1815, Correspondence, American Philosophical Society Archives; "History of the County of Worcester," *Worcester Magazine and Historical Journal* 1, no. 2 (Nov. 1825): 33–34. Russo, *Keepers*, 51.
16. New-York Historical Society, *Constitution*, 8–15; Steenshorne, "Past," 32–36.
17. "Literary Notice," *APS Transactions*, new series, I (1818): viii–x; Oliver Fiske, "Address to the Members of the American Antiquarian Society," *AAS Proceedings*, 139–42.
18. Tilghman, "Report," x–xi; Massachusetts Historical Society, *Act*, 6.
19. "Quarterly Meeting," Jan. 1801, *MHS Proceedings* I (1879): 136. For Hall's donations, see "Annual Meeting, 1795," "Quarterly Meeting," Oct. 27, 1795, and "Quarterly Meeting," Jan. 1803, *MHS Proceedings* I (1879): 83, 88, 152, 155. For Hall's membership see "Annual Meeting," Apr. 1801, *MHS Proceedings* I (1879): 140. Abiel Holmes, "History of Cambridge," and James Freeman, "An Account of the Trade and Shipping of Newfoundland in 1799," *MHS Collections* VII (1801, reprinted 1846): 1–66, 219; Tucker, *Massachusetts*, 474, 498.
20. Alabama Historical Society, *Constitution of the Alabama Historical Society; Organized at Tuskaloosa, July 5th, 1850* (Tuscaloosa: Printed by M. D. J. Slade, 1850), 9–12.
21. Massachusetts Historical Society, *Act of Incorporation*, 5, emphasis in original; Sweet, *Antiquaries*, 280.
22. Callcott, *History*, 42; De Bow, "Account," 5; Richard Bartlett, "Remarks and Documents Relating to the Preservation and Keeping of the Public Archives," *NHHS Collections* V (1837): 8–9.
23. New-York Historical Society, *Constitution*, 9; "Advertisement," *HSP Memoirs* I (1826): [3].
24. New-York Historical Society, *Constitution*, 9; Callcott, *History*, 121–24.
25. "Circular to Individuals," *Annals of the Cincinnati Historical Society* (Cincinnati: Printed by R. P. Donogh, 1845), 6–7, emphasis added.
26. Henry Shapiro, "Putting the Past under Glass: Preservation and the Idea of History in the Mid-Nineteenth Century," *Prospects* 10, no. 10 (1985): 243–86, esp. 259–64; Alea Henle, "The Means and the End: Letters and the Work of History," in *The Edinburgh Companion to Nineteenth-Century American Letters and Letter-Writing*, ed. Celeste-Marie Bernier, Judie Newman, and Matthew Pethers (Edinburgh: Edinburgh University Press, 2016), 103–18.
27. "New York Historical Society, Constitution"; "Catalogue of the Books, Tracts, Newspapers, Maps, Charts, Views, Portraits, and Manuscripts, in the Library of the

New-York Historical Society," (New York: J. Seymour, 1813), 2, or *N-YHS Collections* II (1814): 2.

28. Essex Historical Society, *Essex Historical Society, Incorporated June 11, 1821* (Salem MA: s.n., 1821), 8; "Historical Society. Circular," *Rhode-Island American, and General Advertiser*, Sept. 3, 1822.
29. "Literary Notice," *Transactions of the Historical and Literary Committee of the American Philosophical Society* I (1819), ix; Peter Du Ponceau, "Inaugural Discourse," *HSP Memoirs* IV, part I (1840): 24.
30. Essex, *Essex*, 8; "Historical," *Rhode-Island American*, 1822. Subsection adapted and revised from Henle, "Means," 107–10.
31. The individual who later added the rejected materials to the collection was likely Charles Deane. Thaddeus Mason Harris to Dr. Martin Gay, 22 May 1838, rough draft, *MHS Proceedings*, 2nd series, XI (1897): 221–23; "Monthly Meeting," May 1836, *MHS Proceedings* II (1880): 45n.
32. Jerry E. Patterson, *Autographs: A Collector's Guide* (New York: Crown Publishers, Inc., 1973), iv; John M. Mulder and Isabelle Stouffer, "William Buell Sprague: Patriarch of American Collectors," *American Presbyterians* 64, no. 1 (1986): 1–17.
33. "Trustee Records, 1822–1848," vol. 25, 105, RIHS Archives; J. R. Poinsett to Charles Hosmer, Mar. 29, 1841, and Charles Hosmer to J. C. Smith, Jun. 7, 1843, CHS Archives.
34. Jared Sparks, 8 and 25 May 1826, "Journal of Three Southern Tours made for Historical Researches," MS Sparks 123, Sparks Collection; Alea Henle, "Original / Copy," *Early American Studies* 16, no. 4 (2018): 728–32.
35. Alabama Historical Society, *Constitution*, 10.
36. Edwin M. Stone to T. C. Hartshorn, Jul. 28, 1847, "Correspondence & Reports, 1845–1852," vol. 62 (aka IV), 60, RIHS Archives. Analysis of historical society collections based on accession and donation records, donation acknowledgments, or equivalents for the American Antiquarian Society; American Philosophical Society's historical committee; New England Historic Genealogical Society; Pilgrim Society; and historical societies of Connecticut, Georgia, Maine, Maryland, Massachusetts, New Hampshire, New Jersey, New York, Pennsylvania, Rhode Island, University of North Carolina, and Virginia.
37. Stone to Hartshorn.
38. New-York Historical Society, *Constitution*, 14, emphasis in original; "The Society's Circular, January, 1845," *HSP Memoirs* IV, part II (1850): 109.
39. Rachal, "Early," 17.
40. "Connecticut Historical Society," *Daily Herald* (New Haven), Feb. 28, 1843.
41. Alabama Historical Society, *Constitution*, 10, emphasis added; American Historical Society, *Transactions*, 5.

42. New-York Historical Society, *Constitution*, 13; "Circular Letter of the Historical Society," *Massachusetts Spy*, Feb. 28, 1793; Alabama Historical Society, *Constitution*, 9–10; Essex Historical Society, *Essex*, 7.
43. New-York Historical Society, *Constitution*, 10; De Bow, "Account," 6.
44. "Hints to the Historical Society," *Virginia Historical Register and Literary Advertiser*, Oct. 1, 1849.
45. "Circular," *HSP Memoirs* I, part I (1826): 23–25, and IV, part II (1850): 105–12.
46. Alabama Historical Society, *Constitution*, 12; "Office 'Minnesota Historical Society,'" *Annals of the Minnesota Historical Society*, 2nd ed. (Saint Paul: Printed by James M. Goodhue, 1850), [3].
47. Rachal, "Early," 342; "Library Accession Book I, 1825–1862," vol. I-7-45, HSP Archives; "Acknowledgement of Donations," *MHS Collections*, 3rd series, V (1836): 298; "Trustee Records, 1822–1848," vol. 25, 66, 87, RIHS Archives.
48. Baldwin, *Place*, 149–50, 224; Christopher Columbus Baldwin to John Farmer, Oct. 2, 1833, Farmer Papers; Jaffee, *People*, 222; Harvey Green, "Cultural History and the Material(s) Turn," *Cultural History* 1, no. 1 (2012): 61–82, esp. 64; Dunlap, *American*, 69–78; Gura, *American*, 88–92.
49. John Eliot to [Benjamin Trumbull?], Dec. 11, 1790, *MHS Proceedings* II (1880): viii; David Shields, "The Learned World," in *History of the Book in America* II:247–68.
50. "Circular," *Massachusetts Spy*, Feb. 28, 1793; Massachusetts Historical Society, *Act*; New-York Historical Society, *Constitution*; Orosz, *Curators*, 89–93.
51. Isaiah Thomas, "Account," 18; Isaiah Thomas, *Communication from the President of the American Antiquarian Society to the members, October 24th, 1814, Together with the laws of the Society, as Revised* (Worcester: Printed by William Manning, 1815), 4; American Antiquarian Society, *Address to the Members of the American Antiquarian Society; Together with the Laws and Regulations of the Institution, and a List of Donations to the Society Since the Last Publication* (Worcester: Printed by William Manning, 1819), 7, emphasis added.
52. Orosz, *Curators*, 89–93; Walter B. Hendrickson, "The Western Academy of Natural Sciences of Cincinnati," *Isis* 37 (1947): 138–45.
53. Printed Solicitation, Oct. 23, 1846, Folder 10, Box 1, Dorchester Antiquarian and Historical Society Records (Mss 624), New England Historic Genealogical Society, Boston; Essex Historical Society, *Essex*, 7–8; New Hampshire Historical Society Circular, 1830, "Correspondence & Reports," vol. 59 (aka I), 101, RIHS Archives; New Hampshire Historical Society 1823 Circular, John Farmer to John Kelly, Mar. 30, 1827, and Indiana Historical Society Circular, John Farnham to John Farmer, Oct. 30, 1832, Farmer Papers; "Circular Letter of the Maine Historical Society," May 21, 1824, Container G1, Series G, Maine Historical Society Archives, Maine Historical Society, Portland; "Early Records of the Virginia Historical Society, 1831–1833," 16–18; New Hampshire Historical Society Circular, Jacob B. Moore to William

Plumer Jr., Sept. 10, 1837, Plumer Papers; "Connecticut Historical Society," *Connecticut Common School Journal* 2 (Apr. 1, 1840): 180.

54. "Annual Meeting, 1833," *MHS Proceedings* I (1879): 467; Shields, "Learned," 247–68; Margaret Welch, *The Book of Nature: Natural History in the United States, 1825–1875* (Boston: Northeastern University Press, 1998), 4; Dunlap, *American*, 75; Dorinda Outram, "New Spaces in Natural History," in *Cultures of Natural History*, ed. N. Jardine, J. A. Secord, and E. C. Spary (New York: Cambridge University Press, 1996); Paul Lawrence Farber, *Finding Order in Nature: The Naturalist Tradition from Linnaeus to E. O. Wilson* (Baltimore: Johns Hopkins University Press, 2000), 29.
55. Fritzsche, *Stranded*, 184; Wallace B. Stevens, "Account of the Georgia Historical Society," *American Quarterly* 12 (May 1840): 349; "Constitution," *Transactions of the American Historical Society: Instituted at the City of Washington, October 12, 1835* (1839), 5–6.
56. "Circular of the Louisiana Historical Society," *La. Historical Collections* II (1850): 7; Cincinnati Historical Society, "Individuals," 7.
57. Cincinnati Historical Society, "Individuals," 7; Dagmar Wernitznig, *Europe's Indians, Indians in Europe: European Perceptions and Appropriations of Native American Cultures from Pocahontas to the Present* (New York: University Press of America, 2007), 35; Fritzsche, *Stranded*, 185; "Circular," *Massachusetts Spy*, Feb. 28, 1793; New-York Historical Society, *Constitution*, 13.
58. New-York Historical Society, *Constitution*, 10.
59. John Farmer to Joseph Willard, Dec. 26, 1831, Farmer Papers; John Ross to "Cherokee Antiquarians," Sept. 15, 1835, in *The Papers of Chief John Ross, Volume 1*, ed. Gary E. Moulton (Norman: University of Oklahoma Press, 1985), 353–54; *Transactions of the Historical and Literary Committee of the American Philosophical Society* I–III (1819–43); Steven Conn, *History's Shadow: Native Americans and Historical Consciousness in the Nineteenth Century* (Chicago: University of Chicago Press, 2004), 22; Maureen Konkle, *Writing Indian Nations: Native Intellectuals and the Politics of Historiography, 1827–1863* (Chapel Hill: University of North Carolina Press, 2004), 90; Peter Nabokov, *A Forest of Time: American Indian Ways of History* (New York: Cambridge University Press, 2002), 6.
60. "Circular," *HSP Memoirs* IV, pt. II, 109; O'Brien, *Firsting*.
61. Conn, *History's*, 211–16.
62. William Jenks, *An Address to the Members of the American Antiquarian Society; Pronounced in King's Chapel, Boston, on Their First Anniversary . . .* (Boston: Published by Isaiah Thomas, 1813); Thomas, *Communication*.
63. "The Importance of Preserving Original Mss.," *New England Historical and Genealogical Register*, Apr. 1, 1848, emphasis in original.
64. John Kelly to John Farmer, Nov. 26, 1822, Farmer Papers, emphasis in original. For a list of the manuscript volumes in Farmer's possession on his death, see "Appraisal of Property of John Farmer," 10–12, Farmer Papers.

65. Trustees Report, Jul. 19, 1845, "Correspondence & Reports, 1838–1845," vol. 61, 148, RIHS Archives; Edward Armstrong, printed circular, Mar. 1849, "Correspondence, Vol. IV, 1834, 1837–1849," Box 17, Series I, Corresponding Secretary Records, MHS Archives.
66. Marla R. Miller, "Introduction: Pastkeeping in Another Small Place," in *Cultivating a Past: Essays on the History of Hadley, Massachusetts*, ed. Marla R. Miller (Amherst: University of Massachusetts Press, 2009), 1–24.

CHAPTER FOUR: "DISJOINTED FRAGMENTS"

1. Isaiah Thomas, *The History of Printing in America, With a Biography of Printers, and an Account of Newspapers*, 2 vols. (Worcester, MA: From the Press of Isaiah Thomas, Isaac Sturtevant, Printer, 1810), 106–7; Burnette, *Beneath*, 45, 49.
2. Sweet, *Antiquaries*, 280; Dunlap, *American*, 95–108; Van Tassel, *Recording America's Past*, 64, 101–2.
3. Appleton P. C. Griffin, *Bibliography of American Historical Societies, the United States, and the Dominion of Canada, Second Edition, Revised and Enlarged* (Washington: Government Printing Office, 1907); Jimerson, "Documents," 235–58; Randall C. Jimerson, *Archives Power: Memory, Accountability, and Social Justice* (Chicago: Society of American Archivists, 2009), 83–86; Dunlap, *American*, 95–108; Tucker, *Clio's*, 122–32; Tucker, *Massachusetts*, 28–32; Haberman, "Provincial Nationalism," 162–93; Whitehill, *Independent*, 13, 42; Van Tassel, *Recording*, 64, 101–2; Burnette, *Beneath*, 45, 49; Lester J. Cappon, "American Historical Editors before Jared Sparks: 'They Will Plant a Forest,'" *William and Mary Quarterly*, 3rd series, 30, no. 3 (1973): 385–87, 390–91, 393; Glynn, *Reading Publics*, 66–100; Russo, *Keepers of the Past*, 16–18; David Hall, and Alan Taylor, "Reassessing the Local History of New England," in *New England: A Bibliography of Its History*, ed. Roger Parks, 7 vols. (Hanover: University Press of New England, 1989), 7:xix–xlviii.
4. Jeremy Belknap, "Description of the White Mountains in New-Hampshire," "Extract of a Letter from the Rev. Jeremy Belknap, Containing Observations on the Aurora Borealis," and "A Letter from the Rev. Jeremy Belknap, on the Preservation of Parsnips by Drying," *APS Transactions* II (1786): 42–49, 196–97, and 199–200; David S. Shields, "The Learned World," in *History of the Book in America* II:247–55, esp. 252.
5. Evans, *History*, 146, 214–16; Society of Antiquaries, *Archaeologia: Or Miscellaneous Tracts Relating to Antiquity* I (1770), and 2nd ed., I (1779).
6. Harvard University, *[Triennial Catalogue, 1794] Catalogus Eorum Qui in Universitate Harvardiana, Cantabrigiae* (Bostoniae: Typis Thomae et Johannis Fleet, 1794); Massachusetts Historical Society, *Catalogue of Books in the Massachusetts Historical Society Library* (Boston: Printed by S. Hall, 1796); American Antiquarian Society,

Archaeologia Americana: Transactions & Collections of the American Antiquarian Society I (1820); Gura, *American*, 40–42; Evans, *History*, 214–16.

7. Elisabeth Kaplan, "We Are What We Collect, We Collect What We Are: Archives and the Construction of Identity," *American Archivist* 63, no. 1 (2000): 126–51.
8. John Kelly to John Farmer, Nov. 1, 1822, Farmer Papers; Lynn W. Turner, *William Plumer of New Hampshire, 1759–1850* (Chapel Hill: Published for the Institute of Early American History and Culture at Williamsburg, Virginia, by the University of North Carolina Press, 1962).
9. For a list of Farmer's publications, see "John Farmer and What He Did for New Hampshire," *Historical New Hampshire* (1945), 3–6, or *NHHS Collections* VI (1850): 42–43. François Weil, "John Farmer and the Making of American Genealogy," *New England Quarterly* 80, no. 3 (2007): 418–21.
10. John Farmer to John Kelly, Jan. 9, 1824, Farmer Papers.
11. John Farmer to John Kelly, Jan. 24, 1824, Farmer Papers.
12. John Kelly to John Farmer, Nov. 10, 1823, John Farmer to John Kelly, Nov. 14 and Dec. 12, 1823, William Plumer Jr., to John Farmer, Nov. 17, 1823, William Plumer Sr., to John Farmer, Dec. 6, 1823, and Parker Noyes to John Farmer, Dec. 15, 1823, Farmer Papers; John Farmer to William Plumer Jr., Dec. 11, 1823, Plumer Papers.
13. John Kelly to John Farmer, Oct. 16 and 27, Nov. 3 and 28, and Dec. 8 and 18, 1823, William Plumer Sr., to John Farmer, Dec. 6, 1823, and John Farmer to John Kelly, Oct. 18, 1823, Farmer Papers.
14. "Fourth Meeting" and "Fifth Meeting," *MHS Proceedings* I (1879): 16–17, 23; Tucker, *Clio's*, 122–31.
15. "Introduction," "Fourth Meeting," and "Sixth Meeting," *MHS Proceedings* I (1879): xix–xx, xxii–xxix, 16–17, 24; Lucia McMahon, *Mere Equals: The Paradox of Educated Women in the Early American Republic* (Ithaca: Cornell University Press, 2012), 7–9, 62–63; "Letters relating to the Expedition against Cape Breton," *American Apollo* Oct. 5, 1792, or *MHS Collections* I (1792, reprinted 1806): 5–60; Tucker, *Clio's*, 122–31.
16. "Introductory Address from the Historical Society," *American Apollo* Oct. 5, 1792, 4–6, or *MHS Collections* I (1792): 2–4; Tucker, *Clio's*, 122–31.
17. Massachusetts Historical Society supplements were intended to be separable from the *American Apollo*, to facilitate binding, and were scanned as a long installment versus multiple short; see *American Apollo*, Oct. 5, 1792, in America's Historical Newspapers. "Introductory," *American Apollo*, Oct. 5, 1792, 4–6, or *MHS Collections* I:2–4; "Introduction," *MHS Proceedings* I (1879): xxii–xxix.
18. "Introduction," *MHS Proceedings* I (1879): xxii–xxix; Tucker, *Clio's*, 127–29; Andie Tucker, "Newspapers and Periodicals," in *History of the Book in America* II:289–408, esp. 397.

19. "Introduction," *MHS Proceedings* I (1879): xxix–xxxi; Tucker, *Clio's*, 130–31; Haberman, "Provincial."
20. "Quarterly Meeting," Oct. 31, 1797, *MHS Proceedings* I (1879): 107–9; James N. Green, "The Rise of Book Publishing," in *History of the Book in America* II:75–127, esp. 75, 91–93; Shields, "Learned," 252.
21. Christopher D. Ebeling to Jeremy Belknap, Oct. 1, 1796, *MHS Collections*, 6th series, IV (1891): 607–8, emphasis in original; Levi Whitman, "A Topographical Description of Wellfleet," *MHS Collections* III (1794, reprinted 1810): 117–25; Russo, *Keepers*, 23–24.
22. *MHS Collections*, 2nd series, II (1814).
23. "Society Minutes, 1824–1843," 31, 42, 44, 46, 52, 55, 77, 79, 80, 82, 83, 89, 96, 114, vol. I-7–45, HSP Archives; *HSP Memoirs* I–IV, part II (1826–50); Samuel W. Eager, *An Outline History of Orange County* (Newburgh: S. T. Callahan, 1846–47), 3; Dunlap, *American*, 129.
24. "Extracts from Dr. Stiles' Literary Diary," and "Prospectus of Hubbard's History," *MHS Collections*, 2nd series, II (1814): 260, 282–83; "Annual Meeting," Apr. 1814, "Quarterly Meeting," Aug. 1814, "Annual Meeting," Apr. 1815, and "Quarterly Meeting," Aug. 1815, *MHS Proceedings* I (1879): 239–40, 242–43, 247, 249.
25. "Preface," *N-YHS Collections* I (1811): [iii].
26. "Documents Extracted from the Second Volume of Hazard's '*Historical Collections*,'" *N-YHS Collections* I (1811): 189; Glynn, *Reading*, 74–75.
27. "Preface," *N-YHS Collections* I (1811): vi; *N-YHS Collections* III–IV (1821–26).
28. Russo, *Keepers*, 23–24; *Transactions of the Historical and Literary Committee of the American Philosophical Society* I–III (1819–43); Peter P. Pratt, "Peter Du Ponceau's Contributions to Anthropology," *Ethnohistory* 18, no. 2 (1971): 147–58; American Antiquarian Society, *Archaeologia Americana* II (1836). Other examples include the volumes issued by the Historical and Philosophical Society of Ohio and the New Hampshire Historical Society.
29. Plumer Jr., to Farmer, Dec. 22, 1823, Kelly to Farmer, Nov. 10 and 28, 1823, Farmer to Kelly, Nov. 14, and Dec. 12, 1823, Plumer Sr., to Farmer, Dec. 6, 1823, Noyes to Farmer, Dec. 15, 1823, John Kelly to William Plumer Jr., Nov. 4, 1823, and John Farmer to William Plumer Jr., Nov. 14, 1823, and Dec. 11, 1823, Plumer Papers.
30. *NHHS Collections* I (1824); John Farmer to John Kelly, Jan. 24, Feb. 4, Oct. 12 and 19, 1824, Plumer Sr., to Farmer, Dec. 6, 1823, Nathaniel A. Haven Jr., to John Farmer, Dec. 15, 1823, and Nathaniel Adams to John Farmer, Mar. 1 and 31, 1824, Farmer Papers.
31. "Contents," and "Deposition of Elizabeth Miles, 1754," *NHHS Collections* I (1824): [iii]–iv, 277–79.
32. "Preface," *N-YHS Collections* I (1811): vi, emphasis in original; "Advertisement to the First Edition," *HSP Memoirs* I, part 1 (1826): [v]; Virginia Historical Society, "The

Report of the Executive Committee," *Virginia Historical Register* I, no. 1 (1848), 9, 47, and II, no. 1 (1849), 12, 53.

33. "General Table of Contents of the Ten Volumes, Methodically Arranged," "A Chronological Table of the Most Remarkable Events Recorded in the Ten Volumes," and "A General Index to the Ten Volumes," *MHS Collections*, 1st series, X (1809): 193–302; "Quarterly Meeting," Aug. 1804, and "Quarterly Meeting," Oct. 1809, *MHS Proceedings* I (1879): 165, 214; "General Table of Contents of the Ten Volumes of the Second Series," *MHS Collections*, 2nd series, X (1823): 193–200; "General Table of Contents of the Ten Volumes of the Third Series, Methodically Arranged," *MHS Collections*, 3rd series, X (1849): 237–43.
34. *MHS Collections*, 2nd series, II, III, IV, VII, and VIII (1814–1819); "Quarterly Meeting," Oct. 26, 1809, *MHS Proceedings* I (1879): 214.
35. "General," *MHS Collections*, 1st series, X (1809): 193–202; "General," *MHS Collections*, 2nd series, X (1823): 193–200; "Quarterly Meeting," Oct. 1809, *MHS Proceedings* I (1879): 214; "Letter from King Philip to Governour Prince," *MHS Collections*, 1st series, II (1793): 40.
36. "An Original Letter from Dr. Increase Mather, to Governor Dudley, 1708," "An Original Letter from Dr. Cotton Mather, to Governor Dudley, 1708," "An Original Letter from Governor Dudley, to Dr. Increase and Dr. Cotton Mather, 1708," and "Extract from Dr. Cotton Mather's Private Diary," *MHS Collections* III (1794): 126–38.
37. Shields, "Learned," 252.
38. Meredith McGill, "Copyright," in *History of the Book in America* II:198–211, esp. 199, 202–3.
39. Meredith L. McGill, *American Literature and the Culture of Reprinting, 1834–1853* (Philadelphia: University of Pennsylvania Press, 2003); McGill, "Copyright," 198–210; *Collections of the Georgia Historical Society* I (1840); *MHS Collections*, 3rd series, V–VII; *RIHS Collections* IV (1838); *Transactions of the American Historical Society* I (1839).
40. Plumer Jr., to Farmer, Nov. 17, 1823; Abiel Holmes to John Farmer, Nov. 13, 1823, emphasis in original, and Plumer Sr., to Farmer, Dec. 6, 1823, Farmer Papers; "Collections of the New Hampshire Historical Society, for the Year 1824," *North American Review* XX, no. XLVII (1825): 448–49; "Penhallow's History of the Indian Wars, &c.," *NHHS Collections* I (1824): 13; "Art. X.—Collections of the New-Hampshire Historical Society. Vol. III," *American Monthly Review*, Jan. 1, 1832, 54–55.
41. Plumer Sr., to Farmer, Dec. 6, 1823; "Ancient Documents," *NHHS Collections* I (1824): 297–98.
42. John Farmer to John Kelly, Dec. 25, 1823, emphasis in original, and Plumer Sr., to Farmer, Dec. 6, 1823, Farmer Papers.
43. Plumer Sr., to Farmer, Dec. 6, 1823, emphasis in original; Farmer to Kelly, Dec. 25, 1823.

44. William Plumer Sr. to John Farmer, Dec. 6 and 26, 1823, emphasis in original, Farmer Papers; "Ancient Documents," *NHHS Collections* I (1824): 297–336; William Plumer Sr. to Samuel L. Mitchell, Jan. 1, 1812, letter-book copy, Plumer Papers.
45. John Farmer to John Kelly, Mar. 1, 1824, John Kelly to John Farmer, Feb. 26, 1824, and Nathaniel Adams to John Farmer, Mar. 1, 1824, Farmer Papers.
46. William Plumer Sr. to John Farmer, Jan. 28, 1825, and John Farmer to John Kelly, Feb. 22, 1826, Farmer Papers; "Contents" and "Documents," *NHHS Collections* I (1824): iv, 297–336; "Communication respecting the Wheelwright Deed," *NHHS Collections* II (1827): 137–38.
47. "Contents" and "Documents, Relating to the History of New-Hampshire," *NHHS Collections* I (1824): [iii]–iv, 298.
48. Plumer Sr. to Farmer, Dec. 26, 1823, and Jan. 28, 1825.
49. Albert G. Greene and William G. Goddard, "Preface," *RIHS Collections* IV (1838): 3–4; Publications Committee Report, [1834], "Correspondence and Reports, 1822–1838," vol. 59 (I), 141, RIHS Archives.
50. "Trustee Records, 1822–1848," vol. 25, 52, 57–58, 71, 74, 89, 92, 100, 105, 116, 128, Publications Committee Report [1834], "Correspondence and Reports, 1822–1838," vol. 59 (I), 141, and Publications Committee Reports, Jul. 20, 1835, Oct. 22, 1835, and [1836], "Correspondence and reports, 1835–1838," vol. 60 (II), 8, 62, 85, for examples of Rhode Island Historical Society purchases, see vol. 59 (aka I), 133, or vol. 60 (aka II), 4, RIHS Archives; *RIHS Collections* I–V (1827–43).
51. Greene, "Preface," *RIHS Collections* IV (1838): 3–4; Robert Walsh to Thomas Webb, November 8, 1835, "Correspondence and Reports, 1835–1838," vol. 60 (aka II), 67, RIHS Archives.
52. Romeo Elton, "Memoir of the Rev. John Callendar," *RIHS Collections* IV (1838): 10–23; "Romeo Elton," in Wilson and Fiske, *Appleton's Cyclopædia*, II:338–39.
53. Peter Du Ponceau, "A Grammar of the Language of the Lenni Lenape or Delaware Indians, Translated from the German Manuscript of the Late Rev. David Zeisberger, for the American Philosophical Society," *APS Transactions*, new series, III (1830): 94; Lester Cappon, "Jared Sparks: The Preparation of an Editor," *MHS Proceedings*, 3rd series, 90 (1978): 3–21, esp. 20–21; Joseph Story to Jared Sparks, Oct. 19, 1833, MS Sparks 153, Sparks Collection. See also Butterfield, "Archival," 81–104; Cappon, "American," 375–76, 398–400; Dorothy Twohig, "The Satisfaction I Feel in Having My Papers So Properly Arranged: The Papers of George Washington," *Virginia Cavalcade* 48, no. 4 (1999): 148–57; Scott F. Casper, *Constructing American Lives: Biography and Culture in Nineteenth-Century America* (Chapel Hill: University of North Carolina Press, 1999), 194.
54. J. Francis Fisher, "Inedited Letters of William Penn; Copied, in London, from the Originals in the Possession of the Hon. John Penn," *HSP Memoirs* III, part I (1834): 281–85; Benjamin Chew, "Petition of the Indians to Governor Markham," *HSP*

Memoirs III, part II (1836), 206; J. Francis Fisher, "Inedited letters of William Penn, from the Originals or Authentic copies," *HSP Memoirs* IV, part I (1840): 170.

55. Greene, "Preface," and John Callendar, "Historical Discourse, on the Civil and Religious Affairs of the Colony of Rhode Island," *RIHS Collections* IV (1838): 3–4, 176.
56. "Introduction," *Collections of the Georgia Historical Society* I (1840): vi–ix; W. B. Stevens, "History of Georgia," *Southern Quarterly Review* 13, no. 26 (1848): 470–501.
57. George Wymberley Jones De Renne (attrib.), *Observations on Doctor Stevens's History of Georgia* (Savannah: n.p., 1849), 27–28, emphasis in original; Standing Committee Report, Oct. 7, 1845, Georgia Historical Society Archives, Savannah.
58. "Collections of the Massachusetts Historical Society, for the Year 1792," *Monthly Anthology and Boston Review*, Oct. 1, 1804; "Collections of the Massachusetts Historical Society, for the Year 1799," *Monthly Anthology and Boston Review*, Jun. 1, 1806.
59. George Bancroft, *A History of the United States: From the Discovery of the American Continent to the Present Time*, 10 vols. (Boston: Published by Charles Bowen, 1834–1874) for reference to the Connecticut Historical Society see VI:ix, and for sample footnote references to historical society publications see V:115 and VI:281; "Minutes, 1825, 1839–1857," 58, CHS Archives; Richard Hildreth, *The History of the United States of America: From the Discovery of the Continent to the Organization of Government Under the Federal Constitution*, 3 vols. (New York: Harper and Brothers, Publishers, 82 Cliff Street, 1849), I:v, III:549–64; Dunlap, *American*, 123–33; Tucker, *Massachusetts*.
60. Du Ponceau, "Inaugural," 5–32, esp. 25; Virginia Historical Society, "Report," 9; Carson, *History*, I:174.
61. Virginia Historical Society, "Report," 9; Du Ponceau, "Inaugural," 25; Glynn, *Reading*, 95.

CHAPTER FIVE: "LESS REPULSIVE TO THE GENERAL READER"

1. CHS Logs; "United States Census 1850." Index and images, *FamilySearch*, https://www.familysearch.org/search/collection/1401638, citing NARA microfilm publication M432, Washington, D.C., National Archives and Records Administration, accessed Aug. 4, 2017 (henceforth 1850 Census).
2. U.S. Census Bureau, "Population of 100 Largest Urban Places: 1850," https://www.census.gov/population/www/documentation/twps0027/tab08.txt; "Connecticut Population by Town, 1830–1890," Connecticut Department of Economic and Community Development, https://portal.ct.gov/SOTS/Register-Manual/SectionVII/Population-1830-1890; email, Joe Festa, New-York Historical Society, to author, Oct. 2, 2014; Massachusetts Historical Society, "Massachusetts Historical Society Archives, 1758–1934, bulk 1891–1899, Collection Guide," see series I.A. Vol. OS 1, http://www.masshist.org/collection-guides/view/fa0356. The Massachusetts Historical Society visitor register contains an estimated twenty signatures per page and

320 pages with signatures, per emails, Andrea Cronin, Massachusetts Historical Society, to author, Jul. 13 and 17, 2013.

3. Pfitzer, *Popular*, 6, 22, 42, 57; Casper, *Constructing*, 23–28.
4. "Advertisement to the First Edition," *HSP Memoirs* I, part 1 (1826): [v]; "Introductory Address from the Historical Society," *MHS Collections* I (1792): 2–4; "Preface," *N-YHS Collections* I (1811): iv.
5. Du Ponceau, "Inaugural," 5–32, esp. 25; Virginia Historical Society, "Report," 9.
6. Introductory Note, *Register of Pennsylvania* I, no. 1 (1828), 1; Du Ponceau, "Inaugural," 28.
7. Du Ponceau, "Inaugural," 24–25; Carson, *History*, I:175; "Society Minutes, 1824–1843," 46, Box I-1–3, HSP Archives; Deborah Norris Logan to Samuel Hazard, Feb. 21, 1829, and Apr. 17, 1830, Hazard Family Papers, Historical Society of Pennsylvania, Philadelphia.
8. Most diaries and journals published before 1840 in *American Diaries* did not appear in historical society publications per Laura Arksey, Nancy Pries, and Marcia Reed, *American Diaries: An Annotated Bibliography of Published American Diaries and Journals, Volume 1: Diaries Written from 1492 to 1844* (Detroit: Gale Research, 1983). Cappon, "American," 385–400; Nigel Hamilton, *Biography: A Brief History* (Cambridge, MA: Harvard University Press, 2007), 3–4.
9. William Duane, ed., *Passages from the Remembrancer of Christopher Marshall* (Philadelphia: Printed by James Crissy, 1839), iii–iv; Green, "Cultural," 61–82, esp. 64; Pfitzer, *Popular*, 10–11; David Jaffee, "The Village Enlightenment in New England, 1760–1820," *William and Mary Quarterly* 47, no. 3 (1990): 345–46.
10. John T. Cunningham, "Barber and Howe: History's Camp Followers," *New Jersey History* 102, no. 1/2 (1984): 64–72; Jaffee, "Village," 327–46; John W. Barber, *History and Antiquities of New Haven (Conn.): From Its Earliest Settlement to the Present Time, Collected and Compiled from the Most Authentic Sources* (New Haven: Published and Sold by J. W. Barber, and by the Booksellers in New Haven, 1831); John Warner Barber, *Connecticut Historical Collections, Containing a General Collection of Interesting Facts, Traditions, Biographical Sketches, Anecdotes, &c. Relating to the History and Antiquities of Every Town in Connecticut* (New Haven: Published by Durrie and Peck and J. W. Barber, Printed by B. L. Hamlen, 1836; 2nd ed., New Haven: Published by Durrie and Peck and J. W. Barber, 1846).
11. Barber, *New Haven*, 3–5, 42; Pfitzer, *Popular*, 6, 42.
12. Volumes by Barber and collaborators/imitators: Barber (New Haven, 1832; Connecticut, 1836, 2nd ed., 1846; Massachusetts, 1839; New England, New York, and New Jersey, 1841); Barber and Howe (New York, 1841; New Jersey, 1844); Howe (Virginia, 1845; Ohio, 1847; Great West, 1852); and Day (Pennsylvania, 1843). Despite title similarity, Benjamin F. French's *La. Historical Collections* did not follow Barber's style. Henry Howe, *Historical Collections of the Great West*, 2 vols. (Cincinnati:

Published by Henry Howe, at E. Morgan, 1852), I:8; Cunningham, "Barber," 66–67, 71; Pfitzer, *Popular*, 6, 42.

13. John Warner Barber, *Historical Collections, Being a General Collection of Interesting Facts, Traditions, Biographical Sketches, Anecdotes, &c., Relating to the History and Antiquities of Every Town in Massachusetts, with Geographical Descriptions* (Worcester: Published by Dorr, Howland, 1839), iii–iv; John Warner Barber to Thaddeus Mason Harris, Mar. 30, 1839, "Correspondence, Vol. IV, 1834, 1837–1849," Box 17, Series I, Corresponding Secretary Records, MHS Archives.
14. "Monthly Meeting," Mar. 26, 1839, *MHS Proceedings* II (1880): 127–128; Dorr and Howland to Thaddeus Mason Harris, Mar. 29, 1839, and Thaddeus Mason Harris to Dorr and Howland, Apr. 1839, "Correspondence, Vol. IV, 1834, 1837–1849," Series I, Corresponding Secretary Records, MHS Archives.
15. Dorr and Howland to Harris, Mar. 29 and Apr. 3, 1839; Barber to Harris, Mar. 30, 1839; Harris to Dorr and Howland, Apr. 1839; Cunningham, "Barber," 71.
16. Henry Howe, *Historical Collections of Ohio: Containing a Collection of the Most Interesting Facts, Traditions, Biographical Sketches, Anecdotes, Etc. Relating to Its General and Local History: With Descriptions of Its Counties, Principal Towns and Villages* (Cincinnati: Published for the author by Derby, Bradley, 1847), 3, emphasis in original; Barber, *Massachusetts*; Pfitzer, *Popular*, 3–10; Jaffee, "Village," 345–46.
17. "Forefather's Song," *MHS Collections*, 3rd ser., VII (1838): 29–30; Howe, *Ohio*, 3; "List of Portraits in the Hall of the Historical Society," *MHS Collections*, 3rd ser., VII (1838): 285–91.
18. "Circular," *HSP Memoirs* I, part I (1826): 23–25, and IV, part II (1850): 105–12; Sherman Day, *Historical Collections of the State of Pennsylvania; Containing a Copious Selection of the Most Interesting Facts, Traditions, Biographical Sketches, Anecdotes, Etc. Relating to its History and Antiquities* (Philadelphia: Published by George W. Gorton; New Haven: Durrie and Peck, 1843).
19. Ronald J. Zboray and Mary Saracino Zboray, *Everyday Ideas: Socioliterary Experience among Antebellum New Englanders* (Knoxville: University of Tennessee Press, 2006), 205; "Special Meeting," Jun. 5, 1833, "Monthly Meeting," Jul. 25, 1833, and "Monthly Meeting," Sept. 26, 1833, *MHS Proceedings* I (1879): 471, 473, 477–78; "Monthly Meeting," Mar. 21, 1842, and "Monthly Meeting," Oct. 30, 1845, *MHS Proceedings* II (1880): 226–27, 269, 326; Martin Green, *The Problem of Boston: Some Readings in Cultural History* (New York: W. W. Norton, 1966), 75–76; Bickford, *Connecticut*, 21–29, 31–32; "Minutes, 1825, 1839–1857," 56, 66, 68, 176, 177, CHS Archives; "Historical Lecture," *Connecticut Courant*, Dec. 23, 1843, [2]; Tucker, *Massachusetts*, 67–72; "Trustee Records, 1822–1848," vol. 25, 87, 89, 97, 100, 111, 125, RIHS Archives.
20. Charles Francis Adams, *Diary of Charles Francis Adams, Volume 7, June 1836–February 1838*, ed. Marc Friedlænder, Robert J. Taylor, Celeste Walker, Richard Alan Ryerson (Cambridge: Belknap Press of Harvard University Press, 1986), 158–59, 365, 385–86;

"D'Aulney and La Tour," "Commission to Sir Edmund Andros," and "Papers Relative to His Administration," *MHS Collections*, 3rd series, VII (1838): 90–121, 139–95; Tucker, *Massachusetts*, 67–72, 491, 547.

21. "Minutes, 1825, 1839–1857," 176, 177, CHS Archives; Vail, *Knickerbocker*, 91.
22. Tucker, *Massachusetts*, 39–40; Arius Nye, "A Fragment of the Early History of the State of Ohio—An Address Delivered at Marietta, on the 48th Anniversary of the First Settlement of the State," in *Transactions of the Historical and Philosophical Society of Ohio* (Cincinnati: G. W. Bradbury, 1839), 306; Vail, *Knickerbocker*, 375–82; Bickford, *Connecticut*, 22.
23. Len Travers, *Celebrating the Fourth: Independence Day and the Rites of Nationalism in the Early Republic* (Amherst: University of Massachusetts Press, 1997), 225; "Historical Commemoration," Hartford *Daily Courant*, Apr. 9, 1840; "The Historical Celebration," Hartford *Daily Courant*, Apr. 24, 1840; Bickford, *Connecticut.*
24. "The Historical Celebration," Hartford *Daily Courant*, Apr. 25 and 24, 1840; "Hymn," Hartford *Daily Courant*, Apr. 22, 1840; Bickford, *Connecticut*, 31–32.
25. "The Historical Celebration," Hartford *Daily Courant*, Apr. 24, 1840; Kiracofe, "Jamestown Jubilees," 35–68.
26. Philip Hone, *The Diary of Philip Hone, 1828–1851*, ed. Bayard Tuckerman (New York: Dodd, Mead, 1910), 355–59; "The Historical Celebration," Hartford *Daily Courant*, Apr. 24, 27, 28, and May 1, 1840.
27. Bickford, *Connecticut*, 25–26, 28.
28. "Minutes, 1825, 1829–1857," 7, 15, CHS Archives; Bickford, *Connecticut*, 25–26, 28; Robert B. Downs, *Henry Barnard* (Boston: Twayne, 1977), 16–22.
29. "Com. of Const. of 1639–40 Costume Party in His. Socty Rooms," 1840, Henry Barnard Papers, Connecticut Historical Society, Hartford; "The Historical Celebration," Hartford *Daily Courant*, Apr. 24, 25 and 27, 1849; "Celebration of the Connecticut Historical Society," *Alexandria Gazette*, Apr. 30, 1840; Bickford, *Connecticut*, 27–28.
30. "Com. of Const."; CHS Accessions, 15.
31. "Historical Commemoration," Hartford *Daily Courant*, Apr. 9, 1840, emphasis added; Hannah Whittelsey to Judge Williams, Apr. 20, 1840, Recording Secretary Charles Hosmer Correspondence, CHS Archives.
32. Analysis based on examination of accessions, donation records, or equivalents for the 1840s for the American Antiquarian Society; New England Historic Genealogical Society; Pilgrim Society; and historical societies of Connecticut, Georgia, Maine, Maryland, Massachusetts, New Hampshire, New Jersey, New York, Pennsylvania, Rhode Island, and University of North Carolina.
33. Christopher Columbus Baldwin to John Farmer, Oct. 2, 1833, Farmer Papers; Baldwin, *Place*, 149–50, 224; Bickford, *Connecticut*, 21–29; Downs, *Henry Barnard*, 9–17; "Library Accession Book I, 1825–1862," vol. I, 7–45, HSP Archives; "Trustee Records,

1822–1848," vol. 25, 66, 87, RIHS Archives; Jaffee, *People*, 222; Green, "Cultural," 64; Baldwin, *Place*, 149–50; Dunlap, *American*, 69–78; Gura, *American*, 88–92.

34. Thomas Robbins, *Diary of Thomas Robbins, D.D., 1796–1854,* edited and annotated by Increase N. Tarbox, 2 vols. (Boston: Beacon Press, Thomas Todd printer, 1886–87), II:781; CHS Accessions, for donations of shoes, see 15, 23, 132, 140, 159, 187, 190, 191, 254, 266, 270, 289, 295, 296, 298, 303, 305, 325; tree samples, 157, 201; tongs, plates, and flat iron, 132, 147, 259, 267; military items, 170, 177, 189; and industrialization, 108, 206.
35. "Connecticut Historical Rooms," Hartford *Times*, Sept. 20, 1845; CHS Accessions, for Hosmer's gifts, see 86, 88, 118, for Harriet Johnson's, 138.
36. For discussion of artifacts, see Keith Tony Beutler, "The Memory Revolution in America and Memory of the American Revolution, 1790–1840" (Ph.D. diss., Washington University, 2005); Steenshorne, "Past," 175–225; Briann Greenfield, *Out of the Attic: Inventing Antiques in Twentieth-Century New England* (Amherst: University of Massachusetts Press, 2009), 4.
37. "Minutes, 1825, 1839–1857," 178–79, and Gov. Trumbull's Hat Committee, "Report," [May 1, 1849], Recording Secretary Charles Hosmer Correspondence, CHS Archives; "Man's Hat," (#1950.203.0), CHS eMuseum.
38. Simeon Hart to Charles Hosmer, Mar. 15, 1841, and Maria Ledyard to Simeon Hart, Jan. 25, 1841, Recording Secretary Charles Hosmer Correspondence, and object files for Ledyard waistcoat (# 1841.5.0) and shirt (# 1844.48.0), CHS Archives; CHS Accessions, 68, 214; Susan Campbell, "Ledyard's Legend: Was Revolutionary War Colonel Killed with Own Sword in Battle?" *Hartford Courant*, Sept. 6, 2001.
39. Thomas Day to Gov. John Cotton Smith, Mar. 18, 1841, Recording Secretary Charles Hosmer Correspondence, CHS Archives; CHS Accessions, 68; "Connecticut Historical Rooms," Hartford *Times*, Sept. 20, 1845; "Col. William Ledyard Waistcoat" (#1845.5.0), CHS eMuseum; Jared Sparks, "Journal," Jun. 15, 1847, MS Sparks 141k, Sparks Collection.
40. Ledyard to Hart; Hart to Hosmer; CHS Accessions, 68, 214; "Col. William Ledyard Waistcoat" (#1845.5.0), and "Col. William Ledyard Shirt" (#1844.48.0), CHS eMuseum; Kathleen M. Brown, *Foul Bodies: Cleanliness in Early America* (New Haven, CT: Yale University Press, 2009), 164–74.
41. "Col. William Ledyard Waistcoat" and "Col. William Ledyard Shirt," CHS eMuseum; Brown, *Foul*, 251–90.
42. Robbins, *Diary*, I:iii–v, II:967–68, 971, 988–91; Bickford, *Connecticut*, 28, 35, 37.
43. Robbins, *Diary*, II:791, 956, 969, 979, 986–88, 994; Bickford, *Connecticut*, 28, 35, 37.
44. Robbins, *Diary*, II:986–94; Bickford, *Connecticut*, 28, 35, 37.
45. "A Walk about Hartford," *Boston Courier* Jul. 24, 1845; "Connecticut Historical Society," Hartford *Times*, Sept. 20, 1845; Robbins, *Diary*, II:993–94; Bickford, *Connecticut*, 6–23; Wadsworth Athenaeum Museum of Art, "Wadsworth Athenaeum History," https://www.thewadsworth.org/about/history/; CHS Accessions.

46. Bickford, *Connecticut,* 5–23.
47. David R. Brigham, *Public Culture in the Early Republic: Peale's Museum and Its Audience* (Washington: Smithsonian Institution Press, 1995), 5–9, 83–106; William S. Hendon, Frank Costa, and Robert Allan Rosenberg, "The General Public and the Art Museum: Case Studies of Visitors to Several Institutions Identify Characteristics of Their Publics," *American Journal of Economics and Sociology* 48, no. 2 (1989): 231–43; Kristian H. Nielsen, "'What Things Mean in Our Daily Lives': A History of Museum Curating and Visiting in the Science Museum's Children's Gallery from c. 1929 to 1969," *British Journal for the History of Science* 47, no. 3 (2014): 505–38.
48. CHS Logs.
49. See appendix 2.
50. Total number of actual visitors is unknown, as is whether signers represented a statistically representative sample. Individuals who signed constitute a self-selected set. Therefore, signers are expressed in percentages as representative of known visitors. Census-based data is not a representative sample of either all visitors or known visitors and not expressed in percentages. Robbins, "Diary," 987, 990; CHS Logs, Sept. 5 and Oct. 1, 1850.
51. Hendon, "General," 230.
52. CHS Logs, Jan. 25, Feb. 11 and 16, May 17, Jun. 19, Jul. 13 and 26, Aug. 12 and 21, Sept. 2 and 23, and Oct. 5, 1850.
53. Irish visitors included the Paige family, whose children were baptized in the Episcopal church. CHS Logs, Mar. 14, Aug. 13 and 17, 1850; Thomas M. Clark, Charles J. Hoadly, and Gurdon W. Russell, *Contributions to the History of Christ Church, Hartford* (Hartford: Belknap and Warfield, 1895), 585.
54. CHS Logs, Aug. 30, 1850; Mary Kelley, *Learning to Stand and Speak: Women, Education, and Public Life in America's Republic* (Durham: Published for the Omohundro Institute of Early American History and Culture by the University of North Carolina Press, 2006), 137; McMahon, *Mere Equals*, 59–63.
55. United States Census Bureau, "Chapter B: Population Characteristics and Migration," *Historical Statistics of the United States, 1789–1957,* Jun. 1949, 27; Robbins, "Diary," 987, 990; CHS Logs, Jan. 1, Feb. 9, 16, 21, and 22, May 25, Jul. 25, Sept. 21, and Nov. 16, 1850; Sarah Francis, Wethersfield, CT (#156), Harvey S. White, Middletown, CT (#207), and Sylvester Bliss, Wilmington, NY (#2424), 1850 Census.
56. CHS Logs, Jan. 1, Aug. 30, and Sept. 4 and 6, 1850; Abigail H., Charles P., Emily A., and Elizabeth Frost, Springfield, MA (#1243), Fredrick S., Julia D., and Lucy S. Wildman, Fairfield, CT (#436), and David D. and Fanny Wildman, Fairfield, CT (#642), 1850 Census.
57. *Sherman & Smith's Railroad, Steam Boat, & Stage Route Map of New England, New York, and Canada.* (New York: n.i., 1850); CHS Logs, Feb. 21 and 27, Mar. 5 and 21, Apr. 30, May 4, 6, 11, 13, 17, and 28, Jun. 19 and 27, Jul. 11, 17, and 28, Aug. 7, 8, 16, 19, 24,

and 28, Sept. 5, 11, 12, 27, and 30, Oct. 1, 7, 22, and 30, Nov. 23 and 27, and Dec. 2 and 5, 1850; William P. Palmer, Norwich, CT (#2217), 1850 Census; Frederic Denison, *Notes of the Baptists and Their Principles in Norwich, Conn., from the Settlement of the Town to 1850* (Norwich: Manning, 1857), 84–85.

58. CHS Logs, Apr. 20, Jul. 29, Aug. 9 and 20, Sept. 11 and 25, Oct. 16, 18, and 20, 1850; E. K. Chamberlain, Sarah M. Kendrick, and Kendrick H. Chamberlain, Cincinnati, OH (#1537), Henry, John H., L. Jacob, and Mulford Starr, Medford, NJ (#17), George, Georgianna, Carolina, and Harriet Nock, Windsor, CT (#208), and John S. Charles C., Mary J., and Ellen F. Baldwin, Hartford, CT (#2232), 1850 Census; Francis S. Reader, *History of the Newspapers of Beaver County, Pennsylvania* (New Brighton, PA: F. S. Reader and Son, 1905), 39–40; Ellery Bicknell Crane, ed., *Historic Homes and Institutions and Genealogical and Personal Memoirs of Worcester County, Massachusetts, With a History of Worcester Society of Antiquity* (New York: Lewis, 1907), I:312.

59. CHS Logs, Apr. 27, Aug. 14, 19, 28, and 31, Sept. 5 and 27, and Oct. 11 and 16, Nov. 30, 1850; Abel and Martha Driggs, Vernon, CT (#71), Anne and Susan Lyman, Hartford, CT (#2169), and Oliver B. Hayes, Hartford, CT, 1850 Census; *Vital Records of Bolton to 1854 and Vernon to 1852* (Hartford: Connecticut Historical Society, 1909), 155.

60. Trinity visitors included three on Feb. 9, two on May 25, and one each on Jan. 1, Feb. 11, 16, 21, and 22, and Jul. 25 (a repeat from May 25). CHS Logs, Jan. 1, Feb. 9, 11, 16, 21, and 22, May 25, Jul. 21, Sept. 14, 19, and 21 and Dec. 25, 1850; Charles Hoadley Alumni File, College Archives, Trinity College, Hartford, CT; Charles J. Hoadley, Hartford, CT (#3007), 1850 Census.

61. CHS Logs, Jan. 1, and Sept. 9, 19, and 21, 1850; Charles J. Hoadley, Hartford, CT (#3007), John D. Jones, Cincinnati, OH (#68), William D. Ely, Hartford, CT (#1630), and Eliza L. Butler, Hartford, CT (#1488), 1850 Census; "Supplement to the Obituary Record of Graduates of Yale University, 1909–1910," *Obituary Record of Graduates of Yale University Deceased from June, 1900, to June, 1910* (New Haven: Tuttle, Morehouse and Taylor, 1910), 1345; Moses S. Beach and William Ely, *The Ely Ancestry: Lineage of Richard Ely of Plymouth, England* (New York: Calumet Press, 1902), 311–12; David F. Ransom, "The Butler-McCook House," *Hog River Journal* (now *Connecticut Explored*), https://www.ctexplored.org/the-butler-mccook-house/.

62. CHS Logs, Jun. 17, Jul. 4, and Sept. 5 and 9, 1850; Daniel Cooke, Vernon, CT (#179), Horace Childs, Henniker, NH (#271), Benj. Colby, Henniker, NH (#211), Amos Allan, Norwich, CT (#2230), David L. and Lucinda C. Maples, Norwich, CT (#2117), Orrin M. Rising, Suffield, CT (#384), and William Palmer, Hartford, CT (#2630), 1850 Census; "United States Census 1860," Index and images, *FamilySearch*, https://familysearch.org/search/collection/1473181, citing NARA microfilm publication M653, Washington, D.C., National Archives and Records Administration, accessed Aug. 4, 2017 (henceforth 1860 Census).

63. CHS Logs, Jun. 7 and Aug. 30, 1850; Eleazer R. Crane, Mansfield, CT (#260), and Charles Tudor, Granby, CT (#412), 1850 Census; Eleazer R. Crane, Mansfield, CT (#434), and Charles Tudor, Granby, CT (#84), 1860 Census.
64. CHS Logs, May 2, Jun. 27, Jul. 4 and 15, Aug. 12, Sept. 2, Oct. 30, and Dec. 30, 1850; Nicholas Killam, Hartford, CT (#2603), Samuel Fitch, Somers, CT (#107), Joseph B. and Charles Metcalf, Somers, CT (163), Hatfield Soule, Chicopee, MA (#2338), David N. Northway, Granville, MA (#73), James C. Taylor, Chicopee, MA (2569), George P. Bradley, Stockbridge, MA (#90), and Sophrona and James E. Woodbridge, Canton, CT (#99), 1850 Census; Nicholas Killim, New York City, NY (#801), Samuel Fitch, Stafford, CT (#238), Joseph B. Medcalf, Tolland, CT (#734), Hatfield N. Soule, Lowell, MA (#2213), David N. Northway, Granville, MA (241), James C. Taylor, Woburn, MA (#2597), George P. Bradley, Stockbridge, MA (#657), and James Woodbridge, New Haven, CT (#41), 1860 Census; J. A. Spalding, *Illustrated Popular Biography of Connecticut* (Hartford: Press of Case, Lockwood, and Brainard, Published by J. A. Spalding, 1891), 353; Louis Mitchell, *The Woodbridge Record: Being an Account of the Descendants of the Rev. John Woodbridge, of Newbury, Mass.* (New Haven: Privately Printed, 1883), 210.

CHAPTER SIX: "AN OBLIVIOUS SOCIETY"

1. John Kelly to John Farmer, May 13, 1825, Farmer Papers, emphasis in original.
2. "Report of John Howland," Oct. 1, 1822, "Correspondence and Reports, 1822–1838," vol. 59 (aka I), 5, and Edwin C. Stone to T. C. Hartshorn, Jul. 28, 1847, and William R. Staples to T. C. Hartshorn, Jun. 2, 1848, "Correspondence and Reports, 1845–1852," vol. 62 (aka IV), 60, 80, RIHS Archives.
3. Christopher Columbus Baldwin to John Farmer, Jan. 28, 1832, and Jun. 3 and Oct. 2, 1833, Farmer Papers.
4. Henle, "Means," 103–18, esp. 107–10.
5. Analysis based on manuscript donation records, printed donation notices, and library catalogues for the American Antiquarian Society; American Historical Society; American Philosophical Society's Historical and Literary Committee; New England Historic Genealogical Society; Pilgrim Society; and the historical societies of Connecticut, Georgia, Maine, Maryland, Massachusetts, Missouri, New Hampshire, New Jersey, New York, Pennsylvania, Rhode Island, University of North Carolina, and Virginia.
6. "Circular to Individuals," *Annals of the Cincinnati Historical Society* (Cincinnati: Published by Order of the Society, Printed by R. P. Donogh, 1845), 6; "Fourth Annual Meeting," *Annals of the Missouri Historical & Philosophical Society, No. 1* (Jefferson City: Metropolitan Print, 1848), 24; Virginia Historical Society, "Report," 8–10.
7. Casper, *Constructing*.

8. Alabama Historical Society, *Constitution*, 10; American Historical Society, *Transactions*, 5; Virginia Historical Society, "Report," 10.
9. Alabama Historical Society, *Constitution*, 9; Harriet E. Amos Doss and Sara Frear, "Octavia Walton, Le Vert," *Encyclopedia of Alabama*, http://www.encyclopediaofalabama.org/article/h-2355; "Octavia Walton Le Vert," Alabama Women's Hall of Fame, http://www.awhf.org/levert.html; "Report of the Standing Committee," Oct. 7, 1845, "Correspondence & Reports, 1845–1852," vol. 62 (aka IV), 2, RIHS Archives.
10. Jared Sparks, "Journal," Mar. 7, 1831, MS Sparks 141g, Sparks Collection; Ostrowski, *Books*, 87–89, 103–5.
11. CHS Accessions, 91 (private), 156 (lieutenant); "Stated Meeting, May 4, 1847," *Proceedings of the New-York Historical Society for the Year of 1847*, 60–61; "Donations Announced November 5th, 1846," *NJHS Proceedings* II, no. 1 (1846, reprint 1968): 7; "The Cabinet Keeper of the Northern District Respectfully Reports," "Correspondence & Reports, 1835–1838," vol. 60 (aka II), 143, RIHS Archives; "Catalog of Books, Pamphlets, Manuscripts, Maps, Belonging to the Library of the Maine Historical Society, 1822–1872," 230, Maine Historical Society Archives, Maine Historical Society, Portland, ME; Jabez Haskell Hayden, *Records of the Connecticut Line of the Hayden Family* (Windsor Locks, CT: Case, Lockwood, and Brainard, 1888), 131–32.
12. Deborah Norris Logan, "Diary," Feb. 6 and 8, 1818, vol. 50 (aka 8), 92, Logan Family Papers (collection 379).
13. CHS Accessions, 28 (quitclaim deed), 173 (Bidwell letter); *New England Families, Genealogical and Memorial . . . Compiled Under the Editorial Supervision of William Richard Cutter* (New York: Lewis Historical Publishing Company, 1913), III:1150; "Library Accession Book I, 1825–1862," 11, vol. I-7-45, HSP Archives; "Northern Cabinet Report, for 1824–1825," Jul. 19, 1825, "Correspondence & Reports," vol. 59 (aka I), 47, RIHS Archives.
14. CHS Accessions, 263; "Minutes, 1825, 1839–1847," 135, CHS Archives; Edward Hooker, *The Descendants of Rev. Thomas Hooker, Hartford, Connecticut, 1586–1908*, ed. Margaret Huntington Hooker (Rochester: printed for Margaret Huntington Hooker, 1909), 168.
15. Donations to the Northern District, 1846, "Correspondence & Reports, 1835–1838," vol. 62 (aka IV), 13, RIHS Archives; Susan Zaeske, *Signatures of Citizenship: Petitioning, Antislavery, and Women's Political Identity* (Durham: University of North Carolina Press, 2003); Gerda Lerner, "The Political Activities of Antislavery Women," 112–28 in *The Majority Finds Its Past: Placing Women in History* (New York: Oxford University Press, 1979); Deborah Bingham Van Broekhoven, *The Devotion of These Women: Rhode Island in the Antislavery Network* (Amherst: University of Massachusetts Press, 2002); "Joseph Leonard Tillinghast," *Biographical Dictionary*

of the United States Congress, 1774–Present, http://bioguide.congress.gov/scripts/biodisplay.pl?index=T000272.

16. "Monthly Meeting," Dec. 26, 1834, *MHS Proceedings* I (1879): 498; "Anne Pollard at One Hundred Years of Age," Massachusetts Historical Society, Boston, http://www.masshist.org/database/viewer.php?item_id=1775&pid=15; "Donations to the Cabinet of the Maryland Historical Society," 2, Maryland Historical Society Archives; CHS Accessions, 191 and 315.
17. Julie Des Jardins, *Women and the Historical Enterprise in America: Gender, Race, and the Politics of Memory, 1880–1945* (Chapel Hill: University of North Carolina Press, 2003), 3.
18. "Report of the Cabinet-Keeper of the Northern District," Jul. 19, 1841, and David Benedict to unknown, Rhode Island Historical Society, Apr. 10, 1841, "Correspondence & Reports, 1838–1845," vol. 61 (aka III), 98, 100, RIHS Archives.
19. CHS Accessions, 95 (brocade), 101 (curtain, #1844.21.0), 132 (iron), 153 (tomb), and 251 (embroidery, #1845.30.0).
20. William Bentley, *The Diary of William Bentley, D.D., Pastor of the East Church, Salem, Massachusetts, Volume 3: January, 1803–December, 1810* (Salem, MA: Essex Institute, 1911), 103–4; Henle, "Widow's," 331–32.
21. Logan, "Diary," Mar. 19, Aug. 7, Sept. 12 and 27, 1825, vol. 50 (aka 8), 87, 129, 146–47; Deborah Norris Logan to Peter Du Ponceau, Jan. 1, 1820, Peter Stephen Du Ponceau Collection, American Philosophical Society, Philadelphia.
22. Hannah Mather Crocker, *Reminiscences and Traditions of Boston*, ed. Eileen Hunt Botting and Sarah L. Houser, with Michael Desjardins, Katherine Mastrucci, John Miner, and Courtney Smotherman (Boston: New England Historic Genealogical Society, 2011), xviii–xix.
23. Crocker, *Reminiscences*, xviii–xix, 40–41, 258, 357–58; Henle, "Widow's," 327–28.
24. Hannah Mather Crocker to Abiel Holmes, Oct. 19, 1822, "Letters to the Corresponding Secretary, 1812–1833," Corresponding Secretary Records, 1st series, vol. II, MHS Archives; Henle, "Widow's," 337.
25. AAS Donations, [1], [3], [8], 11, 12–13, 28, 29, 42, 50–51, 53, 62, 134, 253; "Meeting of June 1, 1814," *AAS Proceedings*, 43; Hannah Mather Crocker to Thaddeus Mason Harris, Jun. 13, 1814, American Antiquarian Society Archives; "Adjourned Meeting," Sept. 19, 1792, "Adjourned Meeting," Jun. 11, 1794, and "Special Meeting," Dec. 20, 1794, *MHS Proceedings* I (1879): 43, 69, 78, and 116; "Acknowledgement of Donations," *MHS Collections*, 2nd series, VII (1818): 298.
26. Kelley, *Learning*, 191–244, esp. 202–3; Kate Davies, *Catharine Macaulay and Mercy Otis Warren: The Revolutionary Atlantic and the Politics of Gender* (New York: Oxford University Press, 2005), 231–47, 305; Nancy Rubin Stuart, *The Muse of the Revolution: The Secret Pen of Mercy Otis Warren and the Founding of a Nation* (Boston: Beacon Press, 2008), iii.

27. Hannah Mather Crocker to Thaddeus Mason Harris, Jun. 13, 1814, American Antiquarian Society Archives; Hannah Mather Crocker, "Antiquarian Researches," in Post, *Observations on the Real Rights of Women*, 27–36; Hannah Mather Crocker, "Antiquarian Researches," (3 drafts), Folder 4, Box 10, Mather Family Papers; Eileen Hunt Botting and Sarah L. Houser, "'Drawing the Line of Equality': Hannah Mather Crocker on Women's Rights," *American Political Science Review* 100 (May 2006): 265–87; Henle, "Widow's," 333–34; AAS Donations, 29.
28. Rarity of people donating their own manuscripts based on examination of manuscript donation records, printed donation notices, and library catalogues for the period up to 1850.
29. AAS Donations, 62, 134, 135, 223; Hannah Mather Crocker, "Jephtah's Vow Explained," and "The United Trinity," Folders 1–2, Box 10, Mather Family Papers.
30. James Carnahan Wetmore, *The Wetmore Family of America, and Its Collateral Branches: With Genealogical, Biographical, and Historical Notices* (Albany: Munsell and Rowland, 1861), 308; Hannah Whittelsey to Judge Williams, Apr. 20, 1840, Recording Secretary Charles Hosmer Correspondence, CHS Archives.
31. Whittelsey to Williams, Apr. 20, 1840; CHS Accessions, 23.
32. Whittelsey to Williams, Apr. 20, 1840; Susan P. Schoelwer, *Connecticut Needlework: Women, Art, and Family, 1740–1840* (Hartford: Connecticut Historical Society, 2010), 38–39.
33. CHS Accessions, 23.
34. Whittelsey to Williams, Apr. 20, 1840; CHS Accessions, 23; Kelley, *Learning*, 191–244; Schoelwer, *Connecticut*, 36–37; "Crewel Embroidered Fragment" (Object #1840.7.2), CHS eMuseum.
35. Whittelsey to Williams, Apr. 20, 1840; CHS Accessions, 23; Laurel Thatcher Ulrich, *Age of Homespun: Objects and Stories in the Creation of an American Myth* (New York: Alfred A. Knopf, 2001); Marla R. Miller, *The Needle's Eye: Women and Work in the Age of Revolution* (Amherst: University of Massachusetts Press, 2006).
36. Whittelsey to Williams, Apr. 20, 1840; CHS Accessions, 23.
37. CHS Accessions, 15, 132, 159, 191, 254, 266, 298; "Woman's Shoes" (Object #1843.13.0a,b), CHS eMuseum.
38. James N. Green, "The Rise of Book Publishing," Karen Nipps, "Case Study: Urban Printing," and Jack Larkin, "'Printing Is Something Every Village Has in It': Rural Printing and Publishing," in *History of the Book in America* II:75–127, 137–45, 145–60.
39. Priscilla Maxwell, *The Christian Patriot: Some Recollections of the Late Col. Hugh Maxwell, of Massachusetts; Collected and Preserved by a Daughter* (New York: Published by S. W. Benedict, 1833), [iii]; Thomas Gilpin, *Exiles in Virginia: With Observations on the Conduct of the Society of Friends during the Revolutionary War, Comprising the Official Papers of the Government Relating to That Period, 1777–1778* (Philadelphia: Published for the Subscribers, 1848), vii; William Hunting Howell,

"'Starving Memory': Antinarrating the American Revolution," in *Remembering the Revolution: Memory, History, and Nation Making from Independence to the Civil War*, ed. Michael A. McDonnell, Clare Corbould, Frances M. Clarke, and W. Fitzhugh Brundage, 93–109 (Amherst: University of Massachusetts Press, 2013).

40. Maxwell, *Christian*, [iii]; Beutler, "Memory"; Casper, *Constructing*; Sarah J. Purcell, *Sealed with Blood: War, Sacrifice, and Memory in Revolutionary America* (Philadelphia: University of Pennsylvania Press, 2010); Alfred Young, *Shoemaker and the Tea Party: Memory and the American Revolution* (Boston: Beacon Press, 1999); Alfred Young, *Masquerade: The Life and Times of Deborah Sampson, Continental Soldier* (New York: Knopf, 2004); Stephen G. Hall, *A Faithful Account of the Race: African American Historical Writing in Nineteenth-Century America* (Chapel Hill: University of North Carolina Press, 2009), 17–48.

41. Caroline Gilman, *Letters of Eliza Wilkinson, During the Invasion and Possession of Charlestown, S.C. by the British in the Revolutionary War, Arranged from the Original Manuscripts* (New York: Published by Samuel Colman, 1839), iii; Kelley, *Learning*, 191–244.

42. Abigail Adams, *Letters of Mrs. Adams, the Wife of John Adams, with an Introductory Memoir by her Grandson, Charles Francis Adams* (Boston: Charles C. Little and James Brown, 1840), xii–xxvi; Margaret Morris, *Private Journal, Kept during a Portion of the Revolutionary War, for the Amusement of a Sister* (Philadelphia: Privately printed, 1836), 3–4; Richard Hill, *Letters of Doctor Richard Hill and His Children: Or, The History of a Family, as Told by Themselves, Collected and Arranged by John Jay Smith* (Philadelphia: Privately Printed for the Descendants, 1854), 210; Casper, *Constructing*.

43. The Massachusetts Historical Society collections include a "Branding Iron" (#0461), gift of Azor Gale Archibald, Nov. 25, 1808; "Quarterly Meeting," Jan. 1809, *MHS Proceedings* I (1879): 203; "Extracts from the Society's Circular Letter," *Constitution, By-Laws, Charter, Circular and Members of the Maryland Historical Society* (Baltimore: Printed by John Murphy, 1844), 16; De Bow, "Account," 6.

44. Edward Battle, "Notices of Negro Slavery," *HSP Memoirs* II, part II (1827): 351. O'Brien, *Firsting*; William Law, "Oration Delivered before the Georgia Historical Society at the Celebration of Their First Anniversary," *Collections of the Georgia Historical Society, Volume I* (Savannah: Printed for the Society; Boston: Freeman and Bolles, 1840), 26–27, 33–34.

45. William Plumer Jr. to John Farmer, Apr. 12 and 20, 1836, Farmer Papers; John Farmer to William Plumer Jr. Apr. 15, 1836, Plumer Papers.

46. Richard Bartlett to John Farmer, Dec. 6, 1834 (2 letters), Farmer Papers.

47. Documentation of slavery-related gifts to the Rhode Island Historical Society includes Southern District Cabinet Keeper Report, Jul. 7, 1827, and Northern District Cabinet Keeper Report, Jul. 19, 1825, "Correspondence & Reports, 1822–1838,"

vol. 59 (aka I), 42, 47, Northern District Cabinet Keeper Report, [1837], "Correspondence & Reports, 1835–1838," vol. 60 (aka II), 143, Southern District Cabinet Keeper Report, Jul. 16, 1844, "Correspondence & Reports, 1838–1845," vol. 61 (aka III), 135; and Northern District Cabinet Keeper Report, [1846], and Edwin C. Stone to T. C. Hartshorn, Jul. 28, 1847 "Correspondence & Reports, 1845–1852," vol. 62 (aka IV), 15, 60, RIHS Archives.

48. William Jay, "New York Historical Society," *The New World: A Weekly Family Journal of Popular Literature, Science, Art and News* 6 (Apr. 22, 1843): 482.
49. John H. B. Latrobe, *Memoir of Benjamin Banneker* (Baltimore: Printed by John D. Toy, Published under the Direction of the Society, 1845), 5–6; Maryland Historical Society Second Annual Report, 98–100, Maryland Historical Society Archives; "Extract from the Annual Report of the Maryland Historical Society," *African Repository and Colonial Journal* 22 (1846): 208.
50. Du Ponceau, "Inaugural," 26–28.
51. Report of the Standing Committee, Oct. 7, 1845, "Correspondence & Reports, 1845–1852," vol. 62 (aka IV), 2, RIHS Archives; O'Brien, *Firsting*; Steenshorne, "Past," 54–55.
52. Rhode Island Historical Society to Joseph L. Howard, Mar. 12, 1828, "Correspondence & Reports, 1822–1838," vol. 59 (aka I), 71, RIHS Archives; Amy Lonetree, *Decolonizing Museums: Representing Native America in National and Tribal Museums* (Chapel Hill: University of North Carolina Press, 2012), 9–16.
53. "History Timeline," Cayuga Nation, accessed Sept. 1, 2017, http://cayuganation-nsn.gov/history-timeline.html; New-York Historical Society, *Proceedings of the New-York Historical Society for the Year of 1847*, 64–74.
54. Historical and Philosophical Society of Ohio, *Transactions of the Historical and Philosophical Society of Ohio, Part Second, Vol. I* (Cincinnati: Geo. W. Bradbury, Printers, Published by Order of the Society, 1839), [3]; Alabama Historical Society, *Constitution*, 9–10; Missouri Historical and Philosophical Society, *Annals*, 4–5.
55. "Address by Rev. William Jenks," *AAS Proceedings*, 34.
56. American Historical Society, *Transactions*, 5; see also "Correspondence & Reports, 1835–1838," vol. 60 (aka II), 22–52, RIHS Archives.
57. T. Webb to Edward Bangs, Sept. 9, 1834, Report of the Committee on Antiquities and Aboriginal History, Jan. 6, 1835, T. Webb to [James Stevenson], Nov. 7, 1834, T. Webb. to the Secretary of the Navy, Aug. 9, 1834, T. Webb to Rev. Patten, May 27, 1835, T. Webb to Royal Society of Antiquaries, Oct. 3, 1835, and Charles C. Rafn to T. Webb, Apr. 16, 1835, "Correspondence & Reports, 1835–1838," vol. 60 (aka II), 24, 30, 35, 38, 46, 49, and 52, plus 22–52 generally, RIHS Archives.
58. Report of the Standing Committee; Harlow W. Sheidley, *Sectional Nationalism: Massachusetts Conservative Leaders and the Transformation of America, 1815–1836* (Boston: Northeastern University Press, 1998), 118–68; Kermes, *Creating*.

59. American Antiquarian Society, *Archæologia Americana* I (1820) and II (1836); "Office, 'Minnesota Historical Society,'" *Annals of the Minnesota Historical Society*, 2nd ed. (Saint Paul: Printed by James M. Goodhue, 1850), [3]; "Circular," *Annals*, 7. See also Susan A. Miller and James Riding In, "Introduction," and Susan A. Miller "Native America Writes Back: The Origin of the Indigenous Paradigm in Historiography," in *Native Historians Write Back: Decolonizing American Indian History*, ed. Susan A. Miller and James Riding In (Lubbock: Texas Tech University Press, 2011), 1–6 and 9–24.
60. Du Ponceau, "Inaugural," 26; William Rogers to I. K. Tefft, Jul. 9, 1843, Tefft Correspondence, Box 2, Administrative Records, Georgia Historical Society; Edward Harden to I. K. Tefft, Sept. 4, 1846, Edward Harden Papers, Georgia Historical Society.
61. Carl Benn, *Native Memoirs from the War of 1812: Black Hawk and William Apess* (Baltimore: Johns Hopkins University Press, 2014) xi, 27–28, 36–37; Konkle, *Writing*, 161–62.
62. John Ross to "Cherokee Antiquarians," Sept. 15, 1835, in *The Papers of Chief John Ross, Volume 1*, ed. Gary E. Moulton (Norman: University of Oklahoma Press, 1985), 353–54; Konkle, *Writing*, 90.
63. William W. Warren, quoted in William W. Warren, *History of the Ojibway People*, 2nd ed., ed. Theresa Schenk (St. Paul: Minnesota Historical Society Press, 2009) ix–x; Barry O'Connell, "'Once More Let Us Consider': William Apess in the Writing of New England Native American History," in *After King Philip's War: Presence and Persistence in Indian New England*, ed. Colin G. Calloway (Hanover, NH: University Press of New England, 1997), 162–77; Theresa Schenck, "William W. Warren's *History of the Ojibway People*: Tradition, History, Context," in *Reading Beyond Words: Contexts for Native History*, 2nd ed., ed. Jennifer S. H. Brown and Elizabeth Vibert (Peterborough, ON: Broadview Press, 2003), 193–210, esp. 197; Konkle, *Writing*, 97–223.
64. Elizabeth McHenry, *Forgotten Readers: Recovering the Lost History of African American Literary Societies* (Durham, NC: Duke University Press, 2002), 108–9; Hall, *Faithful*, 17–85; Dorothy Porter Wesley, "Black Antiquarians and Bibliophiles Revisited, with a Glance at Today's Lovers of Books and Memorabilia," in *Black Bibliophiles and Collectors: Preservers of Black History*, ed. Elinor Des Verney Sinnette, W. Paul Coates, and Thomas C. Battle (Washington: Howard University Press, 1990), 3–22.
65. Henle, "Means."

CONCLUSION

1. John Eliot to [Benjamin Trumbull?], Dec. 11, 1790, *MHS Proceedings* II (1880): viii. See also Des Jardins, *Women*; Susan Williams, *Alice Morse Earle and the Domestic History of Early America* (Amherst: University of Massachusetts Press, 2013); Ellen

F. Fitzpatrick, *History's Memory: Writing America's Past, 1880–1980* (Cambridge, MA: Harvard University Press, 2002), 51–97; Lonetree, *Decolonizing*; Robert B. Townsend, *History's Babel: Scholarship, Professionalization, and the Historical Enterprise in the United States, 1880–1940* (Chicago: University of Chicago Press, 2013); Marla R. Miller, "Introduction," in *Bending the Future: Fifty Ideas for the Next Fifty Years of Historic Preservation in the United States*, ed. Max Page and Marla R. Miller (Amherst: University of Massachusetts Press, 2016), 9–27.

2. Nina Baym, *American Women Writers and the Work of History* (New Brunswick, NJ: Rutgers University Press, 1995); Seelye, *Memory's Nation*; Mires, *Independence Hall*; Nash, *First City*; Steenshorne, "Past"; Batinski, *Pastkeepers in a Small Place*.
3. American Historical Association, *Officers, Acts of Incorporation, Constitution, List of Members, Historical Societies in the United States* (Baltimore: Friedenwald, 1896); Griffin, *Bibliography*; Keith Erekson, *Everybody's History: Indiana's Lincoln Inquiry and the Quest to Reclaim a President's Past* (Amherst: University of Massachusetts Press, 2012), 24–36.

Index